Debating the Lewis Turning Point in China

Has China's labor market passed the turning point and thus entered a period of labor shortage? This has been one of the most controversial subjects in economic studies and policy discussion in recent years. This volume brings together studies by a group of prominent Chinese and foreign economists at the forefront of this debate. It includes analyses both in support of and against the case that China has passed the Lewis turning point. Several studies also draw important implications of this change for macroeconomic conditions, growth outlook and economic structure.

This book was originally published as a special issue of the *China Economic Journal*.

Huang Yiping is Professor of Economics at the China Center for Economic Research, National School of Development, Peking University, China. He is also an adjunct professor at the Australian National University and a member of the China Finance 40 Forum. His current research focuses on macroeconomic policy, international finance and rural development.

Cai Fang is Director, Professor and Fellow at the Institute of Population and Labor Economics, Chinese Academy of Social Sciences, China. He serves as Vice Chairman of the China Population Association. His current research focuses on China's labor migration, population and development, economic reform, income distribution and poverty.

Debating the Lewis Turning Point in China

Edited by
Huang Yiping and Cai Fang

Routledge
Taylor & Francis Group

LONDON AND NEW YORK

First published 2014
by Routledge
2 Park Square, Milton Park, Abingdon, Oxon, OX14 4RN

Simultaneously published in the USA and Canada
by Routledge
711 Third Avenue, New York, NY 10017

Routledge is an imprint of the Taylor & Francis Group, an informa business

British Library Cataloguing in Publication Data
A catalogue record for this book is available from the British Library

ISBN13: 978-0-415-83345-5

Typeset in Times New Roman
by Taylor & Francis Books

Publisher's Note
The publisher accepts responsibility for any inconsistencies that may have arisen during the conversion of this book from journal articles to book chapters, namely the possible inclusion of journal terminology.

Disclaimer
Every effort has been made to contact copyright holders for their permission to reprint material in this book. The publishers would be grateful to hear from any copyright holder who is not here acknowledged and will undertake to rectify any errors or omissions in future editions of this book.

Contents

CONTENTS

Citation Information

The following chapters were originally published in the *China Economic Journal,* volume 3, issue 2 (July 2010). When citing this material, please use the original page numbering for each article, as follows:

Chapter 2
Demographic transition, demographic dividend, and Lewis turning point in China
Fang Cai
China Economic Journal, volume 3, issue 2 (July 2010) pp. 107-119

Chapter 3
Discussions on potential bias and implications of Lewis turning point
Yang Du and Wang Meiyan
China Economic Journal, volume 3, issue 2 (July 2010) pp. 121-136

Chapter 4
The rise of labor cost and the fall of labor input: Has China reached Lewis turning point?
Wang Meiyan
China Economic Journal, volume 3, issue 2 (July 2010) pp. 137-153

Chapter 5
Has China passed the Lewis turning point? A structural estimation based on provincial data
Yang Yao and Ke Zhang
China Economic Journal, volume 3, issue 2 (July 2010) pp. 155-162

Chapter 6
The Lewis turning point of Chinese economy: Comparison with Japanese experience
Ryoshin Minami and Xinxin Ma
China Economic Journal, volume 3, issue 2 (July 2010) pp. 163-179

Chapter 7
Macro-economic implications of the turning point
Ross Garnaut
China Economic Journal, volume 3, issue 2 (July 2010) pp. 181-190

Chapter 8

What does the Lewis turning point mean for China? A computable general equilibrium analysis
Yiping Huang and Tingsong Jiang
China Economic Journal, volume 3, issue 2 (July 2010) pp. 191-207

Chapter 9

Will Chinese growth slow after the Lewis turning point?
Ligang Song and Yongsheng Zhang
China Economic Journal, volume 3, issue 2 (July 2010) pp. 209-219

Notes on Contributors

Fang Cai, Institute of Population and Labor Economics, Chinese Academy of Social Sciences, Beijing, China

Ke Zhang, Cornell University, New York City, USA

Ligang Song, Australian National University, Canberra, Australia

Ross Garnaut, Institute of Applied Economic and Social Research, University of Melbourne, Melbourne, Australia

Ryoshin Minami, Department of Economics, Toyo University, Tokyo, Japan

Tingsong Jiang, Center for International Economics, Canberra, Australia

Wang Meiyan, Institute of Population and Labor Economics, Chinese Academy of Social Sciences, Beijing, China

Xinxin Ma, Keio Economic Observatory, University, Tokyo, Japan

Yang Du, Institute of Population and Labor Economics, Chinese Academy of Social Sciences, Beijing, China

Yang Yao, China Center for Economic Research & National School of Development, Peking University, Beijing, China

Yiping Huang, China Center for Economic Research, National School of Development, Peking University, China

Yongsheng Zhang, Development Research Centre of China, Beijing, China

Acknowledgement

This book is a product of collaboration among several institutions. Economists from the Institute of Population and Labor Economics (IPLE) at the Chinese Academy of Social Sciences, the National School of Development (NSD) at the Peking University and the China Economy Program (CEP) at the Australian National University were among the first to research on the Lewis Turning Point (LTP) in China. From as early as 2006, economists like Cai Fang, Ross Garnaut and their collaborators began to make the proposition that labor shortage was forthcoming. The group of labor economists from IPLE worked diligently with other to continue to build the case that China would soon pass the LTP and should be prepared for this new situation.

For years, of course, this remained a controversial subject, even inside these institutions. And economists proposing LTP for China were a minority group in policy discussions both at home and abroad. But what happened in 2012 probably changed many economists' and officials' mind. While GDP growth slowed steadily from 8.1 percent in the first quarter to 7.4 percent in the third quarter, labor shortage continued in large parts of the country. Even wages of migrant workers increased by 11.8 percent from a year earlier. The emerging labor shortage was clearly a result of rapid growth of demand underpinned by the average of 10 percent economic growth and decline of the working age population by 3.5 million in 2012 due to the one-child policy.

In early April 2010, the NSD of the Peking University and the IPLE of the Chinese Academy of Social Sciences jointly hosted the workshop *Debating the Lewis Turning Point in China* at the Fragrance Hotel in Beijing. This workshop was also supported by CEP of the Australian National University. Scholars presented papers both for and against the case of the LTP in China and analyzing its implications. Eight papers discussed at the workshop were later published as a special issue in *China Economic Journal* (CEJ) later that year, with Huang Yiping and Cai Fang as the guest editors. The special issue turned out to be a successful one. So now Taylor & Francis, publisher of the CEJ decided to turn this special issue into a book.

We add two chapters to this volume, the introductory chapter by Cai Fang on new labor market conditions and a concluding chapter by Huang Yiping and Cai Fang to describe a major economy-wide transition primarily triggered by the LTP. We hope that these chapters should not only make the discussions more update but also make discussions interesting to a broader group of readers.

NSD, IPLE and CEP provided funding for the 2010 workshop in Beijing and related research. In this regard, we like to thank Cai Fang of IPLE, Zhou Qiren and Yao Yang of NSD and Ross Garnaut and Song Ligang of CEP for generous supports. Wang Jiao of NSD and many others provided administrative supports for the workshop and research projects. Two editors of China Economic Journal, Wu Homou and Shen Yan, managed the publication process of the special issue. Finally, we would like to thank Taylor & Francis to publish this book, especially assistance provided by Emily Ross and Kimberley Smith.

Huang Yiping and Cai Fang
March 2013, Beijing

Approaching a neoclassical scenario: the labor market in China after the Lewis turning point

Fang Cai

Institute of Population and Labor Economics, Chinese Academy of Social Sciences, Beijing, China

1. Introduction

The three chief characteristics of a neoclassical scenario of labor market, which I contrast with a dualistic scenario of labor market such as described by Lewis (1954), are:

1. Wage is determined by marginal productivity of labor.
2. The labor market can correct its own disequilibrium in labor supply and demand over the long run.
3. There are three basic types of unemployment – cyclical, frictional, and structural – all of which need to be addressed with macroeconomic and labor market policies.

For a long time the Chinese economy exemplified a dual economy characterized by unlimited labor supply, subsistence wage, and the existence of institutional barriers to labor mobility, with the resultant difficulty in labor market clearing. Consequently, employment issues in China were understood exclusively in Lewisian (never in neoclassical) terms. Since the implementation of reform and opening up, and, in particular, China's entry into WTO in the new millennium, an enormous number of surplus laborers from the rural areas have migrated to coastal cities to take up non-agricultural jobs. It was not until very recently that the Lewis turning point arrived, signaled by widespread labor shortage and constant wage increase, particularly for unskilled workers, and facilitated by both demand and supply factors, such as demographic trends and strong growth of employment in urban areas.

While China is moving away from unlimited supply of labor and towards a neoclassical labor market scenario, today's employment problems show both neoclassical and dual economy characteristics. Some of the more prominent of these problems are:

1. Underemployment in the agricultural sectors has yet to be alleviated.
2. The worsening of cyclical unemployment, especially among migrant workers.

3. Higher degree of vulnerability among young people and older workers in urban areas than other groups to forms of natural unemployment, including structural and frictional unemployment.
4. Inadequate protection for workers' rights, including those relating to wage negotiation and labor disputes.

This paper illustrates how China's recent demographic trends, together with fast economic growth and employment expansion, have reshaped the country's employment landscape, which is no longer characterized by unlimited supply but by near equilibrium. In response to this shift, we must also fundamentally change the way we understand China's employment problems and the challenges policy-makers face. In addition to promoting employment, increasingly, policies must try to address problems of cyclical and natural unemployment, particularly among those who have been hardest hit by the transition and, as such, are especially vulnerable.

In this paper, we highlight key employment issues in China by looking closely at three distinct groups: migrant workers, college graduates and the urban working vulnerable. Each of these groups faces its own set of employment-related difficulties. Migrant workers are prone to be affected by cyclical unemployment, because when urban labor markets tighten due to economic slowdowns, many of them end up returning to agriculture work, which is a form of underemployment. College graduates are most vulnerable to structural and frictional unemployment, which partly explains why unemployment rates are often higher among this group than among some other groups. Third, the vulnerability of the vulnerable workers in urban areas is due largely to inadequate education and skill, a situation for which there are deep historical reasons.

This last problem points toward major challenges in institution building, and we will discuss it in some detail in this paper. As a result of the widespread awakening to their rights and entitlements among ordinary workers, brought by the arrival of the Lewis turning point and the continuing stress the labor market is under, labor disputes have been on the rise. The government has been quick to respond to this trend, by passing legislations and implementing policies. This is, in fact, yet another sign that China's labor market is on track to turning neoclassical after being Lewisian for a long time.

The demographic trend and its impacts on labor supply

Thanks to its strict implementation of the one-child policy, China has been able, in a very short time, to complete a demographic transition that took most developed countries much longer to complete. Since reform began, changes in China's demographic profile have gone through the following stages: sharp decline in fertility rate, then in the number of young people as a percentage of total population, decreasing growth rate for people of working age, and then the rapid aging of the Chinese population. When the percentage of young people contracted at a higher rate than the growth rate of the percentage of elderly people, China began to see a sufficient labor supply, a result of productive population structure. As these demographic trends continue, the working age population will grow more slowly, while the aging process will pick up speed. These trends will surely raise many challenges.

Despite the dramatic decline in total fertility rate (TFR) – from 5.8 to 2.3 – in China throughout the 1970s, by the early 1980s China's TFR was still above replacement level. What drastic reduction in fertility rate that China has been able to achieve owes very much to socio-economic development, on one hand, and wide adoption of family planning, on the other, during the reform period. These were highly effective in arresting high fertility rates. By the dawn of the twenty-first century, not only had China successfully carried out the transition towards a modern population growth pattern, but it had been able to do so in under 30 years. By comparison, it took many industrialized countries of comparable income level almost a century to do the same.

There have long been disagreements among scholars and official authority about China's TFR. Figure 1 shows China's TFR from 1950 to 2009. All pre-1998 figures had government sources and were as such 'official', but scholars treat only those for the years after 1998 to be genuinely trustworthy. In Figure 1, we can see that the TFR in China has been below 1.5 for many years, which is quite low in international comparison (Gu and Li 2010).

As the Chinese government began to distance itself gradually from this position, i.e. that TFR in China has been below 1.5 for many years according to census data from the National Bureau of Statistics, the United Nations put China's TFR for 2006 at 1.4 in its newly published *World Fertility Pattern, 2009*, thereby placing the country among those with low fertility rates (United Nations 2010). We may yet be hit by the consequent decline in labor supply, which will happen without warning.

One repercussion of persistently low fertility rates is a commensurate change in the age composition of a population. Since about 1980 the growth of the elderly population has accelerated, while that of the population of people of working age has decelerated – yet the population of young people has shrunk altogether. We can conclude that under the condition of persistently low fertility rates, the growth of the working age population will slow down before stopping altogether. These trends will lead eventually to labor shortages. According to one forecast based on the latest available statistics (United Nations 2011), the number of Chinese people aged between 15 and 64 will peak in 2015, after which it will begin to decrease (Figure 2).

These trends such as just described will lead to concomitant changes to the age structure of China's population. Our argument is based on two assumptions. First, we assume a continual rise in enrolment in higher education, and have left those aged 15 to 19 outside the purview of these analyses. Second, we assume there will be little or no increase in the rate of labor force participation for people 65 or older, and have included in our analysis only people between the ages of 20 and 64. In the next decade we expect to see a rise in the average age of people of working age, a slight decrease in the population size of the very young, a more significant decrease in the population size of people of ages between those of the previous two groups, and the elderly to account for 32% of the nation's total population by 2020.

As many previous studies have shown, among rural laborers, those with a more favorable demographic profile, for example, those who are better educated and younger, are more likely to migrate to settle in places further from home and for longer periods (Du and Wang 2010). Since non-agricultural labor supply is closely linked to rural-urban labor migration, and except in cases where sufficiently strong incentives intrinsic to the labor market or the prospects for professional growth exist, people of working

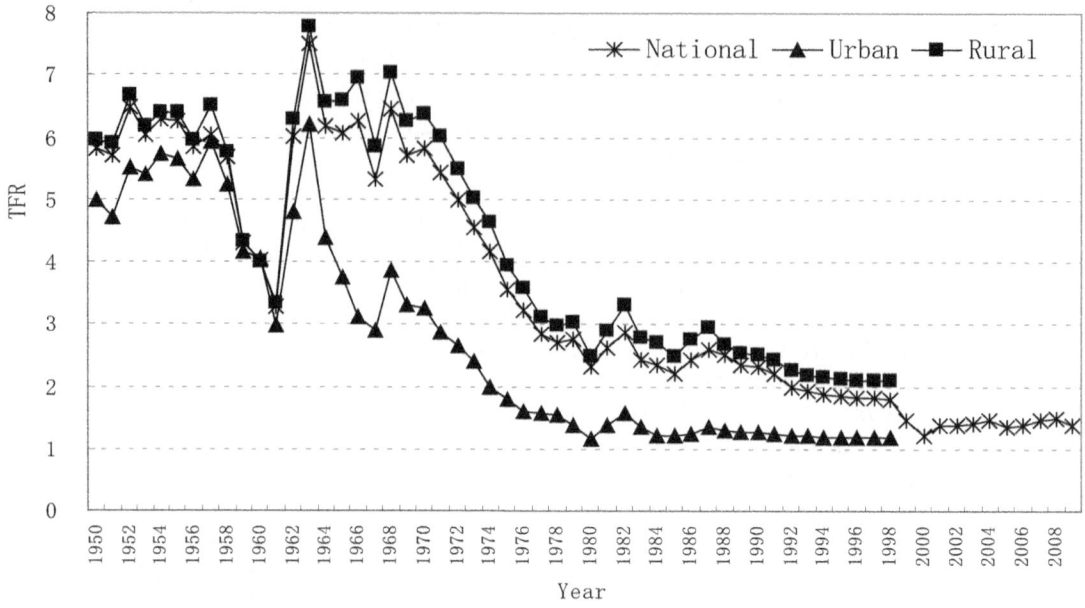

Figure 1. Reduction in total fertility rates

Source: Regional TFR for the period before 1998 was calculated using data from the China Center for Population Information database; national TFR post-1998 is calculated on the basis of various population survey and/or census data

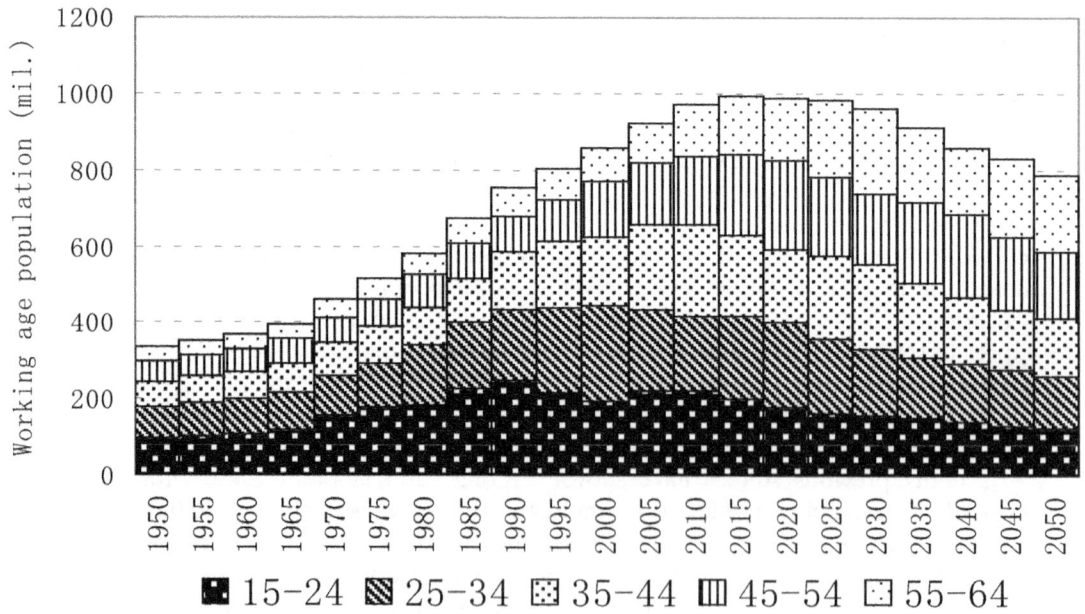

Figure 2. Changing age composition of working age population

Source: United Nations (2011)

age tend to become less mobile as they get older. Moreover, since older urban workers tend to face greater risks for structural and frictional unemployment, and enrolment rate in higher education has continued to rise, an older labor force also means a reduction in labor force participation rates.

Consequences for the labor market

An aging population presents two huge challenges to any society. On one hand, it poses a threat to the sustainability of the pension system and the elderly care infrastructure, and on the other, it reduces labor supply. In the period of reform, when there existed underemployment in both rural and urban sectors, the Chinese government has actively helped promote employment by developing labor market and reallocating people among different sectors and between rural and urban areas. Therefore, China's economic growth is, on one hand, partly attributable to the massive supply of labor, and, on the other, the reallocative efficiency gained by labor mobility from agricultural to non-agricultural sectors, which constitutes the demographic dividend of total factor productivity growth (World Bank 1997; Cai and Wang 1999; Cai and Wang 2005). As China enters a new era demographically, the impact on the labor market is enormous. These changes will shape the course of China's future development

Labor supply and demand: basic characteristics

Even though past forecasts for the annual increase in the number of new entrants to the nation's workforce never put it above 20 million, official figures for the number of new jobs needed each year to absorb the addition workers have been consistently larger. According to calculation done by the Ministry of Human Resources and Social Security, there are a total of more than 24 million people in the labor reserve. This number is arrived at by adding up the numbers for three groups of people: more than10 million new entrants to the labor market, each year, more than 8 million people currently unemployed who are looking for jobs, and over 6 million laid-off workers who need work (Zhang 2008).

This calculation method is problematic, however. First of all, it is missing a temporal dimension and creates the false impression of timelessness. While the landscape of China's labor demand and supply has changed significantly in recent years, some of the basic categories assumed in this calculation no longer exist. For example, the category that used to be labeled 'laid-off workers' was renamed in 2005 and these people are now referred to as the 'registered unemployed'. This means that, at least officially, there were no longer any laid-off workers in China but there was, however, a total of 80 million 'registered unemployed' in 2008. The second problem with this calculation is that it is based on the questionable assumption that all the unemployed must be absorbed. But this intention is neither necessary nor feasible. According to mainstream theories of employment, insofar as there is such a thing as a natural unemployment rate, it tends to stay fairly stable over the long run.

The demographic and economic trends just described have led to a changed relationship between labor supply and demand. Take the annual increase in the number of people between the ages of 16 and 64 on the supply side and annual increase in the number of urban workers on the demand side. When the two trends are examined together, the changing dynamics of the labor market become obvious. Since the number of agricultural workers has been falling while that of non-agricultural workers in rural areas is not expected to expand, we may treat the increases in the number of urban workers, migrant workers included, as representative of the magnitude of the overall labor demand of the Chinese economy.

In what follows, we take a closer look at the general employment situation in China by comparing the demand and the supply of labor for urban sectors. There are two parts to the statistical data on urban employment in China. The first includes the total number of urban employees, which is published by the National Bureau of Statistics (NBS). This number does not, however, cover most migrant workers in urban areas. According to estimation on the basis of micro data from 2009, only 12.5% of the total of 310 million urban employees were migrant workers. The second part includes the total number of people classifiable as migrant workers according to NBS official definition. According to that definition, an individual qualifies as a 'migrant worker' if s/he has been away from the town or township of their household registration for six months or more. Surveys have shown that of all migrant workers, 95.6% work and live in cities of varying sizes. Factoring in the overlap between these two numbers, we can calculate the actual number of urban workers inclusive of both registered urban residents and migrant workers. We can then compare this number with the total number of people of working age in the country (Table 1).

Between 2001 and 2011, labor demand of urban sectors, which encompasses employment among both urban residents and the migrants, grew at an annual rate of 3.2%. During the same period, labor supply, measured by the number of people of working age grew by an annual rate of only 1.1%. For the purpose of this study, we have excluded people older than 60 from working age population because, given retirement age in China – 60 for men and 55 for women – they by default stand little chance of finding a job in the present labor market. A look at people between the ages of 15 and 59 shows that this population had begun to shrink by 2010. This suggests, among other things, that the problem of high rates of underemployment in both the rural and the urban labor markets was finally easing. As such, constant surplus of supply relative to demand no longer accurately describes China's labor market after the arrival of the Lewis turning point.

Wage increases for unskilled workers

Wages have been growing continuously in China since the late 1990s, when a huge number of workers were laid off in urban areas and labor productivity increased as a consequence. Since the beginning of this century, the average wage in major urban sectors has been rising at an annual rate of over 8%, a figure unrivaled by any group anywhere in the world. However, understanding China's official statistical data on wages can be a challenge because of the complex ways in which they are collected and calculated. For example, data on urban wage cover only workers formally employed in formal sectors and leave out information on temporary workers and those who work in the informal sectors, therefore, such data cannot be completely relied on if one wants to understand the dynamics of the situation in China with respect to wage. However, wage

	Urban resident workers		Migrant workers		Working age population	
	Numbers	Growth rate	Numbers	Growth rate	Numbers	Growth rate
2001	236	—	80	—	885	—
2002	241	2.1	100	24.7	901	1.7
2003	246	2.0	109	8.8	914	1.5
2004	250	1.8	113	3.8	929	1.6
2005	254	1.7	120	6.4	944	1.6
2006	259	2.0	126	5.0	952	0.9
2007	265	2.1	131	3.7	960	0.8
2008	268	1.3	134	2.5	968	0.8
2009	272	1.4	139	3.5	974	0.7
2010	277	1.6	146	5.3	981	0.7
2011	280	1.0	152	3.7	986	0.6

Table 1. Increases in demand for and supply of labor force (million, %)
Source: authors' own calculation based on *China Statistical Yearbook* (various years), *China Yearbook of Rural Household Survey* (various years), and *China Population Yearbook* (various years), and Du and Hu (2011)

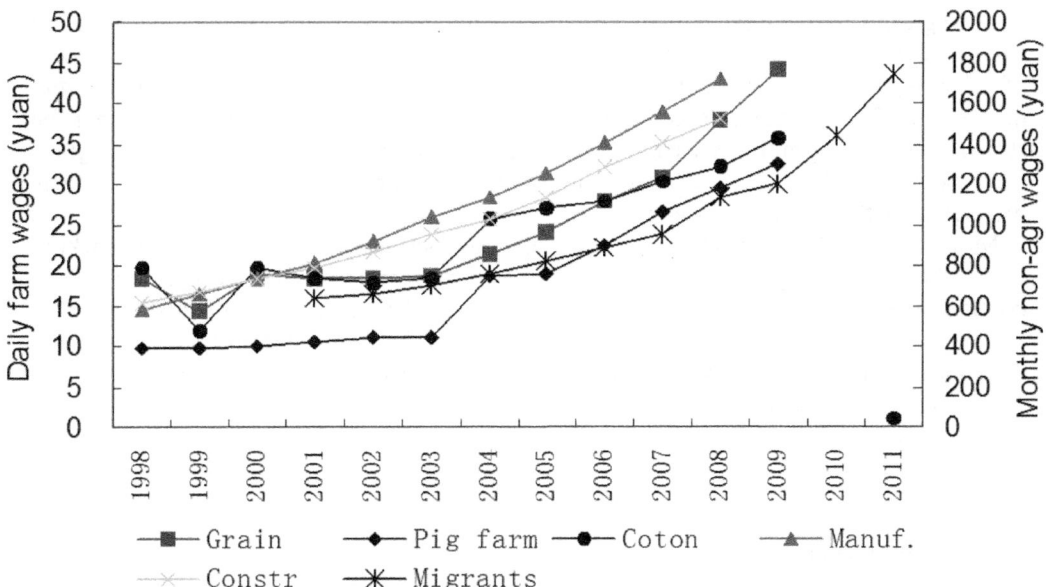

Figure 3. Wages increase in selected sectors
Source: Data on the daily wages for workers in grain and cotton production and on hog farms with more than 50 hogs are from *Compilation of National Farm Product Cost-benefit Data;* monthly wages of manufacturing and construction are from *China Labor Statistics* (various years); monthly wages of migrant workers are from *NBS Statistical Report* (various years)

increases for migrant workers warrant close examination since they not only make up one-third of urban employment but also account for a large percentage of informal workers in non-agricultural sectors,

Until 2004 wages for migrant workers had shown little growth even though wages for urban workers who are local residents had begun to rise. In 2004 the country was hit by the first migrant labor shortage, which triggered a rapid increase in wages. As can be seen in Figure 3, wages for all sectors, including those dominated by migrant workers (such as manufacturing and construction), have been increasing constantly, while wage increase for migrant workers has been particularly impressive. We conclude, therefore, that observed wage increases are mainly attributable to changes in labor demand and supply. We have included here the figures for wage increases in select agricultural sectors as further evidence for the validity of this claim. Indeed, strong wage growth in agricultural sectors signals the decline of the dual economy, which, according to Lewis, is an economy characterized by surplus labor in agriculture.

Wages for migrant workers have been rising continuously since 2004, as a result of migrant labor shortage. Even the global financial crisis did not interrupt this trend. A survey conducted by the National Bureau of Statistics (NBS) shows that average real monthly wage of migrant workers was 1,221 yuan in 2009, which was 90% higher than what it was in 2001. The real wage of migrant workers went up by 19% in 2010 and further increased by 21% in 2011. Other surveys and reports besides the one by NBS have put the figures for migrant labor wage increases even higher. For example, according to a survey conducted in early 2010 by the People's Bank of China, China's central bank, the average wage for migrant workers was 1,783.2 yuan in 2009, a figure that was 17.8% higher than the year before (DSS-PBC, 2010).

In fact, because urban local workers and migrant workers tend to differ considerably with respect to their hours and pay structures, comparative analysis of the wages for the two groups must factor in both wage rates and working hours. According to a 2010 survey ('China Urban Labor Survey', or CULS),[1] migrant workers work for an average of 27% longer than do urban local workers per week, and their hourly wage rates were on average 88.2% of the average wage rate for local urban workers. This means that the reason the average monthly earning for migrant workers was higher (by 5.6% higher) than the number for urban local workers was that the former make up for lower hourly wage rates with longer hours worked.

Moreover, as the demographic profile of this population evolves, so do working habits. For example, younger workers today tend to work fewer hours than their older counterparts used to previously. Findings from CULS show that, in 2010, migrant workers worked an average of almost 12.4 hours less than did migrant workers in 2005. This means that the increase in total monthly earning for migrant workers is a reflection of substantial surge in wage rate (i.e. hourly rate).

Rise in labor disputes

In recent years, particularly since 2008, the year in which several labor-related laws were passed or updated, heightening workers awareness of their rights and entitlements,[2] the number of incidents of labor disputes in China has sharply increased. According to official records, the total number of labor disputes in 2010 was twice what it was in 2003, and the number of severe unrests triggered by conflicts in labor relations has also grown. That is not necessarily a sign of a worsening trend in labor relation, but may be more an indication of stronger demand for labor market institutions.

In his seminal work, Hirschman (1970) named three mechanisms – namely, exit, voice, and loyalty – by which citizens, consumers, and workers can express their dissatisfaction with conditions in the market. Here, we borrow those expressions to describe changed labor relations in China after the arrival of the Lewis turning point. As laborers in general, and migrant workers in particular (especially in China) enjoy more employment opportunities, there has also been greater room for them to exercise their rights by 'voting with their feet', i.e. by choosing 'exit'.

How individual migrant workers use their power of choice depends on what jobs they hold. For example, for workers who are dissatisfied with their jobs in small companies with poor growth prospects, they may simply quit since the odds are reasonably high that they can find a better job elsewhere. But for workers who are dissatisfied with but reluctant to leave a jobs in a sizable company with some industry recognition and growth potential, efforts to seek higher pay and better working conditions may take the form of overt actions such as vocal complaints, collective bargaining, and, in more extreme cases, strikes.

Figure 4 shows the level of labor dispute in different provinces such as measured by the ratio between the number of reported cases and total employment. We can see that they happen more often in the more developed coastal regions than they do elsewhere. Of the total number of labor disputes in China in 2008, a vast majority, or 74.8%, took place in the eastern provinces.

There are several reasons for these regional variations in the occurrence of labor disputes:

1. The Lewis turning point came to more developed regions earlier than it did elsewhere.
2. The more developed regions are also where migrant workers are most concentrated.
3. Since migrant workers are more vulnerable to abuse, they are correspondently more likely to initiate actions in defense of their rights. The rise in labor disputes and the uneven geographical distribution of their occurrence both suggest that there has been a sharp increase both in worker awareness about rights and in the demand for the institutionalization of their protection.

4. Three vulnerable groups

In studying unemployment, scholars in macroeconomics and labor economics have focused mainly on two types of unemployment: cyclical unemployment and natural unemployment (which includes frictional and structural unemployment). In a typical labor market and under normal conditions, macroeconomic fluctuations are associated with temporary changes in the relationship between labor demand and supply, which generate cyclical unemployment. By contrast, natural unemployment, in the form

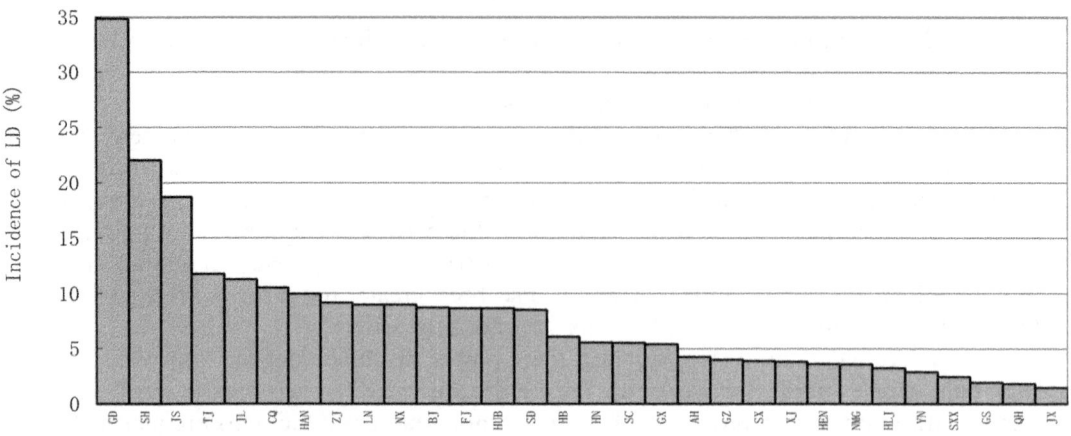

Figure 4. Incidence of labor dispute by province

Note: According to China's official categorization, more developed provinces (the eastern region)
include Beijing (BJ), Shanghai (SH), Tianjin (TJ), Jiangsu (JS), Zhejiang (ZJ), Guangdong (GD),
Shangdong (SD), Fujian (FJ), Liaoning (LN), Hainan (HAN), Hebei (HB), developmentally
intermediate provinces (the central region) include Hunan (HUN), Hubei (HUB), Henan (HN),
Jilin (JL), Heilongjiang (HLJ), Jiangxi (JX), Shanxi (SX), Anhui (AH), and least developed
provinces (the western region) include Guangxi (GX), Shaanxi (SXX), Gansu (GS), Guizhou (GZ),
Inner Mongolia (NMG), Xinjiang (XJ), Yunnan (YN), Ningxia (NX), Qinghai (QH), Sichuan (SC),
Chongqing (CQ) and Tibet (XZ, omitted from the figure due to unavailability of data).

Source: NBS (2009) *China Labor Statistical Yearbook, 2009*

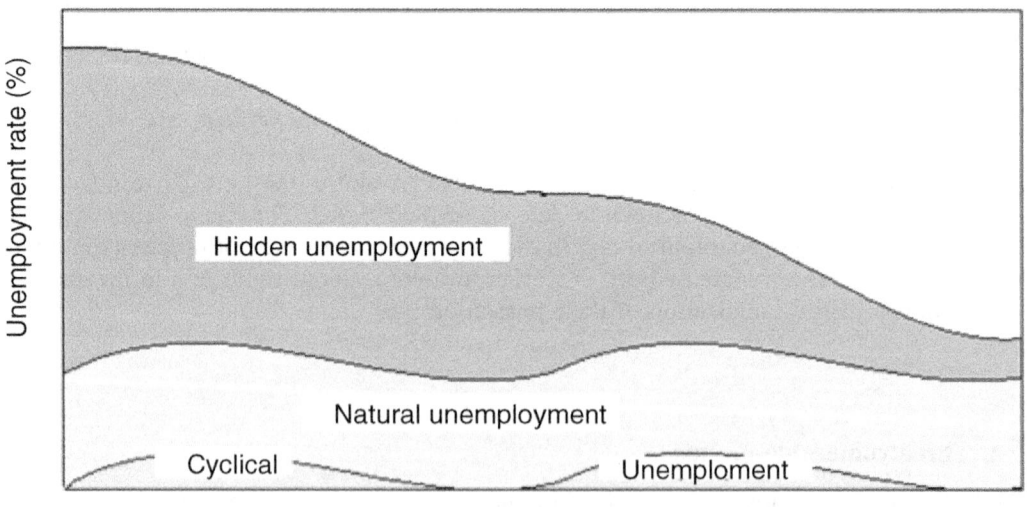

Figure 5. Unemployment types and their changing trends

either of frictional unemployment or of structural employment, is the effect of a mismatch between employment objectives of workers, on one hand, and employment opportunities employers can offer, on the other. More specifically, such mismatch can reflect either the time cost of job search or changes in skill requirements.

As market mechanism plays an increasingly prominent role in labor allocation and macroeconomic business cycles occur in China, both cyclical and natural unemployment have existed in China. According to one estimate (Cai et al. 2004), in the period between 1995 and 2002, roughly 60 to 80% of urban unemployment in China that had been observed was not the result of macroeconomic fluctuations, and should be classified as natural unemployment.

According to Lewis (1954), as a dual economy grows, excess labor supply in agriculture is increasingly absorbed by expanding non-agricultural sectors. It is widely believed that 30 to 40% of China's agricultural labor force during the period between the mid-1980s and the late 1990s constituted excess supply (Taylor 1993; Carter et al. 1996). Similarly, as a legacy of a planned economy, 30 to 40% of total employees of state-owned enterprises (SOE) in urban areas were deemed dispensable (Zhang 2008). Both these forms of underemployment, affecting rural and urban sectors respectively, are tantamount to hidden unemployment. We can distinguish, therefore, three different forms of unemployment: cyclical, natural (frictional and structural), and hidden, and we discuss changes in them separately.

When economic reform began in China, the economy was a typical dual economy characterized by a sharp rural-urban dichotomy, and high rates of hidden unemployment in both spheres. At the same time, both natural unemployment and cyclical unemployment have existed in China. The former is due to a combination of pervasive underdevelopment, inadequate public employment services, and the prevalence of mismatch between job skill and requirement, while the latter is due to macroeconomic fluctuations, which happened throughout the reform period. In order to be able to focus our analytical attention on how the transition away from a dual economy reduced hidden unemployment, the effects of urban employment policy reform, and the breakup of the 'iron rice bowl' in SOE, we shall assume that cyclical unemployment and natural unemployment stay relatively constant.

From Figure 5, we can see that since the beginning of China's reform policies, as the migration of surplus rural labor into urban areas and the reallocation of redundant urban workers continued, hidden unemployment shrank substantially in terms of both aggregate scale and percentage of total 'unemployment'. A number of empirical studies have shown that the massive flows of labor force from agricultural to non-agricultural sectors and from rural to urban areas have contributed tremendously to the reduction in the number of excess labor in agriculture (for example, Cai and Wang 2008; Zhang et al. 2009). Since 2004 when the first nationwide labor shortage took place, the wage rates for ordinary workers have been rising continuously. This was, by definition, a Lewis turning point.

The urban labor market has been experiencing painful adjustments since the late 1990s, and a total of 40 million workers had been laid off up by 2002. As the economy continues to grow and the labor market to evolve, people who had been laid off and were officially registered as unemployed have either found new jobs or retired. It seems, therefore, that while these kinds of adjustment help eliminate hidden unemployment in urban areas, older workers are more vulnerable to frictional and structural unemployment.

Three subpopulations in China are recognized by both the public and the government as being particularly vulnerable with respect to employment. These are migrant workers, college graduates, and urban vulnerable workers who are relatively old and poorly educated, who suffer from unemployment or difficulty in finding a job. By taking a closer look at each of these groups, we can begin to understand better the new challenges China is facing in this transition toward a neoclassical labor market.

A migrant worker is, literally, a 'farmer-turned-worker' in Chinese. And, indeed, much of this population is made up of surplus labor in rural areas. One's status as a migrant worker does not necessarily mean that you are unwanted for agricultural production. More often, agricultural workers who do choose to migrate into the cities do so because they better satisfy the personal conditions for migration than others. In other words, in comparison with those who stay behind, rural migrants have some notable advantages.

First, a higher percentage of migrants, who are mostly between the ages of 20 and 30, would have had some formal education. Many would have completed the nine years of free education legally mandated in China. As such, this population is suitably prepared for most of the unskilled and/or semiskilled jobs available in urban areas. Second, because they invariably lack access to social protection, including employment assistance, they can ill afford to remain unemployed with no income. As a result, they tend to have a higher level of tolerance for poor pay and poor working conditions, and there is a high rate of labor participation among them. Third, since this population tends to suffer from spatial distance between where they live and where they can find a job, institutional exclusion from decision making and informational asymmetry between them and their employers, they tend, at least to a certain extent, to be cut off from market demand.

Today, agriculture is no longer able to reabsorb migrant returnees from the cities whenever urban labor demand crashes during an economic downturn. There are two major reasons for this. First, agricultural production has changed greatly from what it was in earlier times, in part as a result of the great labor hemorrhage; second, the demand for migrant workers in urban areas is now relatively inelastic. They are, therefore, no longer a reserve labor force but rather the pillar of the urban labor market. However, since they tend to receive weaker institutional protection and enjoy less of a social safety net, they are more likely to become victims of labor market volatility caused by macroeconomic fluctuations. As the macro economy goes through cycles of boom and bust, high rates of cyclical unemployment among migrant workers and migrant worker shortage take place alternately.

The difficulties in finding a job facing university graduates are a relatively new phenomenon. Before the massive expansion of university enrolment, university graduates were scarce human resources and tended to be highly valued in the labor market. Even though the system of job placement had largely been phased out by the end of the 1990s, as a group, college graduates had relatively little difficulty securing a job and the unemployment rate among them remained low. This began to change, however, when the first graduates from these classes of enlarged enrolment entered the labor market. In 2001 when this group of students was yet to graduate from universities, the share of new entrants in the total number of unemployed who used publicly run employment services was 16.5%. By contrast, in 2002, when the graduates from the first class of enlarged enrolment who had spent three years or longer in colleges entered the labor market, that number increased to 20.1%. And by 2011 it reached 23.9%. Of these unemployed new entrants, 40.6% were that year's university graduates. According to a 2005 national survey, the unemployment rate was 8% among three-year college graduates and 6.1% for university graduates. Both these numbers were significantly higher than the urban average of 5.2% (Cai and Wang 2009; Wang and Cai 2009).

While the higher unemployment rate and the employment difficulties facing university graduates are no doubt caused, certainly in part, by macroeconomic cycles of boom and bust, to a higher degree, they are cases of frictional and structural unemployment. As human capital, university graduates in general have higher values than and are at an advantage relative to other groups, including migrant workers, (older) urban workers, and new entrants into the labor market with fewer years of formal education. They are, therefore, more likely to work in the formal sectors, to be better paid, and to enjoy more job security. However, since their training is more in specific skills than that of other groups, the job search for university graduates requires a longer time and more sophisticated matching mechanism. As a result, they are more likely to face the risk of structural and frictional unemployment.

Among urban laborers, human capital deficiency is typically associated with older age, less formal education, poorer health, and outdated skills. This is another population that faces greater risks for natural unemployment. Let us consider the effect of education, for example. According to one study (Wang and Niu 2009), for those in the 24 to 64 age range, each additional year in age difference corresponds to a 10.2% drop in education attainment. The correlation becomes more pronounced among older workers. For those in the 44 to 64 age range, each additional year in age difference represents a 16.1% reduction in the level of education attainment. Suppose there is a critical minimum to human capital – say (and not unreasonably), nine years of formal education, which is required for all Chinese citizens, the demarcation separating those who meet it and those who do not would be age 33.[4]

Therefore, this group of laborers is subject not only to the risks of lay-off induced by the campaign to break the SOE 'iron rice bowl' but also to the risks of frictional and structural unemployment. One silver lining for them, however, is that since most of them have urban *hukou*, or household registration, and are already living in urban communities, they tend to be counted properly in official statistics in regard to their employment status. By contrast, migrant workers are often discounted, undercounted, or uncounted altogether. This is evidenced by the fact that they have consistently accounted for a large share of the registered unemployed in official records. On the one hand, since the difficulties those laborers face are longstanding and persistent, registered unemployment in urban areas has been relatively insensitive to macroeconomic fluctuations. But, on the other hand, they are also relatively well protected by the urban social security system and safety net.

5. Conclusions and policy implications

Thanks to rapid economic growth, fundamental changes in society, and strict implementation of family planning policies since the early 1980s, China has achieved a population transition, changing from one characterized by 'high birth rate, low mortality rate and high growth rate' to one characterized by 'low birth rate, low mortality rate and low growth rate', and has done so within a very short time. There have been a number of concomitant demographic changes, most notably with respect to age structure, which, in particular, has generated a demographic dividend during much of this period but that began to dissipate in the early twenty-first century. The labor market has responded to these developments, which can be clearly seen in the nationwide labor shortage and steep rises in worker wage.

According to the literature of development economics, those phenomena signal the arrival of the Lewis turning point. Since this point marks a separation between a dual economic labor market and a neoclassical one, China faces new and fundamentally different tasks and challenges in its effort to maintain good order in its labor market and to keep unemployment rates low. In particular, instead of focusing exclusively on promoting employment, employment policies in China should also address problems of cyclical and natural unemployment problems, and in ways that uniquely suit the situation in China.

First, the household registration (or *hukou*) system, an institution unique to China that makes a sharp distinction between the rural and the urban labor markets, is a key target for reform if China's labor market is to see greater development. More specifically, one important part of this reform is to allow migrants to apply for granted urban resident status so they can gain full access to social services. Not only can this help keep labor supply adequately large and stable, but also can it help reduce the negative effects of cyclical unemployment for migrant workers.

Second, education and training are areas in which more profound vision and more assertive government action are urgently needed. In China, one serious problem is that wage convergence tends to generate a disincentive to complete schooling. To counter this tendency, heavier public spending toward education and better coordination between the education system and the labor market are imperative. Boosting labor force participation through, say, increasing the retirement age can only be effective if accompanied by systematic increases in continuing education and job training for older workers.

Third, the construction of labor market institutions is now of critical importance. Lessons from the experiences of either advanced countries or those of middle-income level suggest that labor market institutions, including industrial relations legislation, minimum wage regime, laws governing collective bargaining and unemployment protection are instrumental for coordinating the demands of different groups and for maintaining social cohesion.

Endnotes

1 China Urban Labor Survey or CULS is a series of surveys conducted by Institute of Population and Labor Economics, Chinese Academy of Social Sciences in 2001, 2005, and 2010, respectively. It representatively sampled laborers in urban households and migrant households and surveyed both individual laborers and households in Shanghai, Wuhan, Shenyang, Fuzhou, and Xi'an.

2 In the year 2008 alone, three labor-related laws were implemented, of which the *Employment Contract Law* emphasizes enhancing employment security and providing better protection for migrant workers and the urban working vulnerable, the *Employment Promotion Law* clearly claims the responsibility of governments in promoting employment and in eliminating various

kinds of labor market discrimination, and the *Labor Disputes Mediation and Arbitration Law* is intended to provide a legal framework for improving labor relations.

3 In 2004, for example, 70% of Chinese migrant workers were in the eastern regions (Sheng and Peng).

4 The critical age here is estimated based on data of the country as a whole. Because education attainment level in rural areas is lower than that in urban areas, it may cause some degree of skew when we examine the urban working age population. The conclusion holds unchanged, however – that is, among the older and less educated, the critical point of nine years of compulsory education arrives well before official retirement age. For a related analysis on education attainments and returns to human capital in both rural and urban areas, see Wang (2009).

References

Cai, Fang. 2004. The consistency of China's statistics on employment: Stylized facts and implications for public policies. *Chinese Economy* 37, no. 5 (September–October): 74–89.

Cai, Fang and Dewen Wang. 1999. The sustainability of China's economic growth and the contributions of labor. *Economic Research Journal*, no. 10: 62–68.

Cai, Fang and Dewen Wang. 2005. China's demographic transition: Implications for growth. In *The China boom and its discontents*, eds. Ross Garnaut and Song Ligang, 34–52. Canberra: Asia Pacific Press.

Cai, Fang and Meiyan Wang. 2008. A counterfactual analysis on unlimited surplus labor in rural China. *China and World Economy* 16, no.1: 51–65.

Cai, Fang and Meiyan Wang. 2009. The Chinese employment situation and youth employment difficulties. In *The China population and labor yearbook volume 10: The sustainability of economic growth from the perspective of human resources*, ed. Fang Cai. Beijing, China: Social Sciences Academic Press.

Cai, Fang, Yang Du, and Wenshu Gao. 2003. Employment elasticity, NAIRU and macroeconomic policies. *Economic Research Journal*, no. 9: 18–25.

Carter, Colin, Zhong Funing, and Fang Cai. 1996. *China's ongoing reform of agriculture.* San Francisco: 1990 Institute.

Department of Survey and Statistics, People's Bank of China (DSS-PBC). 2010. The fifth monitoring report on migrant workers. In *The China population and labor yearbook volume 11: Labor market challenges in the post-crisis era*, ed. Fang Cai. Beijing, China: Social Sciences Academic Press.

Du, Yang and Meiyan Wang. 2010. New estimate of surplus rural labor force and its implications. *Journal of Guangzhou University (Social Science Edition)* 9, no. 4: 17–24.

Gu, Baochang and Jianxin Li. 2010. *The debate on China's population policy in the 21st century.* Beijing, China: Social Sciences Academic Press.

Hirschman, Albert. 1970. *Exit, voice, and loyalty: Responses to decline in firms, organizations, and states.* Cambridge, MA: Harvard University Press.

Hu, Ying. 2009. Predictions on working age population of rural and urban China. Unpublished memo.

Lewis, Arthur. 1954. Economic development with unlimited supply of labor. *Manchester School of Economics and Social Studies* 22.

Taylor, J. R. 1993. Rural employment trends and the legacy of surplus labor, 1978–1989. In *Economic trends in Chinese agriculture: The impact of post-Mao reforms*, eds. Y. Y. Kueh and R. F. Ash, Chapter 8. New York: Oxford University Press.

United Nations. 2009. *The world population prospects: The 2008 revision.* http://esa.un.org/unpp/.

United Nations. 2010. *World fertility pattern, 2009.* http://www.un.org/esa/ population/publications/worldfertility2009/worldfertility2009.htm.

United Nations Department of Economic and Social Affairs, Population Division. 2011. *World population prospects: The 2010 revision*. CD-ROM edition.

Wang, Dewen and Fang Cai. 2009. The education and employment of rural and urban youth in China. In *The China population and labor yearbook volume 10: The sustainability of economic growth from the perspective of human resources*, ed. Fang Cai. Beijing, China: Social Sciences Academic Press.

Wang, Guangzhou and Jianlin Niu. 2009. Composition and development of the Chinese education system. In *The China population and labor yearbook volume 10: The sustainability of economic growth from the perspective of human resources*, ed. Fang Cai. Beijing, China: Social Sciences Academic Press.

Wang, Meiyan. 2009. Universal high school and mass higher education. In *The China population and labor yearbook volume 10: The sustainability of economic growth from the perspective of human resources*, ed. Fang Cai. Beijing, China: Social Sciences Academic Press.

World Bank. 1997. *China 2020: Development challenges in the new century*. Washington, DC: World Bank.

Zhang, Xiaobo, Jin Yang, and Shenglin Wang. 2009. Has China reached the Lewis turning point: Evidence from poor regions. *Journal of Zhejiang University (Humanities and Social Sciences)*, no. 6: 1–18.

Zhang, Xiaojian (ed.). 2008. *The reforms and developments of Chinese employment*. China Labor and Social Security Press.

Demographic transition, demographic dividend, and Lewis turning point in China

Fang Cai

Institute of Population and Labor Economics, Chinese Academy of Social Sciences, Beijing, China

The disagreements on changed stages of demographic transition and the role of a demographic dividend in a dual economy development process often lead to wide debates among scholars about China's development stages. This paper tries to reveal the nexus between demographic transition and dual economy development: the common starting point, close-related processes, and identical characteristics of stages. Based on the empirical evidence of population dynamics, the paper supports the judgment of diminishing demographic dividends and an imminent Lewis turning point in China. The paper also argues that keeping a sustainable and steady economic growth, and becoming a high-income country as early as possible is the key and only way to close the 'aging before affluence' gap. Accordingly, the paper concludes by proposing measures to exploit the potential of the first demographic dividend, creating conditions for a second demographic dividend, and tapping new sources of economic growth.

1. Introduction

One of the hot topics that inspire debates among scholars, policy researchers, and even policy-makers is whether Chinese economic growth is losing its source and momentum from demographic dividends. Another related topic is whether China reaches its Lewis turning point – namely, labor supply is no longer unlimited. In a research paper, Cai and Wang (2005) estimate that the decline in the population dependence ratio, as a proxy for demographic dividend, contributed 26.8% to per capita GDP growth during 1982 to 2000, and warns that such a demographic dividend will disappear after 2013 when dependence ratio stops decreasing and begins increasing. By examining changes in the trend of China's age structure and the demand supply of the labor market, widespread rural labor shortages, wage increase of ordinary workers, Cai (2008a, 2008b) asserts that the Lewis turning point has indeed come, and points out its policy implications in terms of growth pattern transformation, income distribution trends, labor market institutional construction, and human capital accumulation.

While some researchers and even some policy documents support and cite the conclusion about the arrival of the Lewis turning point, others strongly disagree. In previous replies, Cai (2008a) tried to provide a wide range of evidence to defend his arguments. It turns out that people come out with conflicting opinions about economic reality, and explain the same phenomenon in different ways. Many still firmly hold to the conventional wisdom that there is a massive and increasing working age population and thus endless surplus labor force in rural areas, and that this is an unchangeable characteristic of China. Propositions which assert the possibility of labor shortage or disappearance of the surplus labor force in agriculture – namely that the Lewis turning point is arriving – are not widely agreed.[1] Specifically, all skeptical and critical comments on the judgment about an ongoing Lewis turning point, which results from a static understanding of population and labor force in China, are generally puzzled by the Chinese statistics. In what follows, I unveil some aspects of such statistical puzzles.

First, given that the official survey on utilization of agricultural workforce is unable to reflect the fast-changing reality of agricultural production, some scholars are unaware of the changed situation, while others who have tried to understand the statistics are actually trapped in 'the tyranny of numbers' as was Young (1994) when he tried to challenge the 'East Asian miracle'. Either case makes any endeavor of econometric analysis hostage to the data. The point is that economic reform in China has been too fast for the statistical system to catch up (Ravallion and Chen 1999). One of the many examples that cause confusion concerns the accurate numbers of agricultural workforce actually used. In 2008, the reported total labor force engaged in agriculture was 307 million, accounting for 39.6% of the country's total employment, and the figure provided by 2008 Agricultural Census was even higher. However, the actual input of labor in agricultural production, calculated based on agricultural costs survey data, turns out to be much less than any published aggregated figures (Cai and Wang 2008). Comprehensively considering the changing trend of working age population in rural area, the updated situation of labor migration from rural to urban sectors, and the extent to which agriculture is mechanized, one must conclude that the actually used workforce in agricultural production is much less than what official statistical publications declare. Therefore, the declaration that there is large amount of surplus labor to be shifted from agriculture (Lau 2010a) or the conclusion that the marginal productivity of labor in agriculture is still very low (Minami and Ma 2009), which are both based on the aggregated dataset, tend to overestimate the degree of labor surplus in agriculture and conclude that the Lewis turning point has not come to China.

Second, scholars have difficulties in interpreting statistics on labor market and rural and urban employment, and thus they often elicit conclusions that deviate from reality. As the result of sectoral changes and increasing diversification of ownership, especially after the labor market shock in the late 1990s, multifaceted sectors have appeared to absorb labor into urban areas, contrary to the pre-reform period when state and collective sectors dominated employment absorption. Among those sectors of employment, large-scale informal employment, as the byproduct of reemployment of the laid-off and of diversity of employment, is new to China. Meanwhile, massive numbers of rural laborers have transformed their jobs from agricultural to non-agricultural sectors, amounting to 240 million, of which 145 million migrated into cities. In routine statistics, neither informal employment of urban residents nor employment of migrant workers in urban sectors has been authoritatively reported, except for estimated figures of migrant workers based on sampling surveys and aggregated estimate of informally employed urban residents under certain assumptions (Cai 2004). We can view the difference between the number of total employment based on the unit reporting system and the number of employment based on the household survey as a proxy for urban informal employment, which amounts to 95.1 million and accounts for 31.5% of total urban employment in 2008. It is, however, helpless if one wants to do any statistical analysis on structural characteristics of the total employment, because of lack of disaggregated data on it. Moreover, the statistical authority has so far not promulgated an alternative surveyed unemployment rate data series to the discredited registered unemployment rate, and that leads scholars to do various guesstimates on the unemployment rate.

Based on incomplete employment data and unfounded guesstimates, Chinese and international scholars often educed conclusions such as zero growth of employment and a high and increasing unemployment rate (Ru, Lu, and Li 2008, 22; Rawski 2001; Solinger 2001) and doubt the authenticity of the widespread labor shortage.

Third, there is no officially published systematic data and up to date information on the status of demographic change and population dynamics. While various rounds of national population censuses provide information on population changes, no authoritative projections of population change, including predictions of magnitude and the age structure of the population, have been periodically publicized, due to lack of consensus on some important parameters such as the total fertility rate (TFR).[2] The public and academia therefore do not have updated information about the population developments trends and many conceive that the peak of population growth will be reached in or after 2040 and then the total population in China will as many as 1.6 billion (e.g. Lau 2010b). More specifically, most scholars ignore the fact that the growth of China's working age population has been slowing and thus the demographic foundation of unlimited labor supply has been shrinking, and therefore they are unwilling to accept the assertion of an ongoing Lewis turning point associated with a diminishing demographic dividend.

It is obvious that an undistorted understanding of status and trends of demographic transition will help scholars and policy researchers better understand the state of labor market and will serve as a foundation for policy decisions on how China can sustain its economic growth. The following sections of the paper will argue that the demographic transition and dual economy development have a common starting point, related and similar characteristics during successive development stages. To a large extent, they share overlapping processes. Consequently, the demographic dividend period brought about by the population change is one stage in the dual economy development. Accordingly, the theoretical and empirical work and reasoning about a diminishing demographic dividend and incoming Lewis turning point kill two birds with one stone. The rest of the paper is organized as follows. Section 2 reveals a stylized fact about relationship between demographic transition and dual economy development based on international experiences. Section 3 depicts the China's process of demographic transition and its impact on economic growth. Section 4 tries to answer the question of how the 'aging before affluence' gap can be narrowed. Section 5 concludes by drawing policy implications of the issues discussed in the paper.

2. Stages of demographic transition and development of dual economy

The theory of dual economy coined by Lewis (1958) divides a typical developing economy into two sectors: the agricultural and modern sectors. Because labor force is superfluous relative to capital and land in agriculture, its marginal productivity in the sector is very low, even as low as zero or below. As the modern sector expands surplus labor in agriculture is transferred to modern sector without substantial rise of wages, and the whole process is typically called the development of dual economy. Such a process continues until it reaches a point at which the growth of labor demand succeeds growth of labor supply and further labor transfer requires increase in unskilled workers' wage rate. That point is generally called Lewis turning point. In spite of its ups and downs in economics history (Ranis 2004), Lewis theory of dual economy has remained as a key theoretical model in development economics.

However, the demographic transition theory had been formally established before Lewis's prominent paper.[3] Corresponding to pre- and post-industrialization periods, demographic transition is categorized into three stages, characterized (1) high birth rate, high mortality and low natural growth rate of population, (2) high birth rate, low mortality and high natural growth rate of population, and (3) low birth rate, low mortality and low natural growth rate of population. Although whether Lewis was aware of the literatures on demography is unknown, Lewis did provide assumptions similar to those used in demographics. In the definition of agriculture the important sector in a dual economy, he explains: 'population is vast relative to capital and natural resources, so that . . . marginal product of labor is negligible or even zero', therefore, 'there exists an unlimited supply of labor'. The implicit assumption of this statement is that a typical dual economy characterized by unlimited supply of labor is at the second stage of demographic transition – that is, natural growth rate of population is high as the result of declined mortality and inertial high birth rate. Since agriculture is primary sector in the sectoral chain, it is the place where the abundant population and surplus labor force roost.

The key of understanding the logical and empirical relationship between demographic transition and development of dual economy is to explore how demographic dividend is engendered and obtained. In early literature on demography and economics, the relationship between population and economic development was mostly explored by studying the relationship between the economic growth rate and the population growth rate, while the discussion on demographic transition went no further beyond fertility rate, birth rate, mortality, and population quantity. Besides, mainstream of growth theory, while incorporating population into endogenous growth, usually neglects characteristics of demographic transition of dual economy. After long negligence of economic development and structural characteristics of population, particularly the relation between population age structure and labor supply, as all developed countries and many newly industrialized economies successively completed their demographic transition process, demographers became conscious of population aging and its consequences. Economists further unveil the change in working age population going with fertility decline and its effect on sources of economic growth (Williamson 1997). That is, in the interval between a sooner decline of death rate and later decline of birth rate, natural growth rate of population is usually at its fast rise, youth dependence ratio is also increasing. After a certain period of time, as fertility decreases and the baby boomers grow up, the proportion of working age population enhances accordingly. The further decline in fertility as a result of economic and social developments causes slowdown of natural growth rate of population, and the structural consequence of such a dynamics is population aging. In short, following a reversed U shape pattern – namely, natural growth rate of population first increases and then declines after a turning point, with an interval of about one generation, growth rate of working age population presents a similar pattern of changes.

During the period in which population age structure is most productive, adequate supply of labor and high savings rate afford an extra source of economic growth and thus form demographic dividend. Consequently, once demographic transition exceeds this stage – namely, population age structure becomes less and less productive, because of the rapid aging, such conventionally defined demographic dividend gradually disappears. Since the stages in demographic transition can be sufficiently characterized by changes in TFR, one can theoretically expect the following relation between demographic transition and economic growth (Figure 1): the stage of high TFR coincides with steady state of low growth rate; as TFR falls, a more productive population age structure emerges, and demographic dividend promotes higher economic growth rate; when TFR further drops while and population ages, economic growth rate declines to lower steady state. Correspondingly, the specific stage that TFR declines but and population age structure is dominant by productive workers forms a demographic window of opportunity.

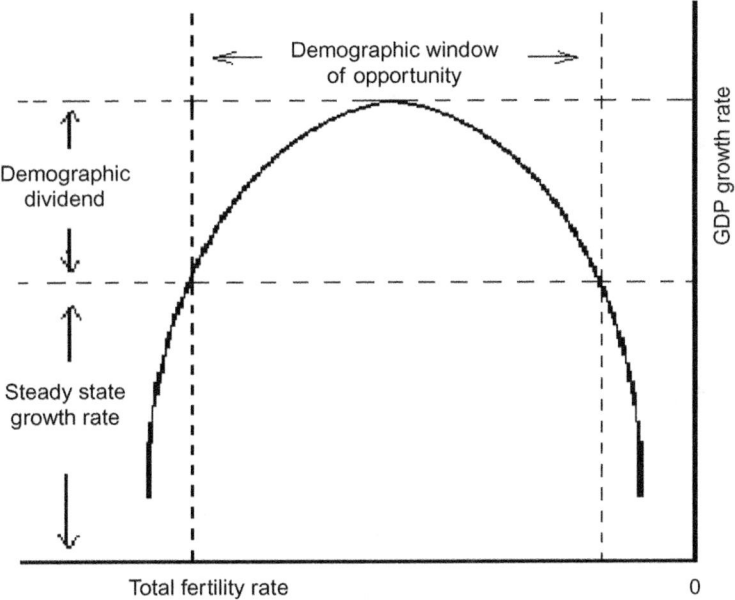

Figure 1. Relationship between fertility and economic growth.

It is worth noting that factors impacting the performance of economic growth are multifold, not just of population. This is also true in explaining both the steady state of growth rate of low-income economies, known for poverty trap, and the steady state of growth rate of high-income economies struggling in technological innovation frontier. For example, in the empirical works of defending neoclassical growth theory, economists have found more than one hundred explanatory variables, which are statistically significant in unveiling determinants of growth performances, but none is sufficient and exclusive (Sala-i-Martin 1997). For simplicity, we also put aside the retroaction effect of economic growth on demographic transition[4] and focus on the straightforward relationship between fertility and economic growth. Under the assumption made above, this fertility-growth nexus can be deduced from the theory of demographic dividend and confirmed empirically.

The panel data from World Development Indicators enable us to provide a descriptive statistics between annual GDP growth rates and TFR levels at the country level since 1960. In this dataset annual GDP growth rates ranged from −51% to 106%. To avoid the complexity in dealing with outliers, we focus on investigating growth rates between 0% and 10%, to better reflect normal range of annual GDP growth rate. Our theoretical model predicts that the relationship between economic growth rate and fertility is not a simple linear one but follows a complex nonlinear relationship. That is, as TFR declines, the economic growth rate increases first and then declines. In Figure 2, according to the function relations between GDP growth rate and TFR and square term of TFR, we present the fitted value of annual growth rate of GDP with 95% confidence interval.

Figure 2 intuitively presents a reversed U shape pattern of GDP growth rate against decline in TFR – countries at the lower stage of demographic transition characterized by high TFR usually suffer poor economic performance; as their TFR levels fall, economic growth speeds up; after a certain point, as TFR further declines and demographic transition enters later stage characterized by very low TFR, economic growth tends to slow down.

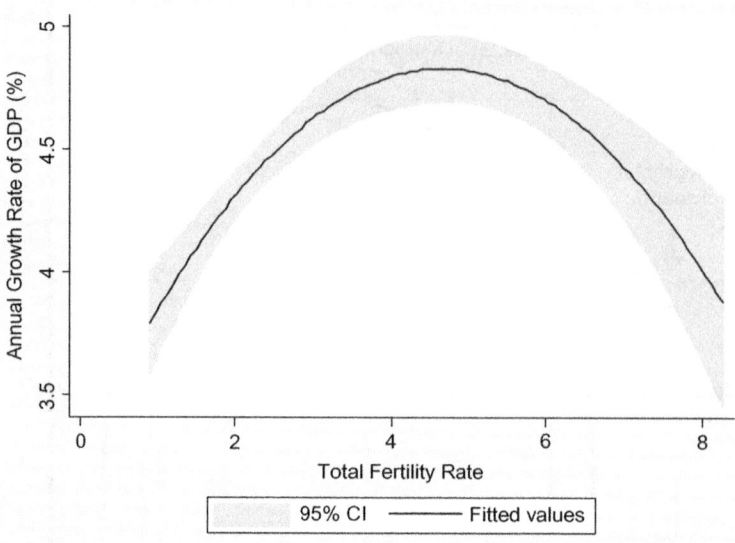

Figure 2.   Empirical relationships between TFR and GDP growth.
Source: Calculation based on dataset of *World Development Indicators.*

Such a simplified empirical curve is consistent with the theoretical prediction described previously.

To further examine the statistical significance of the nonlinear relationship between TFR and economic growth, we regress GDP growth rate on TFR and squared term of TFR (Table 1). The regression results show the reverse U shape relation between GDP growth and TFR by revealing the significantly positive sign of TFR coefficient and negative sign of squared term of TFR. Once we can establish the relationship between fertility rate and economic growth from the perspectives of economic theory as well as international experiences, we can better understand the demographic transition studied in demography, and the relationship between population dividend and the Lewis turning point in economic development. Therefore, we can further analyze the occurrence and disappearances of population dividend in economic development to judge whether the Lewis turning point has arrived.

3.   The economic impacts of Chinese demographic transition

After the founding of the People's Republic of China in 1949, China's demographics transitioned into the second stage accompanied by economic development and improvement in people's living standard. With the exception of the abnormal years between late 1950s and

Table 1.   Regression results: the relation between TFR and growth.

	Coefficient	Standard error	*t* value	P > | *t* |
TFR	0.6852	0.1133	6.05	0.000
TFR square	−0.0736	0.0137	−5.38	0.000
Constant term	3.2359	0.1909	16.95	0.000
Observations		3380		

early 1960s, the second stage of transition manifested itself through significantly declining mortality rate while birth rate remained at a sustained high level. As a result, natural population growth rate was excessively high. Correspondingly, TFR had constantly remained as high as 6(%) until 1970s. However, unlike what many people had imagined, the decline of TFR was NOT the result of the one-child policy. As a matter of fact, the fastest decline of TFR had happened before the one-child policy was strictly implemented. TFR dropped by 3.5 percentage points, from 5.8 to 2.3 in the decade of 1970 to 1980. If we can assume the current TFR to be in the range of 1.6 to 1.8, TFR only declined 0.5 to 0.7 percentage point after 1980. This empirical fact confirms the consensus reached by economists and demographers on demographic transitions. That is, the three major sequential demographic transitions are primarily the result of economic growth and social development. In the period of demographic transition from second to third stage, working age population grows faster than dependent population; hence the proportion of working age population increases gradually. This releases the demographic dividend that upgrades economic growth rate to a level above the steady state.

Although China's population dependence ratio – namely, the ratio of dependent population aged 14 and younger and 65 and older to working age population aged 15 to 64, declined as early as in the middle of 1960s, the substantial increase of working age population and its share in total population, associated by dramatic fall of population dependence ratio, started in the mid 1970s (Figure 3). Such favorable age structure of the population has been translated into demographic dividend that spurred unprecedented performance of economic growth in the Open and Reform period. A series of publications (for example, Cai 2009; Cai and Wang 2005) explain the rationale, process, and empirical tests of the demographic dividend in the development of dual economy of China. In these studies the authors also reach the conclusion of the arrival of the Lewis turning point, and provide empirical tests and proofs of theories. In this paper we discuss demographic transition, demographic dividend, and Lewis turning point in one framework, we intend to explain the logical and historical relations among these three concepts, and to elaborate the challenges China faces in economic development.

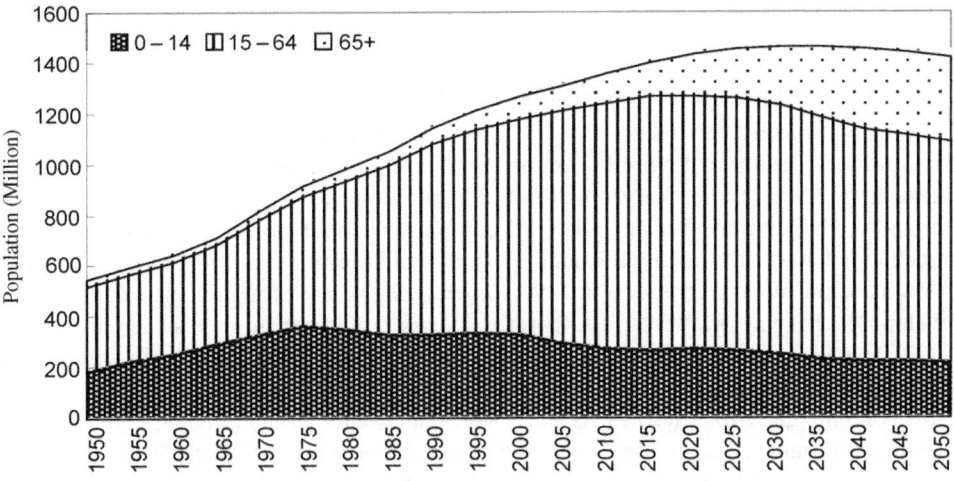

Figure 3.   Changing trends of population age structure.
Source: United Nations, 2009.

The forecast of China's population and its age composition by United Nations, shown in Figure 3, is based on the Fifth Census that was conducted in 2000, the 2005 1% Sample Census, and the official estimates of TFR and other variables. The forecast was the medium estimate and most recently updated in 2008. It is fairly consistent with those made by various Chinese institutions. According to this forecast, China's total population will reach its peak in 2030 and amount to 1.46 billion. Before then, the working age population aged 15 to 64 will reach its peak, 998 million, in 2015. Although these two forecasts on population peak can be obtained from public source at any time, it is obvious that they are unknown not only to the general public but also to a fair number of economists. However, familiarizing oneself with the changing trends of Chinese population is definitely required for scholars who are studying the future of Chinese economic development, especially for those who often voice their opinions and greatly influence the public.

Upon further examining the forecasted results in Figure 3, one can find that the growth rate of working age population was faster than that of total population in the period of 1970 to 2010, and then the trend will reverse – namely, the age structure of Chinese population will no longer evolve to be more productive. From the perspective of labor supply, since urban areas are the centers of development for non-agricultural industries, the employment created by China's fast economic development mostly took place among urban entities, and labor supply in urban areas more and more rely upon rural-to-urban migration.

According to another forecast, which takes into account the impacts of rural-to-urban migration (Hu 2009), by 2015, the amount of incremental working age population in urban areas will be less than that of reduced working age population in rural areas. This implies that without substantial enhancement of incentives that encourage rural-to-urban migration, the migrant workers will not fill up the gap vacated by rapid reduction of urban labor force. Before reaching this point, according to how we calculate urban residents, that is, after taking into account rural-to-urban labor migration, the reduction in rural working age population is approaching the increase in urban working age population year after year (the point where two populations equal to each other is when, China's working age population, in aggregate, stops increasing). The labor market has gradually responded to this situation, which has manifested itself through, on the one hand, nationwide labor shortage and on the other, annual wage increase of migrant workers. By definition, these are the characteristics of Lewis turning point.

4. How to close the 'aging before affluence' gap?

The worldwide experiences show that economic growth and social development are major driving forces behind demographic transition, while population policy plays an external and relatively minor role. Very much like China, countries (or regions) such as Korea, Singapore, Thailand, and Taiwan, where no compulsory population control policy has been implemented, have seen their TFR decline, from a high level similar to China in 1950s to as low as below replacement level in 1990s. Even India, where economic growth and social development have not grown as fast, therefore demographic transition has been lagged relatively behind, has also followed a similar demographic path (Lin 2006). In spite of the unprecedented economic growth in the past 30 years, due to the fact that China set off its high economic growth in the 1980s, much later than the four Asian Tigers, China entered into the new stage of demographic transition at relatively low income per capita, which is characterized as 'aging before affluence'. In 2000, the proportion of ages 65 and over in total China's population was 6.8%, identical to the world average, whereas China's per capita GNI was only 17.3% of the world average based on official exchange rate and 56.3% of the world average based on purchasing power parity. While one must admit that the strict implementation of one-child policy is an accelerator pushing down the fertility, the demographic transition, conclusively, is the result of economic growth and social development. The difference of income level between China and developed countries is therefore the root cause of the 'aging before affluence' gap.

Most developed countries are facing the challenges of population aging to sustainable economic growth and pension insurance scheme, and the efforts in confronting such challenges vary from country to country. However, overall, since developed countries are at a high-income level and technological innovation frontier, they have dealt the aging population crisis so far by sustaining economic growth with elevated productivity. Correspondingly, the key for China to tackle the challenges of shrinking working age population and expanding aging population is to sustain its fast economic growth. In other words, since demographic transition is an irreversible process and cannot be stopped even if one-child policy is modified, aging population trend will continue. The already formed 'aging before affluence' gap can only be narrowed and eventually closed through sustained economic growth.

As the Chinese economy ascends itself in the world's economic pecking order and is expected to surpass Japan and become the second largest economy in 2010, given its low growth rate of population, per capita GDP level of China will rapidly step up. One long-term forecast on China's economic size and per capita GDP conducted by Japanese Center for Economic Research (JCER 2007) predicts that based on PPP and the constant US dollar of 2000, China's aggregate GDP will reach $17.3 trillion in 2020, $25.2 trillion in 2030, and $30.4 trillion in 2040. The projected per capita GDP in the three reference years are $12 thousand, $18 thousand, and $22 thousand, respectively. An even more optimistic forecast by Fogel (2007) expects that China's total GDP will reach $123.7 trillion in 2040, and based on the projected population of 1.46 billion, per capita GDP will be as high as $85 thousand then. It is worth pointing out that these two forecasts are widely different in terms of methodology and data sources. In particular, the calculations involving purchasing power parity are inconsistent with official Chinese entities and scholars. In fact, the gigantic gap between the two forecasts highlighted the limitations of such projections.

Nonetheless, the afore-mentioned forecasts reveal the fact that beginning from the second decade of twenty-first century, as the second largest economy of the world, China will speed up its transformation from a middle-income country to a high-income one. Suppose China can maintain the same pace of or slightly lower than the growth rates of both total and per capita GDP realized in the past 30 years, a significant convergence of wealth level between China and developed countries will be realized. In this regard, the predictions made by these economists reflect a correct direction and futuristic vision. Therefore, under the assumption of unchanged demographic transition, the gap between economic development level and population aging will eventually be closed.

In Figure 4, we compare China's age structure of population with developing countries in year 2000 and 2010 to show the characteristic of 'aging before affluence', whereas we compare China's age structure of population with more developed countries in year 2020 and 2030 to show the pronounced narrowing of 'aging before affluence' gap. This demonstrates that the fundamental solutions in dealing with population aging in the post Lewis turning point eras are threefold: tap the potential of remaining demographic dividend, create new demographic dividend, and find new sources sustaining long-run economic growth.

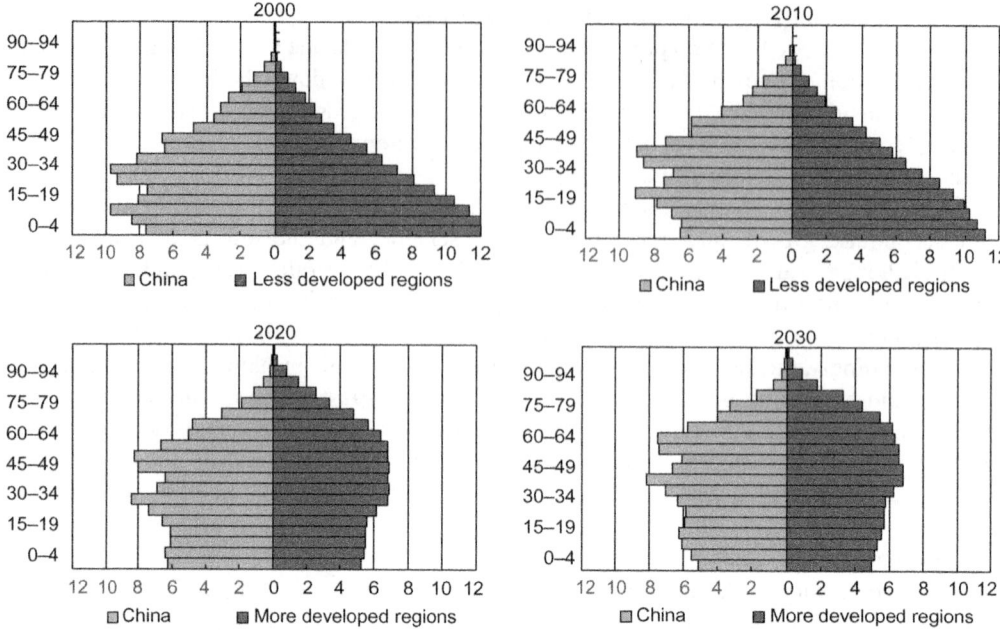

Figure 4.   Narrowing the 'aging before affluence' gap by economic catching up.
Source: United Nations, 2009.

5.   Conclusion and policy implications

The analysis on China's demographic transition and its economic impacts convince us of the close relationship between demographic transition and economic development, and thus the conclusion of diminishing demographic dividend and ongoing Lewis turning point is pursuant with both economic theory and empirical evidence. Even the debates about these conclusions, to some extent, clue to that the arrival of Lewis turning point, discussed in this article, has important policy implications.

The arrival of Lewis turning point is vitally important for a developing economy, because only when it does pass through this point that the marginal productivity of labor in traditional economic sectors begins to converge with that of modern economic sectors. When eventually the productivity gap among sectors disappears, the economy as a whole reaches the point of commercialization and the structural characteristics of dual economy disappear. Therefore, the conclusion of the arrival of Lewis turning point should not raise any concerns. In contrast, being cognizant of this turning point has not only theoretical meaning but also practical significance. That is, in order to find long-lasting sources of growth to sustain and deepen economic development, correctly forecasting the arrival of Lewis turning point and recognizing new challenges and opportunities in this new development stage has important implications in regard to government's economic development policy, decision making among private enterprises, and labor behavior among individuals. In the following we examine the potential sources of China's sustained economic growth in post-Lewis turning point period from the short-term, medium-term and long-term perspective, based on experiences of other economies.

First, there still is potential of the existing demographic dividend to exploit in the short run. Let us first divide demographic dividend into two types: first demographic dividend and second demographic dividend. While the first demographic dividend can be defined as the scenario where labor supply is abundant and savings rate is high, thanks to the increasing magnitude and proportion of working age population, the second demographic dividend can be associated with new motivations of savings and new supply of human resources, resulted from an aging population. Based on this division of demographic dividends, the first dividend has yet to be fully explored. The exploitation of first demographic dividend has been mainly manifested in labor transformation from agricultural to secondary and tertiary sectors. In 2009, migrant workers who lived in cities for 6 months or longer reached more than 150 million, contributing significantly to the urbanization rate, which has reached 46% in the same year, after taking into account these migrant workers. While according to the definition, part of the longer-stayed rural-to-urban migrants are counted as urbanites, since they do not legitimately have urban *hukou* or urban resident status, from the perspectives of a stable source of labor supply, newly created demand for consumption and urban infrastructure, and contributors to the social welfare system, these migrants have not fully made their contributions to the first demographic dividend. In 2007, China's urbanization rate was 45% while the population with urban *hukou* was only 33%, a 12% gap between the nominal and actual urbanization rate. This suggests that further *hukou* reform and equitable provision of public services can exploit the other half of the first demographic dividend on a continuous basis (Cai 2010).

Second, there is vast potential of exploring the second demographic dividend. An aging population structure can also possess advantages, namely second demographic dividend, as long as necessary institutional conditions are met (Cai 2009). As one of the important causes for population aging, the increase of life expectancy, people live longer and healthier, is the foundation to generate the second demographic dividend. This kind of demographic dividend includes three major sources. A first source comes from the demand of old-age supports and supply of pension institutions. As long as there is fully funded pension scheme instead of pay-as-you-go or family support system, the workforce will have larger incentive to accumulate assets for retirement purposes, and then high savings rate can be maintained by investing in capital market and capital appreciation. A second source comes from the expansion of education resources. As the quantity of youth population reduces and its proportion in total population declines, the capacity of working age population supporting school-age population improves, relatively speaking, which is a window of opportunity for extending education and training and hence accumulating human capital. A third source comes from the expansion of labor force participation. Extension of retirement age is a major measure to expand workforce and alleviate the burden of supporting the senior population. In China, the major obstacle of extending retirement age is that the working elderly have relatively less human capital. Before this situation changes, extension of retirement age may put them in a vulnerable situation. Therefore, the key in exploiting such a dividend is to continuously expand education, especially that at the senior high school level, general and vocational education, and on-job-training. As conditions mature, we can then gradually extend the retirement age in order to provide abundant labor supply.

Third, transformation of economic growth model can provide a brand new source for economic growth. Assuming scarcity of labor and thus diminishing return to capital, the neoclassical theory of growth developed based on Western experiences argues that the only way to maintain sustained economic growth is to enhance the contributive share of total factor productivity (TFP) (Solow 1956). Based on this basic assumption, a few economists doubted the existence of East Asian miracle and, if there is, its sustainability (for example, Young 1992; Krugman 1994). In reality, thanks partially to the characteristics of unlimited supply of labor and partially to adequate economic policies favorable for exploiting demographic dividend, the East Asian economies had long averted the crisis of diminishing return of capital. As some major economies passed through their Lewis turning points,[5] at the same time, the newly entered stage of demographic transition rendered their economic growth no longer dependent upon the traditional demographic dividend, those economies transformed their economic growth pattern from capital and labor driven to more TFP driven. Those experiences indicate that as first demographic dividend diminishes and Lewis turning point passes through, driving forces of the Chinese economic growth will be eventually transformed to a reliance on technological advancement and productivity enhancement. The assurance of changed stage of development requires us to speed up the pace of growth pattern transformation.

Notes

1. This existing paper does not intend to discuss the various views caused by different definitions of Lewis turning point. According to Lewis (1972) and Ranis and Fei (1961), Lewis turning point can be referred to as the period of time at which expansion of labor demand exceeds that of labor supply and, as a result, wage rate of ordinary workers starts to rise, while wage of agricultural sector is not yet determined by its marginal productivity of labor and the difference of marginal productivity of labor between agricultural and non-agricultural sectors remains. And the time when the wage rates in agricultural and non-agricultural sectors are both determined by their marginal productivity of labor and the gap in productivities disappears can be called the commercial point. Only at this time, dual economy ends.
2. The 5th National Population Census conducted in 2000 shows that China's TFR was 1.32, which is even lower than policy allowable level of 1.51. Many doubt such a result (e.g. Yu 2002). Since then the debates on what is the actual TFR of China have existed among scholars and policy researchers. Generally speaking, the government departments responsible for implementing the population control policy tend to believe in a higher TFR, whereas scholars believe in a lower TFR. In spite of the disagreement, the estimates mostly fall in the range of 1.6 to 1.8, which are all significantly lower than the replacement level of 2.1.
3. Whereas Thompson (1929) first identified the three stages of demographic transition and another scholar added two more later stages, they were both not considered as the father of the theory of demographic transition, because they did not provide standard theoretical explanation on the decline of fertility. The honor was later awarded to Notestein (1945). Please see Caldwell (1976) for a brief history of this field.
4. In an econometric study, Du (2004) found that population policy, per capita GDP and level of human capital are decisive factors driving down China's fertility and empirically identified the different effects of the three factors.
5. It is commonly believed that the Japanese economy in 1960 and Korean and Taiwan economies reached their Lewis turning point, respectively (for example, Minami 1968; Bai 1982).

References

Bai, Moo-ki. 1982. The turning point in the Korean economy. *Developing Economies* 20, no. 2: 117–140.

Cai, Fang. 2004. The consistency of China's statistics on employment: Stylized facts and implications for public policies. *The Chinese Economy* 37, no. 5 (September–October): 74–89.

Cai, Fang. 2008a. *Lewis turning point: A coming new stage of China's economic development.* Beijing, China: Social Sciences Academic Press.

Cai, Fang. 2008b. Approaching a triumphal span: How far is China towards its Lewisian turning point? UNU-WIDER Research Paper No. 2008/09.

Cai, Fang. 2009. Future demographic dividend – tapping the source of China's economic growth. *China Economist*, no. 21: 17–24.

Cai, Fang. 2010. From farmers-turned workers to migrants-turned residents: Urbanization in next decades, Chinese style. *International Economic Review*, no. 2: 40–53.

Cai, Fang, and Dewen Wang. 2005. China's demographic transition: Implications for growth. In *The China boom and its discontents*, eds. Ross Garnaut and Ligang Song, 34–52. Canberra: Asia Pacific Press.

Cai, Fang, and Meiyan Wang. 2008. A counterfactual analysis on unlimited surplus labor in rural China. *China & World Economy* 16, no. 1: 51–65.

Caldwell, John C. 1976. Toward a restatement of demographic transition theory. *Population and Development Review* 2: 321–366.

Du, Yang. 2005. The formation of low fertility and its impacts on long term economic growth in China. *The World Economy*, no. 12: 14–23.

Fogel, Robert W. 2007. Capitalism and democracy in 2040: Forecasts and speculations. NBER Working Paper, No. 13184.

Hu, Ying. 2009. Predictions on working age population of rural and urban China, unpublished memo.

Japan Center for Economic Research (JCER). 2007. *Demographic change and the Asian economy*. Tokyo: Long-term Forecast Team of Economic Research Department, Japan Center for Economic Research.

Krugman, Paul. 1994. The myth of Asia's miracle. *Foreign Affairs*. 73, no. 6: 62–78.

Lau, Laurence. 2010a. Expansion of domestic demand is fourfold. *China News Website*, January 21, http://www.chinanews.com.cn/cj/cj-ylgd/news/2010/01-18/2077952.shtml.

Lau, Lawrence J. 2010b. The Chinese economy: The next thirty years, presented at The Institute of Quantitative and Technical Economics, Chinese Academy of Social Sciences, Beijing, January 16.

Lewis, Arthur. 1958. Unlimited labour: Further notes. *Manchester School of Economics and Social Studies* XXVI (January): 1–32.

Lewis, Arthur. 1972. Reflections on unlimited labour. In *International economics and development*, ed. L. Di Marco, 75–96. New York: Academic Press.

Lin, Justin Yifu. 2006. Development strategy, population and population policies. In *China's population and economic development in 21st century*, eds. Yi Zeng, Li Ling, Gu Baochang, and Lin Yifu, 3–9. Beijing, China: Social Sciences Academic Press.

Minami, Ryoshin. 1968. The turning point in the Japanese economy. *The Quarterly Journal of Economics* 82, no. 3: 380–402.

Minami, Ryoshi, and Xinxin Ma. 2009. The turning point of Chinese economy: Compared with Japanese experience. *Asian Economics* 50, no. 12: 2–20 (in Japanese).

Notestein, Frank W. 1945. Population – the long view. In *Food for the world*, ed. Theodore W. Schultz. Chicago: University of Chicago Press.

Ranis, Gustav. 2004. Arthur Lewis' contribution to development thinking and policy. Yale University Economic Growth Center Discussion Paper No. 891(August).

Ranis, Gustav, and John C.H. Fei. 1961. A theory of economic development. *The American Economic Review* 51, no. 4: 533–565.

Ravallion, Martin, and Shaohua Chen. 1999. When economic reform is faster than statistical reform: Measuring and explaining income inequality in rural China. *Oxford Bulletin of Economics and Statistics* 61, no.1: 33–56.

Rawski, Thomas G. 2001. What's happening to China's GDP statistics? *China Economic Review* 12, no. 4: 298–302.

Ru, Xin, Xueyi Lu, and Peilin Li. 2008. *Analysis and prospects on China's social situation, 2009*. Beijing, China: Social Sciences Academic Press.

Sala-i-Martin, and Xavier X. 1997. I just ran two million regressions. *American Economic Review* 87, no. 2, Papers and Proceedings of the Hundred and Fourth Annual Meeting of the American Economic Association, pp.178–183.

Solinger, Dorothy J. 2001. Why we cannot count the unemployed? *The China Quarterly*, no. 167 (August), 671–688.

Solow, Robert M. 1956. A contribution to the theory of economic growth. *Quarterly Journal of Economics* 70, no. 1: 65–94.

Thompson, Warren S. 1929. Population. *American Journal of Sociology* 34, no. 6: 959–975.

United Nations. 2009. *The world population prospects: The 2008 revision*. http://esa.un.org/unpp/.

Williamson, Jeffrey. 1997. Growth, distribution and demography: Some lessons from history. NBER Working Paper, No. 6244.

Young, Alwyn. 1994. The tyranny of Numbers: Confronting the statistical realities of the East Asian growth experience, NBER Working Paper No. 4680 (March).

Yu, Xuejun. 2002. Estimation on magnitude and structure of 5th National Population Census. *Population Research* 26, no. 3: 9–14.

Discussions on potential bias and implications of Lewis turning point

Yang Du and Wang Meiyan

Institute of Population and Labor Economics, Chinese Academy of Social Sciences, Beijing, China
(Final version received 31 July 2010)

Thanks to the fast economic growth and quick demographic transition, long-term factors have dominated the Chinese labor market. Therefore, with a short-lived shock in employment due to the global financial crisis, the labor shortage reappeared in the spring of 2010. Taking advantage of the recent aggregated data, this paper predicts the potentials of employment demand in the coming years. Also, the impact of demographic transition is discussed. In addition to quantity shortage, the rising wages for migrant workers characterize the labor market in recent years. Using the national representative data, this paper discusses the trend of labor cost changes when the Chinese economy approaches the Lewis turning point. The implications of large-scale migration to inequality are explored by using 1% population sampling data. This paper also tries to clarify some misunderstandings incurred by misuses of data.

Although labor shortage has been frequently reported in China in the past few years, there still exists disagreement on whether China has achieved the *Lewis Turning Point* (LTP). In fact, as a theoretical model describing general trend of economic development, it is hard to apply LTP into the Chinese economy at the specific time point. Therefore, the debates on precise timing are less policy impressive than discussions on how to improve policies in the era of post-LTP.

There are two purposes for this paper. One of them is to shed light on how to better understand the Chinese labor market by discussing the difference of various sources of data. The other tries to explore the possible implications of LTP to labor costs and inequality in China.

1. Understanding the resurgent labor shortage

After a brief break caused by the global financial crisis, the Chinese labor market has returned to its normal path since the spring of 2009. According to the rural household survey conducted by NBS, total migrant workers in the first three quarters of 2009 were 147 million, 151 million, and 152 million, respectively. With increasing migration flow, labor shortage has been more and more serious. In addition to discussions on current data, this paper explains the phenomenon of labor shortage through a simple supply-demand analysis.

Data discussions

Most studies evaluate the employment situations based on the data from China Statistics Yearbook. However, the employment data released from these Yearbooks have been from three main sources. Since the quality of data from different sources varies, we must be careful in judging the labor market situation by choosing relatively reliable information.

The first one is from the reporting system. In this case, each level of NBS sums up the reported data from its subordinate agencies and then report to the higher authorities. At a first glance, this system strictly covers all employment units and should produce reliable aggregated data. However, this system is notorious as it lacks monitoring and quality control, and it is hard to appraise how reliable the data are. The annual employment by sector is from this system.

The second source is census, including population census in every 10 years, minicensus in every 5 years, and two economic censuses in 2004 and 2008. Compared to the reported data, more resources have been used on census data and the quality is improved in terms of quality control.

The third one is from sampling surveys. Some aggregated data are estimated based on those national representative surveys. For instance, the number of total migrants is based on the rural household survey and the total urban employment is estimated from the labor market survey. The sampling survey provides most reliable information on the Chinese labor market.

Labor market demand

Although a simple supply-demand analysis is helpful to recognize the labor market situation in China, it is still important to choose reasonable data sources. According to the above discussions, the judgment based on reported data that China has more than 300 million labor forces working in primary sector is misleading.

We first look at the demand-side effect. Thanks to the steady and rapid economic growth in the past decades. Chinese economy has ranked at a very top level globally, which provides a large amount of employment demand in total. The growing body of economy implies that one percentage point of economic growth provides more jobs than before.

The relations between employment and economic development are determined by many factors, including industrial structure, wage, benefits level, labor market institutions, and so forth. However, in the short run, those are relatively stable, which allow us to predict employment demand based on the employment elasticity with respect to GDP in the previous years.

Nevertheless, as discussed above, the accuracy of aggregated data is a constraint when doing the prediction through employment elasticity. In particular, the data of employment by sector that are collected through reporting system are reluctant to reflect the actual changes in the Chinese labor market while the prediction based on employment elasticity is sensitive to the changes.

The two rounds of Economic Census in 2004 and 2008 give more reliable information on the aggregated employment. The Economic Census investigated the employment for all legal units and individual employment in both secondary and tertiary sectors. According to the Economic Census in 2004, employment in secondary sector for all the units and registered individual employment was 139.01 million, and 130.20 million for the tertiary sector. In 2008, the employment in secondary and tertiary was 173.39 million and 181.68 million, respectively. Hence, the average rate of employment growth per annum from 2004 to 2008 is 5.68% for the secondary sector and 8.69% for the tertiary sector, and annual growth rates for value added in the two sectors are 12.15% and 11.46%, respectively. The employment elasticity based on the above growth rate is 0.468 for the secondary sector and 0.758 for the tertiary sector.

Assuming that the employment elasticities are kept stable in the coming few years, we may predict the employment growth in various scenarios of growth by sector. This assumption implies a small fluctuation of employment per unit GDP. Although this assumption is not reasonable in the long run because of the technical progress, it is reasonable in the short run.

Table 1 presents the predictions of demand for labor in various scenarios. If the above assumptions are plausible, in 2010 the net increase of employment demand in secondary and tertiary sector will be 18.42 million when both the sectors grow at 8%. The growth of total off-farm employment will be 25.8 million if the two sectors grow at 11%. If 8% and 11% are taken as the lower and upper bound of growth, the newly increased labor demand could be various combinations of the following tables.

It is worth noting here that even 11% of growth in off-farm sectors is not an over-optimistic scenario. For instance, the average annual growth rate for secondary sector in the past three decades is 11.5% with standard deviation of 4.5%, for tertiary sector the average growth per annum is 10.9% with standard deviation 3.4%. If one looks at the economic performance in the past two decades, the average growth rate for the tertiary sector is 12% with standard deviation of 4.3%. In the most recent decade, the tertiary average annual growth rate is 11% (standard deviation of 2%) for 10.5% the secondary sector (standard deviation of 1.4%). In other words, economic growth in China has converged rather than diverged. According to the historical data, 11% annual growth for secondary sector or 10% for tertiary sector is by and large possible. If this scenario comes true, the

Table 1.   Aggregate demand for labor in various scenarios of economic growth.

	Secondary		Tertiary	
	Employment growth	Total employment	Employment growth	Total employment
Annual growth rate at 8%				
Annual employment growth rate	3.74%		6.06%	
2009	649	17,988	1102	19,270
2010	673	18,661	1169	20,438
2011	699	19,360	1239	21,678
Annual growth rate at 9%				
Annual employment growth rate	4.21%		6.82%	
2009	730	18,069	1239	19,408
2010	761	18,830	1324	20,732
2011	793	19,623	1414	22,146
Annual growth rate at 10%				
Annual employment growth rate	4.68%		7.58%	
2009	811	18,150	1377	19,545
2010	849	19,000	1482	21,027
2011	889	19,889	1594	22,621
Annual growth rate at 11%				
Annual employment growth rate	5.15%		8.34%	
2009	893	18,231	1515	19,683
2010	939	19,170	1641	21,324
2011	987	20,157	1778	23,102

Source: National Bureau of Statistics (2009), *the Bulletin of the Second Economic Census, the Statistical Bulletin of Economic and Social Development in 2009, and China Statistical Yearbook in 2009.*

newly increased employment demand in off-farm sectors will reach 24.21 million, which is enough to strengthen the current labor shortage. In turn, the price adjustment in the labor market is inevitable.

Supply-side effects

In fact, the labor supply is also determined by multifactors, including size and structure of labor forces, wage rates, participation rates, and unemployment rates. Therefore, when the labor shortage appears, the price for labor goes up and the quantity adjustment in the labor market keeps going. With increasing wages, those who quit from the labor market previously will participate because the market wage rate might be higher than their reservation wages. The increased participation will result in more labor supply. Meanwhile, with increasing job vacancies, the unemployment declines, which means that the current unemployed persons could be the source of labor supply in the future.

Compared to the dynamics in the labor market, the demographic variables are more stable and insensitive to price changes. According to the population census and population sampling survey, we may estimate the number of newly increased population at labor age in the coming years. As presented in Figure 1, thanks to the rapid demographic transition, the increased number of labor-aged population is declining dramatically. During the period of '11th Five Years Plan', the average increased population at labor age is 7.41 million while the number will decline to 3.12 million in '12th Five Years Plan'. Combining with the above marginal analysis on labor demand, it is not hard to understand why the labor shortage has been more and more serious. It is also good to believe that this trend will exist in the long run, with the development of the Chinese economy.

In addition, the low participation of young labor force reinforces the above demographic effect on labor supply. With dramatic expansion of higher education in the past decade, the extension of years in schooling lowers the participation rate for those who were supposed to be in the labor market between the age of 16 and 22 years. Figure 2 clearly depicts this trend. The participation rate by age presents a typical U-shaped curve. Labor force participation rate for person aged 16 was 20% in 2005 and average participation rate for labor between age of 16 and 22 years was 55%. Considering that the higher education

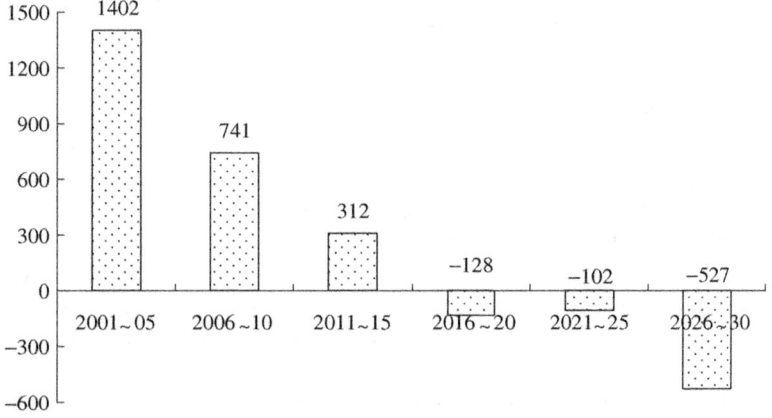

Figure 1.   Annual increased population at labor age: 2001–2030.
Source: Hu, Cai, and Du (2010).

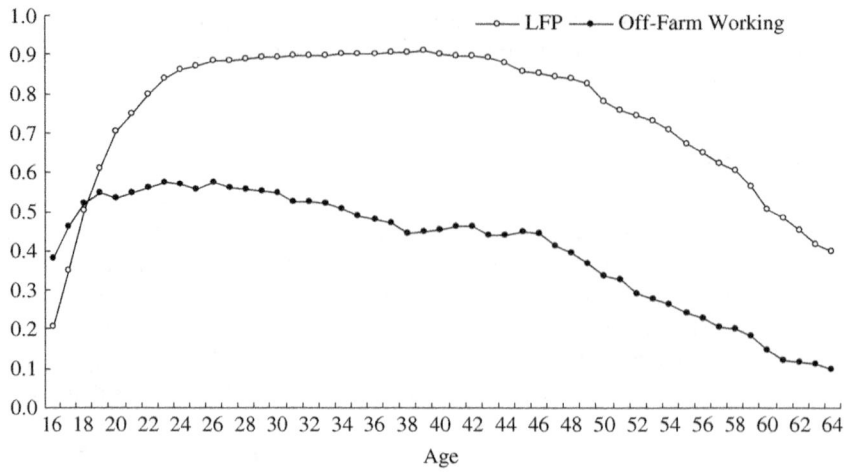

Figure 2.   Labor force participation and share of off-farm working by age.
Source: Author's calculation based on 1% population sampling survey in 2005.

has been going on expansion since 2005, current participation rate for young labor could be lower.

The other factor exacerbating labor supply is that old labor forces have a low probability of being engaged in off-farm activities. As Figure 2 displays, the off-farm working share is stable between the age of 20 and 30 years and starts declining since the age of 40 years, and the probability engaged in off-farm activities drop sharply for cohort aged above 45 years.

The increasing labor costs after LTP

China had witnessed a long period with unlimited labor supply. Due to the large size of rural surplus labor, the wage rate for unskilled workers had been stagnant for a long time although the migration flow had been increasing. With the appearance of labor shortage, the price adjustment in the Chinese labor market has followed up and the rising wages for unskilled workers have been the main drivers to push up labor cost.

Growing wages for unskilled workers

Although wage rates for migrant workers vary across different data sources, they indicate the same growing trend. Three large surveys provide empirical evidences. First evidence is from the rural household survey conducted by NBS nation wide. The sample includes 68,000 rural households, distributed in 7100 villages, 857 counties, and 31 provinces. Given its national representative, the sample could serve to estimate the overall migration and average wage. The second source is the fixed household survey conducted by the Research Center of Rural Economy. The sample covers 22,000 rural households in 31 provinces. The other more recent survey is conducted by People's Bank of China, which includes 4,400 rural households in nine provinces. Although its sample is hard to represent the whole rural China, it is fine to observe the wage trend through this survey given its consistency in terms of survey operation. All three surveys investigate rural households through survey forms.

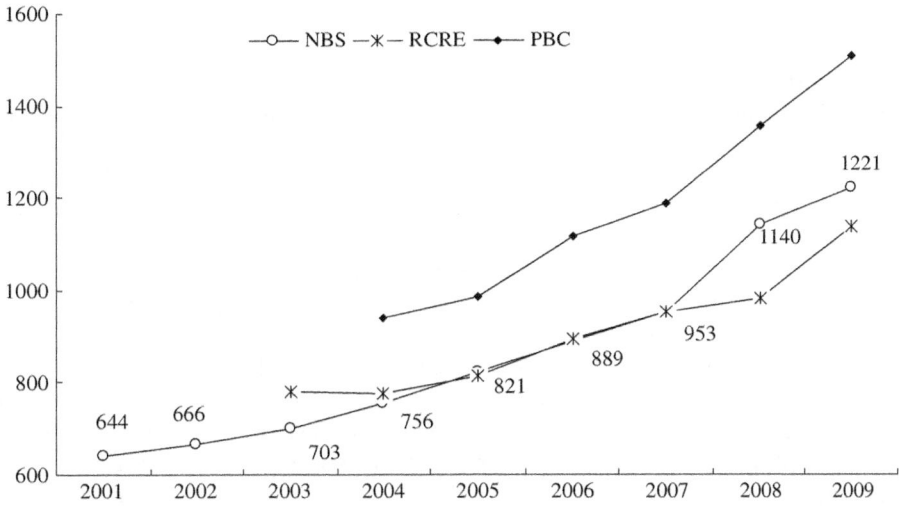

Figure 3.   Real wages for migrant workers.

Note: NBS refers to wage for migrant workers from the survey by National Bureau of Statistics; RCRE refers to wage for migrant workers from the survey by Research Center for Rural Economy; PBC refers to wage for migrant workers from the survey by People's Bank of China.
Source: Wage for migrant workers of NBS and RCRE is updated from Du (2008); wage for migrant workers of PBC is from the Department of Survey and Statistics, People's Bank of China (2010).

Both NBS and RCRE surveys have enough samples to estimate national averages. However, the RCRE survey does not rotate its samples, which might not be able to capture the demographic changes in rural China. Sample rotation is done by NBS survey. One limitation is common to all the three surveys, that is, all of them are conducted in rural areas and investigate migrants' information through their left behind family members. This indirect information, particularly on migrant wages, might cause inaccuracy that underestimates their actual earnings.

Figure 3 reflects the real wage in 2001 price in recent years, adjusted by urban CPI. All the three curves in the picture indicate an increasing trend of migrant wages in the past few years. Even in 2008, when labor-intensive sectors were seriously affected by the global financial crisis, the real monthly wage for migrant workers grew nearly 20%. In 2009, average monthly income for migrant workers reached 1221 yuan in 2001 price, 1.9 times of that in 2001. Considering that migrant workers consist of most of the employees in labor-intensive sector, their rising wages will push up labor costs accordingly.

Unit labor costs

Unit labor cost is measured by hourly labor compensation for workers. To calculate the unit labor cost, one has to have the information on working hours, wages, and other benefits to workers.

In the Chinese labor market, working hour is an important indicator for employer to respond to the labor demand change. When the impact of financial crisis was serious, firms tended to reduce working hours, however, even then they did not fire workers. In 2003, workers in the manufacturing sector worked 46.4 hours per week, and 47.9 hours in 2008. Although there are limits to extend working hours, in order to save hiring costs and other benefit expenditures, the employers are more inclined to adjust working hours when facing a labor shortage.

Labor costs that were measured in hourly terms were reduced when extending the working hours. For example, the average monthly income in the manufacturing sector weighted by manufacturing employment in both work units and migrants was 882 yuan in 2003 and 1612 in 2008, an increase of 34.2%. When measured by hourly wages, it increased from 4.44 yuan per hour in 2003 to 7.85 yuan per hour in 2008, that is, an increase of 76.9% (Table 2).

Although wage is the main component of labor compensation, labor costs include more than wages. In addition to wage, other expenditures related to hiring should be included in labor costs, including bonus, subsidy to food, housing, transportation, and the like, free health care, social insurance, etc. Unfortunately, there is no direct information for us to calculate the labor costs. According to Banister (2006), wage accounted for 78.7% of labor cost in manufacturing. If this coefficient is true, we may estimate the labor costs in manufacturing as displayed in Figure 4. Several factors contribute to the rising hourly labor compensation measured by US dollar, including the growth of wages for unskilled workers, appreciation of RMB, and increasing coverage of social insurance that is not even measured explicitly.

Regarding the labor costs, a wide concern is whether China will keep its advantageous position in labor-intensive sectors. Also, has China been on the track with increasing labor costs when the economy passed through the *Lewis Turning Point*? It is hard to predict the trend in the coming decades, but the economic history of other economies that have witnessed a transition from LTP may provide us with a useful insight. Industrial upgrading induced by increasing labor costs has been observed in developed countries, like Japan, and NIEs, like Hong Kong, Korea, Singapore, and Taiwan. As evidenced by Figure 5, the timing of increasing labor costs coincides with shifting their labor-intensive industries to mainland China. It is good to believe that rapid increasing wages for unskilled workers symbolize the beginning of industrial upgradation in the coming decades.

Table 2. Hourly wages in manufacturing.

	2003	2004	2005	2006	2007	2008
Weekly working hours	46.4	46.9	51.1	50.4	49.40	47.9
Average wage						
Urban unit	1055	1188	1313	1519	1740	2034
Migrant workers	702	780	861	946	1060	1339
	882.3	967.5	1052.3	1183.9	1333.6	1611.5
Employment						
Migrant employment	11390	11823	12578	13212	13697	14041
in manufacturing	0.252	0.303	0.348	0.357	0.376	0.379
Migrant employment	2870.3	3582.4	4377.1	4716.7	5150.1	5321.5
Manufacturing employment in urban unit	2980.5	3050.8	3210.9	3351.6	3465.4	3434.3
Exchange rate	827.70	827.68	819.17	797.18	760.40	694.51
Weighted hourly wages in nominal term (USD)						
	0.54	0.58	0.59	0.69	0.83	1.13

Source: Updated from Du (2008).

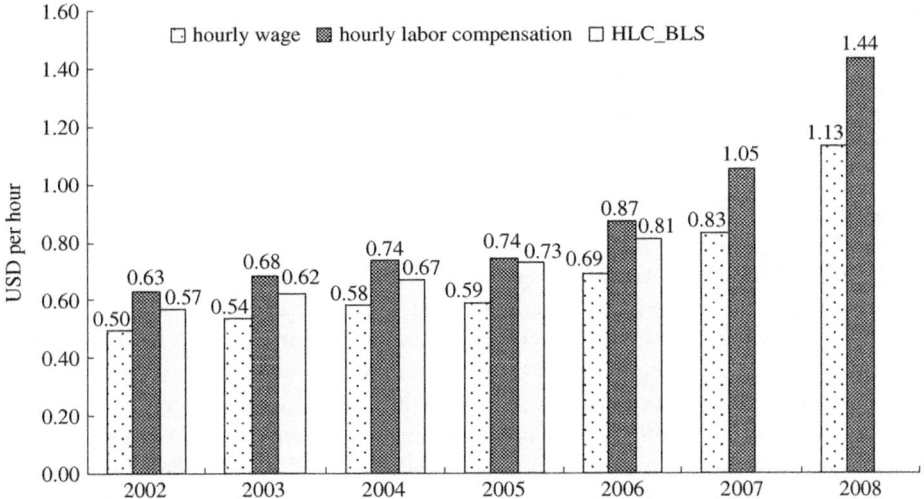

Figure 4.   Labor costs in manufacturing.

Note: HLC_BLS is hourly labor compensation from the Bureau of Labor Statistics (2010), www.bls.gov.

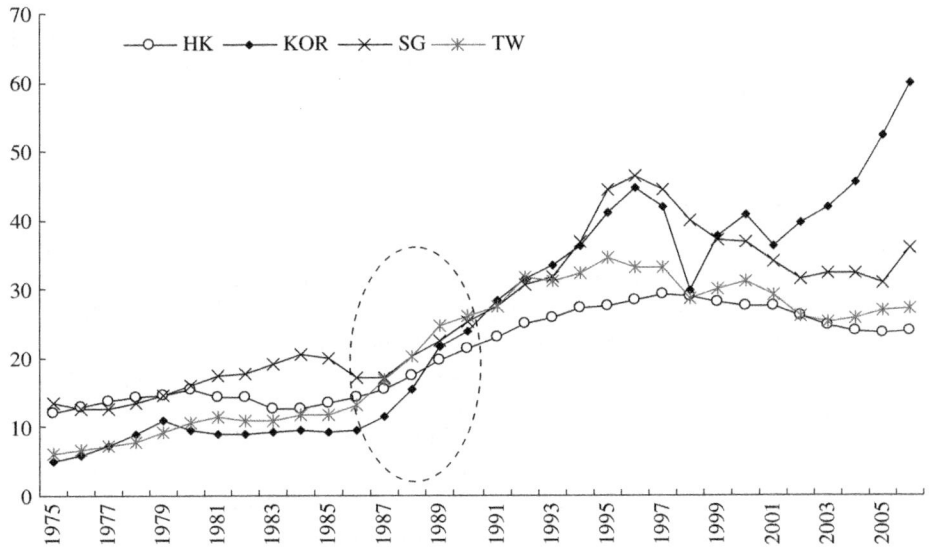

Figure 5.   NIEs' unit labor costs relative to the United States (US = 100).

Source: US Department of Labor, Bureau of Labor Statistics, March 2009.

3.   The implications of labor mobility to income inequality

Unskilled workers' wage growth is helpful to equalize the income distribution. Increasing migration implies that more and more people who previously worked in low-productivity sector get higher incomes. However, limited by segmented statistical system between rural and urban areas, current statistics hardly reflect the impacts of migration on income, which brings about bias to estimate the inequality.

Potential bias of current estimations

Rural-urban differences in China have persistently contributed to a large share of income inequality. According to the World Bank (2009), rural-urban differences accounted for 40% of the total income inequality in 2003, a percentage similar to that in 1995. Sicular et al. (2007) find that rural-urban differences explain one-fourth of the overall inequality in 2002.

As pointed out by Park (2008), current measurements of inequality are subject to a number of sources bias, including sampling bias, exclusion of some categories of income, classification of rural and urban areas, and differences in the cost of living.

Some previous studies have already noticed that the rural-urban migration created sources of bias when measuring the income inequality. Until 2002, NBS urban sample excluded migrants living in urban areas. After they were included, they represented less than 2% of the sample (Park 2008), even though the 2005 1% population sampling survey found that 22% of the population living in cities were migrants. Using rural data from 19 provinces and urban data from 11 provinces, Sicular et al. (2007) find including migrants in calculating urban per capita income reduces the urban-rural income ratio from 2.27:1 to 2.12:1. Ravallion and Chen (2007) also realized that rural-urban migration could be a source of migration although their measurement was based on UHS and RHS.

Some surveys, for instance, CULS1, CULS2, and CHIP,[1] include migrants into the samples, which makes it possible to observe the overall inequality in urban areas. However, they were only conducted in a few cities and therefore lack national representation. More importantly, the rural-urban inequality cannot be reflected in those surveys. The 1% population sampling survey is the only national representative data with information on income (even if there is only one question on it). By exploring these data, it is possible to see the bias of not including migrants well.

Inequality and its composition

For the purpose of pointing out the bias, the population is categorized as rural residents, rural-urban migrants, and urban residents with *hukou*. The key issue here is to observe the impacts of rural-urban migration on urban inequality, rural-urban inequality, and overall inequality. Based on the calculation including migrants, this study is going to point out the direction of bias when migrants are ignored. Considering that 1% of the population sampling survey in 2005 only asked the labor income, the discussion here is focused on those who are aged 16 years and above and are working (rather than to the whole population).

It should be noted that this restriction makes comparisons with the other measures of inequality difficult. The most obvious one is that income inequality is typically measured by household income per capita. Unfortunately, there is no identification code by household for migrants in this 2005 census data, so it is impossible to combine the information of migrants together with their family members. To some extent, this leads to an over-estimation of inequality, in particular, the rural-urban inequality, because this grouping strategy puts more able individuals (migrants) together and the left-behind family members together. Following Brandt and Holz (2007), incomes are deflated spatially for both rural and urban areas. It is worth noting here that those whose incomes are reported zeros are not included when calculating the inequality indices.

The first observation shows the impacts of rural-urban migration on urban inequality. According to the previous studies (Du, Cai, and Wang 2006), due to low social protection, migrants tend to work more intensively in urban areas than their urban local counterparts. Therefore, migrant workers have similar level of earnings on average to local workers

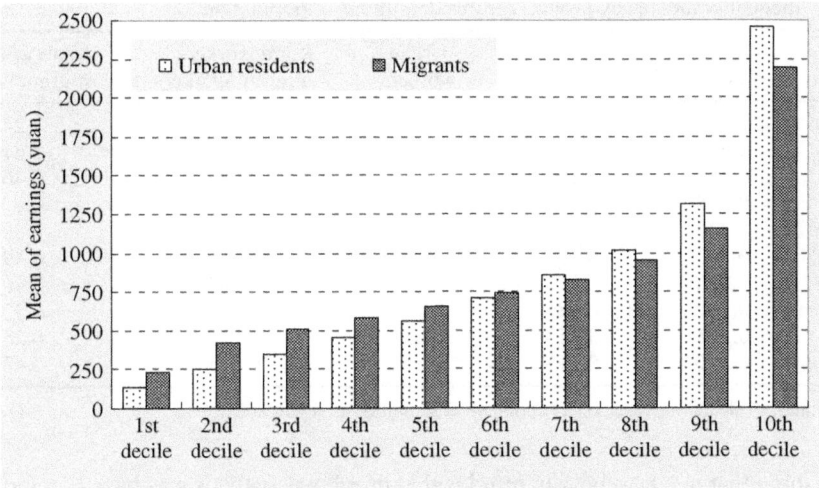

Figure 6.   The mean of earnings by deciles for local and migrant workers.

Source: Author's calculation based on 1% population sampling survey in 2005.

although their hourly wage rates are much lower. In addition, the observation on migrant workers' wage is strongly selective, which means that migrants would return to hometown once they cannot make enough earnings in the urban labor markets.

The 1% population sampling survey supports the same argument. Figure 6 presents the mean of earnings by deciles for both local workers and migrant workers. For low- and middle-income groups, migrant workers have higher earnings than locals, while they earn lower incomes in high-income groups. On average, the monthly income is 811 yuan for local workers and 828 yuan for migrant workers. The two medians are 624 yuan and 718 yuan, respectively.

Table 3 displays the inequality indices by group. The first column represents workers in the rural areas, the second migrant workers, and the third urban local workers. Column 5 is relevant to the current definition of urban population, but most existing studies were based on the third column. Two findings are interesting here. First of all, the migrants' earnings exhibit more even distribution than local workers. For instance, the Gini coefficients for urban local workers and migrant workers are 0.424 and 0.31, respectively. Second, taking account of migrants into urban residents decreases the inequality in urban areas, which reduces the Gini from 0.424 to 0.405, and more significantly, GE(-1) from 0.523 to 0.461.

It is possible that the rural-urban migration increases the inequality in rural areas if rural migrants are still counted as rural population. Based on the 1% population sampling survey, the average monthly earnings for people working in agriculture in rural areas is only 271 yuan and the local off-farm workers can make 739 yuan monthly earnings (the medians being 227 yuan and 636 yuan, respectively). Hence, the income difference between farm work and off-farm work accounted for most inequality within the rural areas. Table 3 also presents the inequality indices in rural areas based on various definitions of rural population, see column 1 and column 4. In fact, the earnings difference among rural residents is quite substantial, mostly contributed by the difference between farm work and off-farm work. Also, taking migrants as rural people increases the Gini coefficient from 0.426 to 0.444.

Table 3.   Inequality indices by group: Various definitions of population.

	Rural workers	Migrant workers	Urban workers	Rural workers + migrant workers	Urban workers + migrant workers
P90/P10	7.678	3.656	7.912	8.623	7.247
P75/P25	2.695	1.777	2.824	3.088	2.618
GE(−1)	0.455	0.193	0.523	0.523	0.461
GE(0)	0.318	0.166	0.329	0.350	0.299
GE(1)	0.330	0.197	0.324	0.357	0.302
GE(2)	0.582	0.405	0.516	0.655	0.497
Gini	0.426	0.310	0.424	0.444	0.405
A(0.5)	0.149	0.085	0.149	0.161	0.138
A(1)	0.273	0.153	0.281	0.295	0.259
A(2)	0.477	0.278	0.511	0.511	0.480

Source: Author's calculation based on 1% population sampling survey in 2005.

One thing that needs to bear in mind is that the above analysis was based on individual information. Typically, rural households allocate their labor forces into farm work and off-farm work in order to maximize household incomes, so more productive household members tend to migrate and work in urban areas. For such a reason, one may infer that per capita household income should be more equal than individual income measures.

The next question is what is the impact of rural-to-urban migration on the overall inequality? According to Table 4, migrant workers are the most homogenous group in terms of labor income, with Gini coefficient of 0.310. The income difference within urban and rural areas is at the similar level when measured by Gini, as evidenced by column 1 and column 3 in Table 2. Most existing studies missed migrant workers when calculating the overall income inequality, which would produce an upward bias for inequality measurement. In this case, when migrants are included, the overall inequality reduces from 0.484 to 0.474 for Gini, and from 0.425 to 0.407 for Theil entropy index (see Table 4).

The final question is to what extent the rural-urban inequality explains the overall inequality? As noted above, most existing studies find that rural-urban differences explain the most part of inequality in China. Table 5 displays different calculations. The first column is a definition neglecting migration, which is the case of current sampling strategy based on *hukou* locality. In this case, the rural-urban inequality accounted for 13.8% of overall inequality in 2005 when looking at GE(2). This proportion is lower than most studies that are subject to data limitations pointed out by Park (2008).

Table 4.   Overall inequalities: Biased and unbiased.

	Rural workers + urban workers	Rural workers + urban workers + migrant workers
P90/P10	10.642	10.145
P75/P25	3.604	3.694
GE(−1)	0.668	0.657
GE(0)	0.422	0.408
GE(1)	0.425	0.407
GE(2)	0.740	0.705
Gini	0.484	0.474
A(0.5)	0.190	0.183
A(1)	0.344	0.335
A(2)	0.572	0.568

Source: Author's calculation based on 1% population sampling survey in 2005.

Table 5. Decompositions of overall inequalities.

	Urban workers + rural workers			Urban workers + (Rural workers + migrant workers)			Rural workers + (Urban workers + migrant workers)	
	Overall	Within	Between	Overall	Within	Between	Within	Between
GE(−1)	0.668	0.566	0.102	0.657	0.592	0.065	0.552	0.105
%	100	**84.73**	**15.27**	100	**90.11**	**9.89**	**84.02**	**15.98**
GE(0)	0.422	0.323	0.099	0.408	0.343	0.066	0.310	0.098
%	100	**76.54**	**23.46**	100	**84.07**	**16.18**	**75.98**	**24.02**
GE(1)	0.425	0.326	0.099	0.407	0.339	0.067	0.311	0.095
%	100	**76.71**	**23.29**	100	**83.29**	**16.46**	**76.41**	**23.34**
GE(2)	0.740	0.638	0.102	0.705	0.635	0.071	0.610	0.096
%	100	**86.22**	**13.78**	100	**90.07**	**10.07**	**86.52**	**13.62**

Source: Author's calculation based on 1% population sampling survey in 2005.

The last two groupings include migrants but in different categories: one includes migrants into rural sample, and the other into urban sample. Including migrants into the analysis, the inequality index is slightly reduced, which is evidenced by a smaller GE(2) in the last two groupings compared to the first. Both categorizations are of relevance. The second grouping is based on *hukou* definition, which reflects the institutional differences between urban and rural residents. In this case, the rural-urban inequality explains about 10% of overall inequality. The final grouping is based on the definition of residence, which has been used by NBS to define urban population since 2000. According to such definition, the proportion of rural-urban inequality is slightly lower than the case in the first grouping and explains 13.6% of overall inequality.

Institutional changes after LTP and implications to inequality

With coming LTP, labor market institutions tend to be more regulated than that in the era of unlimited labor supply. It is also of importance to evaluate their impacts on inequality. Although it is not an easy thing to measure institutional changes in the Chinese labor market, we can still look at them regionally since there are some variations of those institutions across regions.

The following model is applied to analyze the impacts of some labor market institutions on wage inequality. The left-hand side is wage inequality index of city, and the explanatory variables include labor market institutional variables, minimum wage in city, proportion of workers with contract, and proportion of workers with social insurance, and some structural variables that may affect wage inequality, such as proportion of migrants, the ratio of employment in secondary to tertiary sector. Provincial dummies are added to control some unobservable regional factors. Descriptive statistics of the variables are listed in Table 6.

$$ineq_i = \alpha_0 + \alpha_1 MW_i + \alpha_2 CNT_i + \alpha_3 SI_i + \beta_1 EDU_i + \beta_2 SCT_i + \beta_3 MIG_i + PROV + \varepsilon_i$$

Regression results are presented in Table 7. Two categories of institutional variables are concerned here, minimum wage and contracting enforcement. Saint-Paul (1994) argues that minimum wage may have an adverse effect on the income distribution because it redistributes income from skilled to unskilled labor, as well as from the poorest to the lower-middle quintiles by generating unemployment. Unfortunately, the model here cannot capture the effect of unemployment but reveal its impacts on the working population.

Table 6. Descriptive statistics of city-level variables in 2005.

	Mean	Standard deviation	Min.	Max.
Wage inequality measures				
Theil Entropy	0.178	0.047	0.095	0.419
Gini Coefficient	0.310	0.031	0.238	0.438
Labor market institutions				
Ratio of minimum wage to average wage	0.485	0.082	0.215	0.705
Proportion of workers signing contract	0.350	0.125	0.079	0.710
Proportion of workers with UI	0.118	0.065	0.015	0.394
Proportion of workers with pension	0.189	0.067	0.039	0.419
Proportion of workers with medical insurance	0.214	0.083	0.059	0.431
Other labor market and economic indicators				
Averages years of schooling (years)	9.16	0.73	7.26	11.25
Proportion of migrants in population	0.182	0.109	0.019	0.838
Ratio of secondary employment to tertiary	0.651	0.416	0.127	3.967

Source: Calculation from 1% population sampling survey in 2005 and data collected by the Institute of Population and Labor Economics, Chinese Academy of Social Sciences.

Table 7. The role of labor market institutions on wage inequality.

	Gini		Theil	
	Coeff.	T	Coeff.	T
Ratio of minimum wage to average wage	−0.087	−2.61***	−0.134	−2.51***
Proportion of workers signing contract	−0.087	−3.09***	−0.150	−3.36***
Proportion of workers with UI	0.110	1.92*	0.132	1.44
Proportion of workers with pension	−0.016	−0.38	−0.023	−0.34
Proportion of workers with medical insurance	0.015	0.73	0.453	1.38
Average years of schooling	0.006	1.34	0.005	0.61
Proportion of migrants in population	0.097	3.22***	0.156	3.23***
Ratio of secondary employment to tertiary	−0.015	−2.34**	−0.008	−0.75
Province dummies	Yes		Yes	
Adj. R^2	0.37		0.33	
No. of observations	261		261	

Note: ***, significant at 1%; **, significant at 5%; *, significant at 10%.
Source: Calculation from 1% population sampling survey in 2005 and data collected by the Institute of Population and Labor Economics, Chinese Academy of Social Sciences.

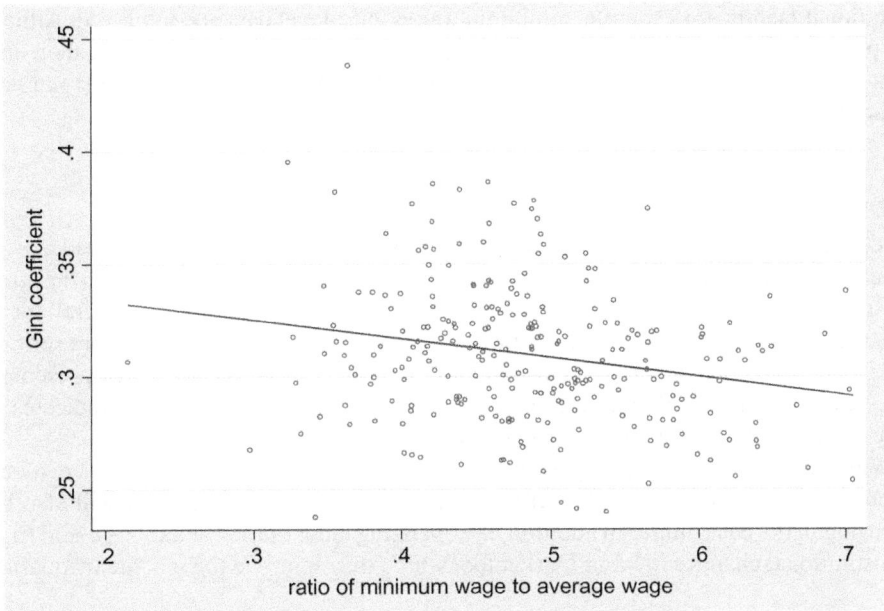

Figure 7.　Wage inequality and minimum wage across cities in 2005.

Source: Calculation from 1% population sampling survey in 2005 and data collected by the Institute of Population and Labor Economics, Chinese Academy of Social Sciences.

As indicated in Table 7, high ratio of minimum wage to average wage is associated with low-wage inequality measured both by Gini coefficient and Theil entropy. Figure 7 depicts the same pattern. Even without controlling for other determinants to wage inequality, scatters of Gini coefficients across cities show downturn with the increase of the ratio of minimum wage to average wage. It seems that the minimum wages have a small impact on inequality among the unskilled because income is shared equally among unskilled workers and they tend to have high job turnover. But, again, the effect of minimum wage on employment is not reflected in wage inequality analysis since the unemployed are not included in the sample at all.

The case for contracting enforcement is similar to that for minimum wage. The enforcement seems to decrease the wage inequality among working population but its effect on income inequality is not clear because the impact of contracting on demand for labor is not captured by the model.

However, some limitations of this empirical exercise have to be noted. First, the data employed in the following model were collected in 2005. Nevertheless, the most significant change of labor market institution, *Employment Contract Law*, took place in 2008, so the data are not able to reflect the change. Second, there is only individual wage information in 1% population sampling survey, which makes it difficult to capture income inequality and the effects of household variables. More importantly, wages are only reported among working population, so wage inequality is incapable of capturing the effects of unemployment on income inequality. However, unemployment is believed to be one of the major sources of inequality (Jenkins 1995; Jenkins 1996). In the China case, when employment growth serves as one of the most important instruments to reduce poverty and inequality, omission of this effect could cause a significant bias. Third, to observe variations of institutional factors, for example, minimum wages, city-level data are employed. Although it is plausible to explore the impacts of institutional factors, it is not about their influences on inequality between regions, while the latter is supposed to be the most important component of inequality in secular China.

Recap

The Chinese labor market has been more and more integrated in the past decade, as evidenced by a large proportion of migrant workers in urban employment. Ignoring this group, which is the case in current statistical system, could cause overestimation to overall income inequality. With increasing size of off-farm employment, the bias could be more serious.

In this section, we did analysis to cover all the groups based on national representative data. Although our calculation does not exhaust the sources of bias also, it indicates that many existing studies could overestimate the inequality.

With coming LTP, the wage growth for unskilled worker could speed up, as evidenced by the case in recent labor market. If this trend is kept, income inequality will also keep improving in the near future. In addition, the changing labor market situations could trigger the institutional changes in labor market too, which may improve the income inequality.

4. Conclusions

Due to the data limitations in China, it is not easy to evaluate the labor market situations based on the current statistics. Before going through the labor market situations in China, this paper discusses various sources of aggregated data and their reliability. Clarification on data may partly help us to understand why the disagreement exists on the judgment of China's labor market situations.

On the merits of various data sources, this paper tries to explain labor shortage that has taken place in the Chinese labor market for several years. Both demographic transition and the strong labor demand induced by fast economic growth dominate the phenomenon while these two fundamental factors will keep stable trend in the medium and long run. During the period of '12th Five Years Plan', average annual growth of population between the age of 16 and 64 years will be 3.7 million, while newly increased demand for labor will be more than 16 million per year even based on the prudent assumption of economic growth rate. It is also good to believe that this trend in China will not be reversible. Therefore, China has to live with labor shortage since then.

When discussing LTP, given the growing trend of Chinese economy is accepted by most people, its implications to public policies should be more addressed than its timing. In this paper, its impacts on wage growth for unskilled workers and income inequality are discussed. According to our analysis, China still has advantage in labor costs although wages for unskilled workers have been increasing rapidly in recent years. Thanks to this change, low-income group can share more from economic growth, which will improve equality eventually.

Acknowledgment

The authors are indebted to Fang Cai, Lixing Li, Yiping Huang, Ross Garnaut and Ligang Song for their valuable comments and suggestions.

Note

1. CULS1 and CULS2 refer to the China Urban Labor Survey, surveys conducted in 2001 and 2005 by the Institute of Population and Labour Economics of the Chinese Academy of Social Sciences. CHIP refers to the China Household Income Project survey.

References

Banister, J. 2006. Manufacturing earnings and compensation in China. *Labor Economics* 3, no. 2: 1–20, China Labour and Social Security Publishing House.

Brandt, L., and C. Holz. 2007. Spatial price differences in China: Estimates and implications. *Economic Development and Cultural Change* 55, no. 1: 43–86.

Du, Y. 2008. Wage level, wage differences and labor cost. In *Reports on China's population and labor no.8: Linking up Lewis and Kuznets turning points*, ed. Fang Cai. Social Sciences Academic Press, Beijing.

Du, Y., F. Cai, and M. Wang. 2006. Marketization and/or informalization? New trend of China's employment in transition. Report for the World Bank. Working paper.

Hu Y., F. Cai, and Y. Du. 2010. Population changes in the twelfth five-year plan period and projection of future population development trends. In *Reports on China's population and labor no.11: Labor market challenges in the post-crisis era*, ed. Fang Cai. Social Sciences Academic Press, forthcoming.

Jenkins, S.P. 1995. Accounting for inequality trends: Decomposition analysis for the UK, 1971–86. *Economica* 62, no. 245: 29–63.

Jenkins, S.P. 1996. Recent trends in the UK income distribution: What happened and why? *Oxford Review of Economic Policy* 12, no. 1: 29–46.

Park, A. 2008. Rural-urban inequality in China. In *China urbanizes*, eds. S. Yusuf and T. Saich, 41–64. Washington, DC: The World Bank.

Ravallion, M., and S. Chen. 2007. China's (uneven) progress against poverty. *Journal of Development Economics* 82: 1–42.

Saint-Paul, G. 1994. Do labor market rigidities fulfill distributive objectives? Searching for the virtues of the European model. *IMF Staff Papers* 41: 624–642.

Sicular, T., X. Yue, B. Gustafsson, and S. Li. 2007. The urban-rural income gap and inequality in China. *Review of Income and Wealth* 53, no. 1: 93–126.

World Bank. 2009. *From poor areas to poor people: China's evolving poverty reduction agenda, an assessment of poverty and inequality in China*. Washington, DC: World Bank.

The rise of labor cost and the fall of labor input: Has China reached Lewis turning point?

Wang Meiyan

Institute of Population and Labor Economics, Chinese Academy of Social Sciences, Beijing, China
(*Final version received 5 July 2010*)

With the emergence and expansion of a shortage of migrant workers, there is much debate over whether China has reached Lewis turning point (LTP). This paper uses China's national farm product cost-benefit survey data to analyze changes of labor cost, labor input, capital input and marginal labor productivity in the agricultural sector. This paper finds that rapid rise of labor cost has happened in the agricultural sector since 2004, accompanied by rapid and significant wage increases for unskilled workers. Total labor input and labor input per unit of three major grain crops have been falling and capital-labor ratio has risen rapidly since the mid-1990s. Output elasticity of labor and marginal labor productivity of japonica rice has risen by a large extent between the period 1980–2004 and 2005–2008. The evidence provided in this paper can help people clarify the debate on whether China has reached LTP.

1. Introduction

The shortage of migrant workers first emerged at Pearl River Delta in 2004. At that time most scholars and policy researchers asserted that it was just a short-term phenomenon which happened occasionally. However, the shortage of migrant workers did not disappear as people expected. Instead, it has in turn expanded to Yangtze River Delta regions and then to inland provinces, from which migrant workers are generally exported. Gradually, it became a national phenomenon in China (Cai and Wang 2005; Liu 2008; Zhang 2008; Wang 2005; Wang 2006).

With the emergence and expansion of this shortage of migrant workers, there is much debate over whether China has reached Lewis turning point (LTP). The academic community and policy makers have very conflicting opinions on this point. Cai (2008, 2010) examined many issues which are related to LTP such as trend of population age, structure, labor market supply and demand situation, continuous labor shortage and wage increases for unskilled laborers. He affirmed that China has reached LTP and has been transitioning from an era of unlimited labor supply to that of finite labor supply. Some other studies also confirm that China has reached LTP (Zhang, Yang, and Wang 2010).

In contrast, some studies deny the coming of LTP in China. For example, Minami and Ma's study shows that there still exist many surplus laborers in China's agricultural sector and China has not reached LTP (Minami and Ma 2009). Chen, Lu, and Chen (2008) believe that the era of labor shortage has not been reached in China. There are also some other researches who deny that China has reached LTP (Jiang 2007; Song 2009; Liu 2009).

Although they have seen labor shortage and labor cost increase all over China, policy makers insist that labor supply is still larger than labor demand, which is given as the reason why much attention is paid to the employment issue. They worry that if LTP arrival is admitted, employment will lose its significance in the government's agenda.

According to Lewis economic development theory, the developing countries with unlimited labor supply will experience a long-term dual economic development process. During this process, there exist numerous surplus laborers in the agricultural sector and the marginal labor productivity in the agricultural sector is very low. Modern sectors can recruit numerous laborers from the agricultural sector with unchanged wage rates and labor supply is higher than labor demand (Lewis 1954).

When labor demand of the modern sector exceeds labor supply from the agricultural sector, the wage rate of the modern sector starts to increase. After economic development passes through the stage of unlimited labor supply with unchanged wage rates, it reaches an important turning point, LTP (Lewis 1972; Ranis and Fei 1961). With the arrival of LTP in an economy, agricultural employment will have a significant and continuous decline.

According to Lewis (1954), wage rates in the agricultural sector are determined by subsistence level before LTP. After LTP, wage rates in the agricultural sector are determined by marginal labor productivity of the sector instead of subsistence level. If we assume subsistence level is constant, obviously, the stage with unchanged wage rate in an agricultural sector is the stage of unlimited labor supply and the stage with rapid wage increase in that sector is the stage of finite labor supply. Thus, we can say that the transition period from stagnated wage to rapid wage increase in the agricultural sector is LTP.

In reality, however, the subsistence level has been increasing. Due to this circumstance, it would be hard to conclude the coming of LTP on the basis of wage increases in the agricultural sector alone. We can assume that compared with the increase of wages after LTP which is determined by marginal labor productivity, increase of subsistence level in the agricultural sector is very slow. Under this assumption, the period with rapid wage increase in the agricultural sector is the period reaching LTP (Minami 2008). In other words, with the coming of LTP, rise of labor cost happens in the agricultural sector.

According to Minami (2008), before LTP, the supply of skilled workers is finite and that of unskilled workers is unlimited. Accordingly, the wage increases for skilled workers are rapid whereas those for unskilled workers are very slow. After LTP, as the unskilled workers become finite, their wages also show a significant and rapid increase.

In development economics, there is a hypothesis called induced technological change. It postulates that technology choices and technological progress direction are induced by changes of relative prices and scarcity of production factors (Hayami and Ruttan 1980). Under the market-oriented resource allocation system, rural households base their decisions on technology choices, production structure, input quantity, input quality and input structure keeping in view the relative prices in the product and production factor market. When LTP arrives, due to labor shortage the labor cost increases, it makes more sense for the rural households to reduce their labor input and increase the capital input in agricultural production. Accordingly, capital-labor ratio will begin to show an increase.

According to Ranis and Fei (1961), before LTP is attained, the marginal productivity of labor is very low in the agricultural sector and therefore the decline in labor input is not likely to cause the corresponding decline in agricultural output. However, once LTP is reached, the agricultural output declines with the continuous outflows of rural laborers from the agricultural sector and the marginal labor productivity in the agriculture sector becomes positive. Afterward, with more and more rural laborers moving out from the agricultural sector, the marginal labor productivity in the agricultural sector continues to rise.

Based on the above analysis, we can expect that the coming of LTP introduces dramatic changes on various aspects related to the agricultural sector, such as the decline of agricultural employment, rise of labor cost in the agricultural sector, wage increases for unskilled workers, fall of labor input in the agricultural sector, rise of capital input in the agricultural sector, rise of capital-labor ratio in the agricultural sector, increase of marginal labor productivity in the agricultural sector and many more.

If we can clarify some of these kinds of facts in the agricultural sector, it would be instrumental in facilitating the debate on whether China has reached LTP. This paper analyzes changes of labor cost, labor input and marginal labor productivity in the agricultural sector in China. Our null hypothesis is that China has not reached LTP. If we find evidence against the null hypothesis, we will reject the null hypothesis.

Although a shortage of migrant workers emerged in 2004, many other phenomena such as wage increase of migrant workers, which might be one of the indicators of the arrival of LTP, came into prominence before that year (Cai 2008). Minami suggested that the arrival of LTP is a starting point for the long-term economic development trend in the process of economic development rather than a swing phenomenon. Whether it just emerges or it has appeared for some time, it should be treated as a component of the long-term economic development. Nevertheless, it is a time period rather than a time point (Minami 1968). The time period that this paper analyzes is the new century.

The rest of this paper is organized as follows: the second section analyzes the shortfalls of data on agricultural employment; the third section discusses the rise of labor cost in the agricultural sector and wage increases for unskilled workers; the fourth section investigates the fall of labor input, the rise of capital input and the increase of capital-labor ratio of the three main grain crops; section five examines the increase of marginal labor productivity in the agricultural sector. The last section concludes.

2.   Shortfalls of data on agricultural employment

As mentioned before in the first section, when an economy reaches LTP, agricultural employment will show a significant and continuous decline. In this section, we will examine the changes that take place in agricultural employment in China. Figure 1 illustrates the number of total employment, the number of agricultural employment and the proportion of agricultural employment in total employment in China 1990 onward.

Figure 1 depicts that before 2003 there were fluctuations in the number of agricultural employment, which is manifested in the general trend of shrinkage. Since 2004, the number of agricultural employment began to decline substantially and steadily. In 2004, it fell by 12 million compared with the previous year. Meanwhile, the number of total employment has increased. The proportion of agricultural employment has been declining 1990 onward and the period before and after 2003 mark a significant difference. Before 2003, the decline was more or less above 50%, however, after 2003 it showed a substantial decrease. It dropped by 9 percentage points from 49% in 2003 to 40% in 2008.

However, we must point out that, employment data shown in Figure 1 are collected through the reporting system of National Bureau of Statistics. We are well aware that there are many problems with these data. Furthermore, the definition of employment in these data does not seem to be precise. Among employed persons in the agricultural sector, we cannot predict how much time they live in countryside and are engaged in agriculture, let alone their actual and exact time input in agriculture. But in reality, there exists a huge difference

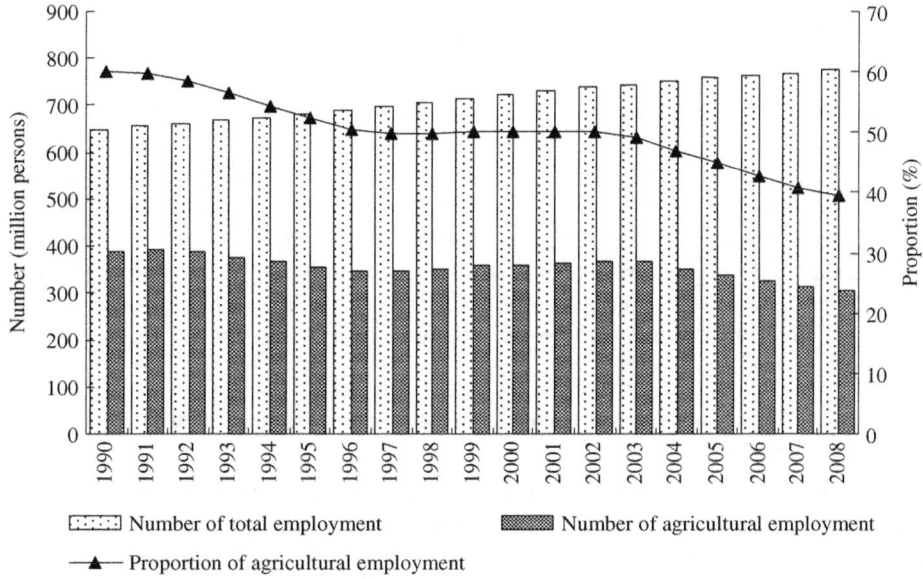

Figure 1. Number and proportion of agricultural employment.
Source: National Bureau of Statistics, *China Statistical Yearbook* (various years), China Statistics Press.

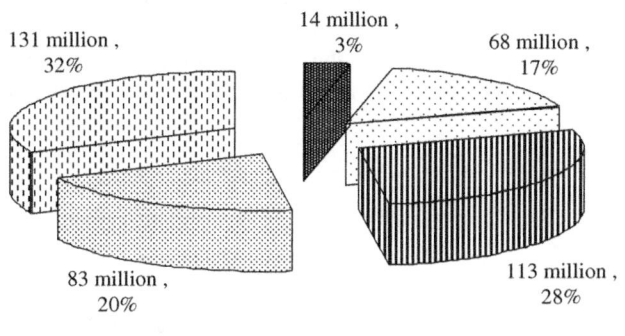

■ 1 month ☐ 2–3 months Ⅲ 4–6 months ☒ 7–9 months ☑ 10 months and above

Figure 2. Time spent on agriculture among employed persons in agriculture.
Source: *Compilation of China's Second National Agriculture Census Data.*

in the actual time spent on agriculture among employed persons in the agricultural sector according to the second agricultural census in 2006 (Figure 2).

From the Figure, among 409 million agricultural employed persons in residing households, only 3% (14 million) spent only 1 month on agriculture within a year, 17% (68 million) spent 2–3 months and 28% (113 million) spent 4–6 months. In total, 48% of the employed persons in agriculture spent less than 6 months on agriculture within a year. That is, actual labor input devoted to agriculture by persons who are considered as 'employed persons in agriculture' is much less than what the number of 'employed persons in agriculture' shows.

So, through the employment data in Figure 1, one could hardly measure the actual labor input in agriculture. Minami and Ma (2009), thus, declined the arrival of LTP, because they overestimated labor input in agriculture by using this kind of aggregated data. For this purpose, China's national farm product cost-benefit survey data are more reliable.

This survey was started in 1953 and now it covers more than 60 thousand rural households. The sample rural households are located in 1553 counties from 31 provinces. Sixty-eight kinds of farm products are included such as grains, oil plants, cotton, fruits and vegetables and so on. The survey instruments include detailed information on land, labor and capital during the process of agricultural production. In the following sections of this paper, the data we have mainly utilized are China's national farm product cost-benefit survey data. We have also employed some other data besides these when required.

3. The rise of labor cost in the agricultural sector and wage increases for unskilled workers

With the arrival of LTP, there is a rise of labor cost in the agricultural sector and the wages for unskilled workers will correspondingly show a significant and rapid increase. In this section, we have examined the changes of labor cost in the agricultural sector and the wages for unskilled workers. Minami examined the labor cost in agriculture by looking at the wages for hired workers in agriculture when he studied Japan's LTP (Minami 2008). We have followed his way here.

Figure 3 provides the daily wage for hired workers of grains, oil plants, raising pigs in large farms, vegetables and cotton, which are taken as representatives of agriculture.[1] Rural consumer price index is used to adjust the wage for hired workers in order to get the comparable wage. The wage mentioned in the Figure is at the 1998 price level.

From Figure 3 it can be inferred that the wage for hired workers for all the listed farm products has been increasing since the beginning of the new century and there has been a

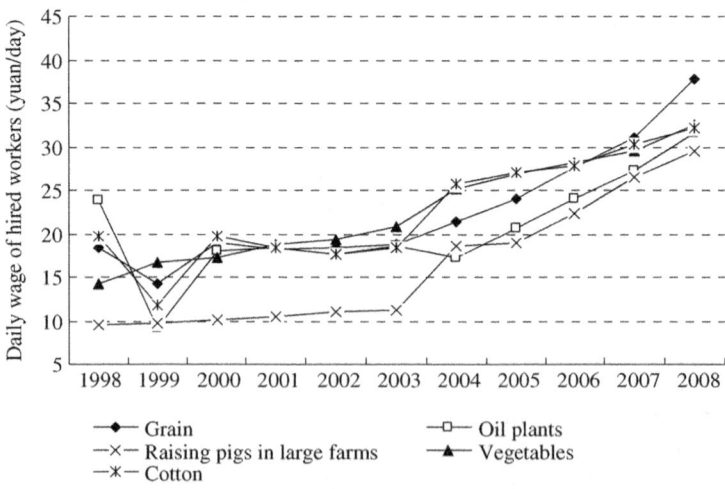

Figure 3.   Wage changes of hired workers in agricultural sector.

Note: Grain refers to the average of rice, corn and wheat; oil plants refer to the average of peanut and rapeseed; vegetables refer to vegetables in medium- and large-sized cities.
Source: Calculated according to data from *Compilation of National Farm Product Cost-Benefit Data* and *China Statistical Yearbook*.

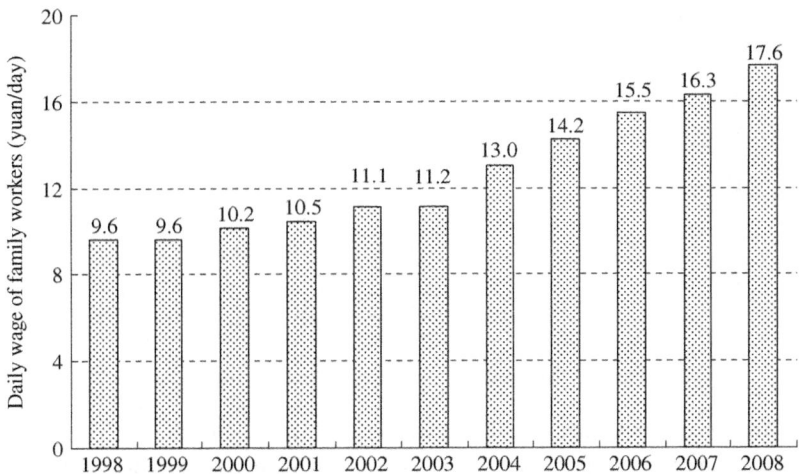

Figure 4. Wage changes of family workers in agricultural sector.
Source: Calculated according to the data from *Compilation of National Farm Product Cost-Benefit Data*.

significant jump in 2004. Daily wage for family workers in agriculture can also reflect the agricultural labor cost though it is just a theoretical remuneration for the family workers.[2] Figure 4 shows the changes in daily wages for family workers in the agricultural sector. The rural consumer price index is used to adjust wage for family workers in order to get a comparable wage. The wage provided in the Figure is at the 1998 price level.

From the Figure, the trend of wage for family workers in agriculture is very similar to that of hired workers. Before 2004, the wage for family workers has been although rising very slowly; however, since 2004, it has increased very rapidly. In 2004, it was just 13 yuan and reached 17.6 yuan in 2008, an increase of 35%.

Wage increase of hired and family workers in the agricultural sector, that is, the rise of labor cost in the agricultural sector, is consistent with the wage increases for unskilled workers in other sectors. As we have already mentioned in the first section of this paper, after LTP, unskilled workers become finite and the wages for unskilled workers show a significant and rapid increase. If rapid wage increases for unskilled workers are found, they could be taken as evidence to reject our null hypothesis that China has not reached LTP. In what follows, we have looked at the wage changes for unskilled workers.

China has witnessed labor migration from rural to urban areas since the beginning of the reform era and the opening up of its economy. Over the years, more and more rural laborers moved to cities in order to work. In 2009, the number of rural to urban migrants who had lived in urban areas for more than 6 months reached 145 million. Most of the rural migrant workers were unskilled workers and worked in the informal sectors of the urban labor market. It makes sense that migrant workers are considered to be the typical representative of unskilled workers.

There had been a long stagnation of migrant workers' wage before the latest change in migrant workers' wage was introduced. From Figure 5, we can observe a significant increase of wages for migrant workers. Since 2004, the growth rate of migrant workers' wage has been showing an upward trend. In 2008, it even reached 19.6%.

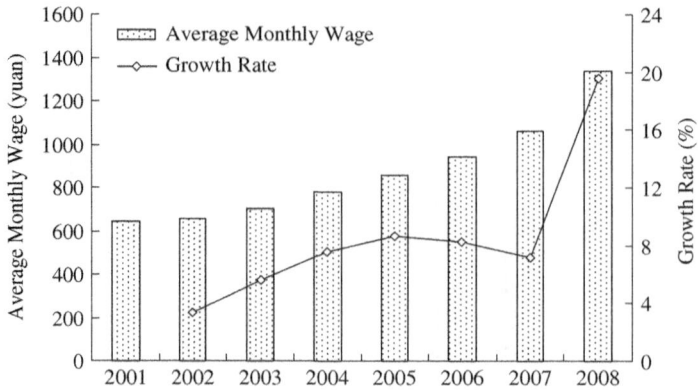

Figure 5.   Average monthly wage for migrant workers and its real growth rate.

Note: We use urban consumer price index to adjust wage of migrant workers in order to calculate its real growth rate.

Source: Average monthly wage for migrants is from the Statistical Reports of National Bureau of Statistics. Growth rate of average monthly wage for migrants is calculated by the author.

Besides rural migrant workers, most of the workers in the mining, manufacturing and construction sector could also be considered as unskilled workers. Figure 6 depicts changes in the real growth rate of average wages in these sectors. Apparently, the average wage in all those sectors began to show a significant and rapid growth since 2000. For mining and manufacturing, the growth rates of wages in most years were above 10%.

To be precise, both the wages for hired workers and for family workers have been increasing rapidly since 2004. We also see a rapid wage increase of migrant workers and a high wage growth rate of workers in the mining, manufacturing and construction sector. That is, the rapid and significant wage increase has been there for the unskilled workers.

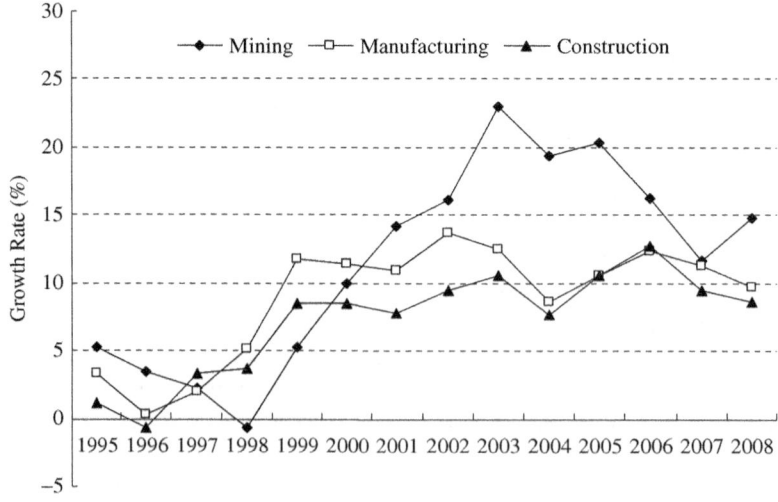

Figure 6.   Annual real growth rate of average wage in selected sectors.

Source: Calculated according to data from *China Labor Statistical Yearbook* (various years).

4. The fall of labor input, the rise of capital input and the increase of capital-labor ratio in the agricultural sector

As a consequence of the rise of labor cost in the agricultural sector, labor input would fall and capital input would increase provided the two factors are normally substituted. Also, the capital-labor ratio will increase accordingly. If the fall of labor input, the rise of capital input and the increase of capital-labor ratio in the agricultural sector are simultaneously found, we could feel more confident to reject the null hypothesis that China has not reached LTP. In this section, we have examined the changes of labor and capital input in the agricultural sector.

Rice, corn and wheat are the three major grain crops in China. The sown area of these three grain crops occupies a majority of sown area of grain crops and also a large share of the total sown area of all farm crops. In 2008, the sown area of these three grain crops was 77% of the sown area of grain crops and 53% of the sown area of all farm crops. In this part, we have analyzed the labor input, capital input and capital-labor ratio of these three grain crops.

(1) The fall of labor input in the agricultural sector

Figure 7 gives the total labor input of rice, corn and wheat over the years. Since the mid-1990s, the total labor input of all these three grain crops has been falling rapidly. In the mid-1990s, there was a large gap in the total labor input between these three grain crops. With the different declining rates, the total labor input of these three grain crops became very close in 2008. Among these three grain crops, rice required the largest total labor input.

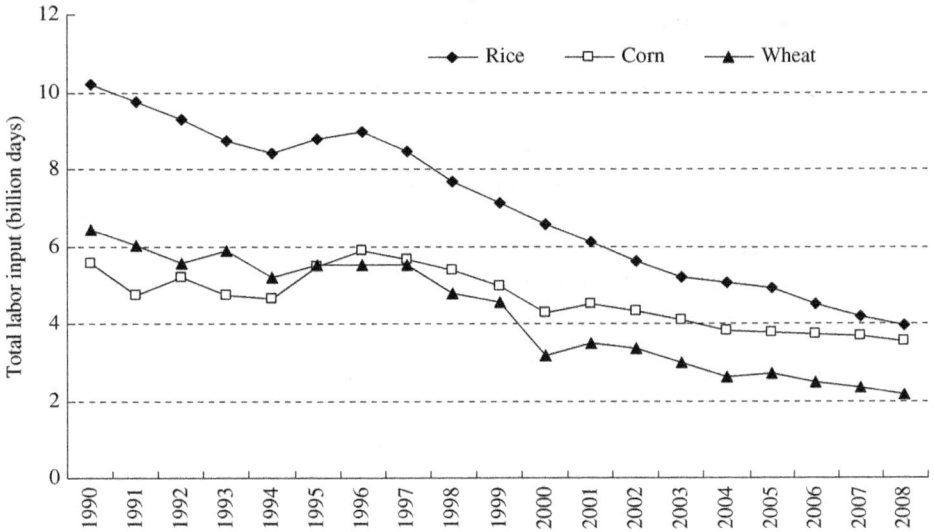

Figure 7. Total labor input of three grain crops.
Note: Total labor input of each grain crop is equal to labor input per unit multiplied by sown area.
Source: Calculated according to data from *China Rural Statistical Yearbook* and *Compilation of National Farm Product Cost-Benefit Data*.

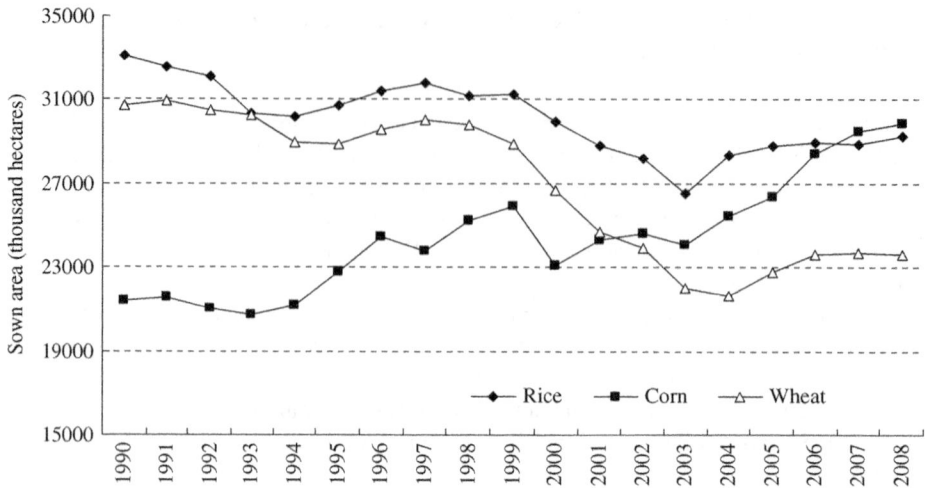

Figure 8.　Sown area of three grain crops.

Source: Calculated according to data from *China Rural Statistical Yearbook*.

Obviously, the total labor input is determined by two factors: sown area and labor input per unit. We do notice in Figure 7 the declining trend of the total labor input of these three grain crops since the mid-1990s. To examine the causes of this trend, we need to analyze changes of sown area and labor input per unit.

We have foremost examined the changes of the sown area of these grain crops (Figure 8). For rice and wheat, their sown area has showed a declining trend since the beginning of the new century and reached the lowest points in 2003 or 2004. After that, both of them began to increase. In contrast, the sown area of corn has showed an increasing trend over the years. In 2007, the sown area of corn was the largest among these three grain crops.

The increase of sown area of the three grain crops in the past several years might be related to the increase of comparative returns in agriculture. In 2004, in the Government Work Report, Premier Wen Jiabao declared that agricultural tax rate will be reduced by more than 1 percentage point per year on average from 2004 and the agricultural taxes will be rescinded in 5 years. On 1 January 2006, China rescinded the agricultural taxes completely. The decreasing and rescinded agricultural taxes, along with various subsidies directly to grain production, have brought the rise of comparative returns in agriculture.

With the fall of total labor input of all these three grain crops and the rise of sown area of the crops in the past several years, we can postulate that the labor input per unit should have been ideally falling. That is exactly what happened. Figure 9 provides labor input per mu of rice, corn and wheat.

Before the mid-1990s, labor input per mu for all these three grain crops has shown a higher and stable level; since the mid-1990s, labor input per mu for all these three grain crops has been declining rapidly. Since 2004, labor input per mu for all these three grain crops has been declining more rapidly. Among these three grain crops, rice has the highest labor input per unit, corn is in the middle and wheat has the lowest.

(2)　The rise of capital input in the agricultural sector

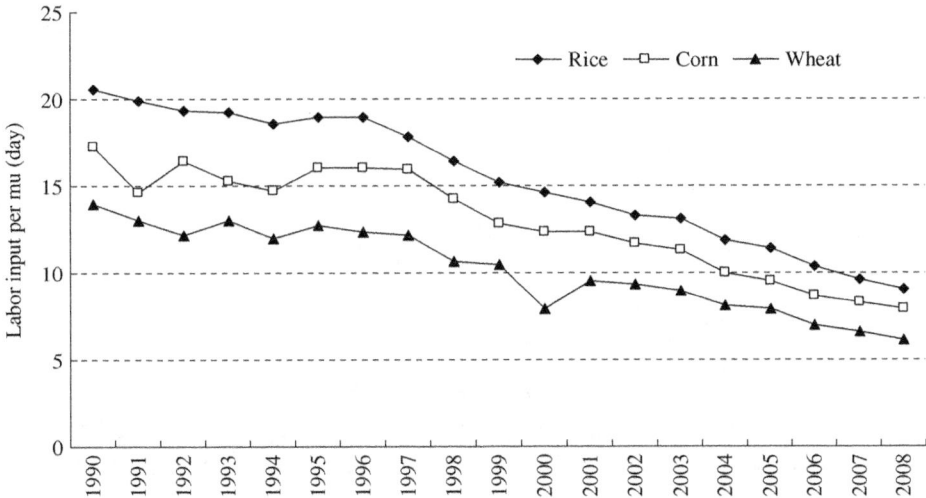

Figure 9.   Labor input per unit of three grain crops.
Source: *Compilation of National Farm Product Cost-Benefit Data.*

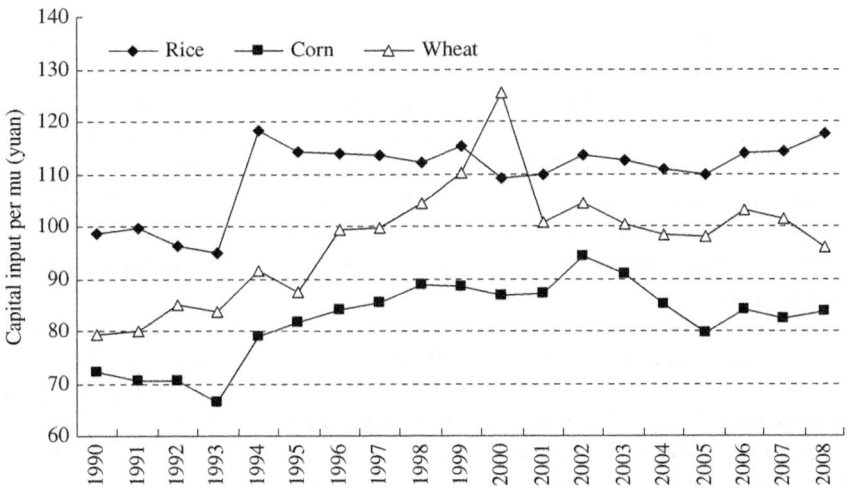

Figure 10.   Capital input per unit of three grain crops.
Source: *Compilation of National Farm Product Cost-Benefit Data.*

Figure 10 provides capital input per unit of rice, corn and wheat.[3] We use the general price index of agricultural means of production to adjust the capital input in order to get a comparable capital input. Capital input given in the Figure is at the 1990 price level. During 1990s, capital input per unit of all these three crops has been increasing steadily. In the new century, capital input per unit of rice and corn has been increasing since 2006. Capital input per unit of wheat has been fluctuating in this period.

Figure 11 shows the total capital input of rice, corn and wheat over the years. It also shows a very similar trend as capital input per unit. The total capital input of all these three crops has showed an increasing trend during 1990s. In the new century, the total capital

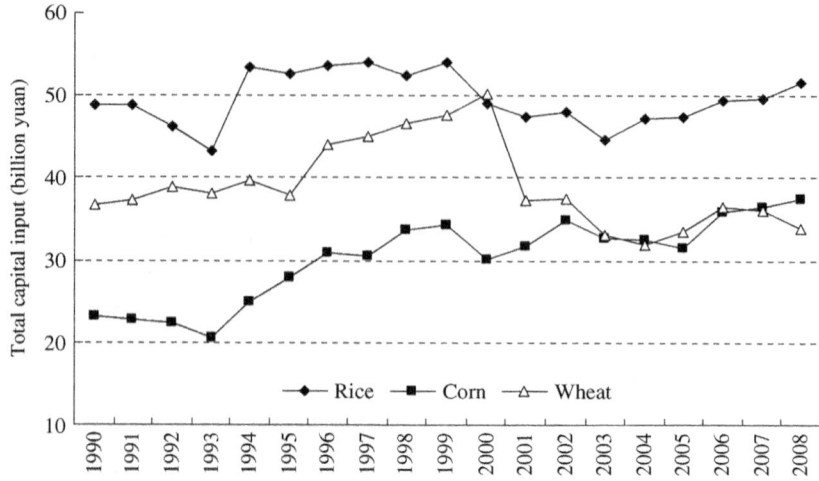

Figure 11.   Total capital input of three grain crops.

Note: Total capital input is equal to capital input multiplied by sown area. Source: Calculated according to data from *China Rural Statistical Yearbook* and *Compilation of National Farm Product Cost-Benefit Data.*

input of rice has been increasing steadily since 2004; the total capital input of corn has been increasing steadily since 2006; and the total capital input of wheat has been fluctuating.

We have to point out that there are some factors which might cause decline or underestimation of capital input. First, tax cut and elimination is a factor-reducing capital input. Tax has been increasing for all these three grain crops and has reached the peak in 2002. The proportion of tax in capital input was 14.4%, 13.4% and 12.6% for rice, corn and wheat, respectively this year. Since 2003, the tax has been rescinded gradually and in 2006 completely. The gradual decrease and final abolition of tax is one of the factors which could have caused the decline of capital input.

Second, the general price index of agricultural means of production underreported the significant deflation of some categories of capital input. Since price index for some categories of capital input is not available, the price index we have used to adjust capital input is the general price index of agricultural means of production. However, when we compare the available price index of categories of capital input with the general price index of agricultural means of production,[4] we find that there exists a huge difference over the years between them, especially for some categories of capital input which occupy large shares in capital input.

Machinery expense is a very typical example. In 1990, the proportion of machinery expense in capital input was 5.1% for rice and corn and 8% for wheat. By 2008, the proportion increased to 24% for rice, 17.7% for corn and 29.4% for wheat.[5] The extent of price increase of machinery from 1990 to 2008 is only about 60% of the general price index of the agricultural means of production, which will cause the underestimated machinery expense when the general price index of agricultural means of production is used to deflate the machinery expense.

If we investigate the changes of agricultural machinery over the years from power and number rather than from expense point of view, it is found that the number of agricultural machinery has been increasing very rapidly. Figure 12 provides the total power of agricultural machinery and the number of tractor-towing farm machinery.

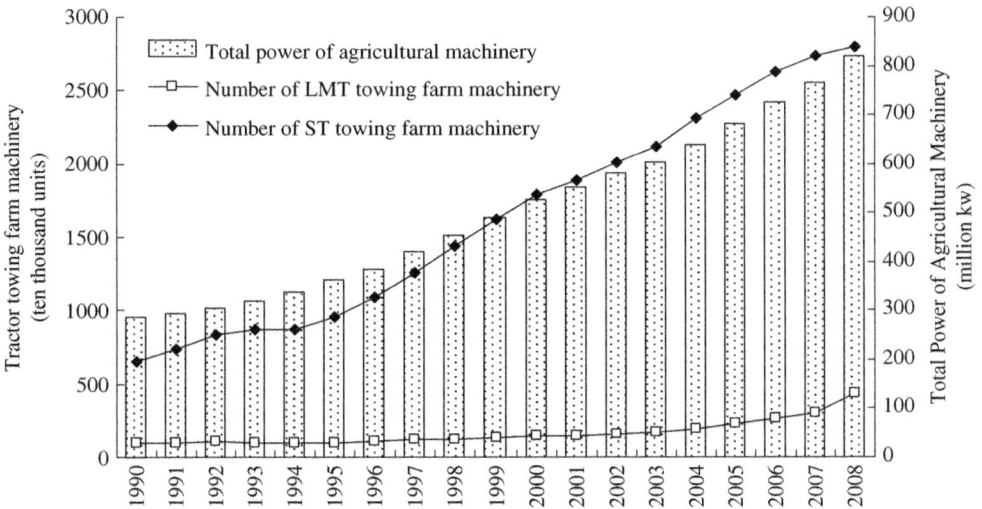

Figure 12.   Changes of major agricultural machinery.

Note: Number of LMT towing farm machinery refers to the number of large- and medium-sized tractor towing farm machinery; Number of ST towing farm machinery refers to the number of small tractor towing farm machinery. Source: *China Statistical Yearbook*.

From the Figure, the total power of agricultural machinery has been increasing steadily and rapidly with an annual growth rate of 6.02% during the period 1990–2008. On one hand, the number of large- and medium-sized tractor-towing farm machinery increased from 0.97 million to 4.35 million with the annual growth rate being 8.67%, whereas on the other, the number of small tractor-towing farm machinery increased from 6.49 million to 27.95 million with the annual growth rate 8.45%.

(3) The increase of capital-labor ratio in the agricultural sector

Figure 13 shows capital-labor ratio of rice, corn and wheat. A steady and rapid increase of capital-labor ratio is manifested in all these three grain crops since the mid-1990s, among which, wheat has the highest capital-labor ratio, rice is in the middle and corn has the lowest capital-labor ratio. As we know, the mechanization of wheat production is much easier compared to that of rice and corn production. So the highest capital-labor ratio of wheat does make sense.

In summary, the total labor input and the labor input per unit have been falling since the mid-1990s. The capital input per unit of rice and corn has been increasing and that of wheat fluctuating in the past several years. The total capital input of these three grain crops has showed a very similar trend as capital input per unit. Agricultural machinery has been increasing very rapidly. We see a rapid and significant increase of capital-labor ratio for all the three grain crops since the mid-1990s.

5. Increase of marginal labor productivity in the agricultural sector

As is expected, according to Lewis theory, the arrival of LTP can be characterized by positive and increased marginal labor productivity in agriculture. Afterward, with more and more rural laborers moving out from the agricultural sector, marginal labor productivity in

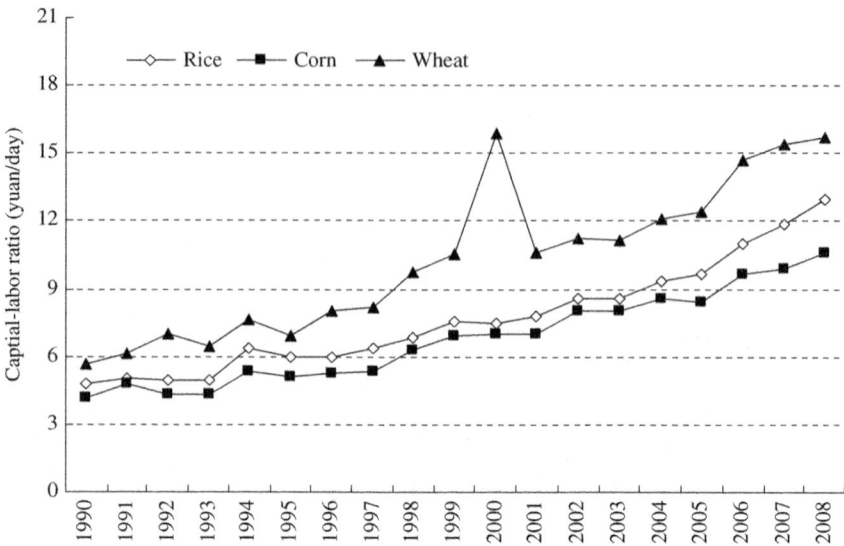

Figure 13.   Capital-labor ratio of three grain crops.
Source: *Compilation of National Farm Product Cost-Benefit Data.*

the agricultural sector continues to increase until the end of the development of dual economy. In this section, we have examined the marginal labor productivity in the agricultural
sector.

We have described labor input of rice, corn and wheat in the previous section. As we
saw, rice has the highest total labor input and labor input per unit among these three grain
crops, and the total labor input and labor input per unit of rice have declined more rapidly
and to a larger extent compared with that of corn and wheat. That is, the most dramatic
changes have happened to labor input of rice among these three grain crops. Therefore, we
expect that the marginal labor productivity of rice will have more significant changes.

So here we select rice as the representative of grain crops to estimate production function. However, rice includes indica rice, in indica rice, late indica rice and japonica rice.
The indicator of rice that we have discussed in the earlier sections is actually the average
of these four grain crops. Here we have chosen japonica rice as the representative of rice
when estimating the function of production.

The data we have used are the national farm product cost-benefit data. We have a
panel dataset for japonica rice in 14 provinces from 1980 to 2008. The production function will take Cobb-Douglas form. The dependent variable includes output (yield per mu)
and the independent variables the capital (capital input per mu) and labor input (labor input
per mu). We have used the general price index of agricultural means of production to adjust
capital input to get a comparable capital input.

As we know, the idea of Cobb-Douglas production function is that output is determined
by capital input, labor input and technological progress. The form of the Cobb-Douglas
production function is

$$Y = AK^{\alpha}L^{\beta}. \tag{1}$$

Here, Y is output, K is capital input, L is labor input. α and β are output elasticity of
capital and output elasticity of labor, respectively.

The log form of the model is

$$\ln Y = \ln A + \alpha \ln K + \beta \ln L. \qquad (2)$$

Here we assume $\alpha + \beta = 1$, that is, the production function of japonica rice is constant returns to scale.

Then we have $\beta = 1 - \alpha$. So (2) can be transformed into

$$\ln Y/L = \ln A + \alpha \ln K/L. \qquad (3)$$

Here, α is output elasticity of capital. Output elasticity of labor will be equal to $1 - \alpha$. The estimated production function form is as follows:

$$\ln Y_{i,t}/L_{i,t} = \ln A + \alpha \ln K_{i,t}/L_{i,t} + prov_i + u_{i,t}. \qquad (4)$$

Here, $Y_{i,t}$ is output per mu of province i in year t, $K_{i,t}$ is capital input per mu of province i in year t, $L_{i,t}$ is labor input of province i in year t. α is output elasticity of capital input. $prov_i$ is provincial dummy variables, which reflect province-specific differences; $u_{i,t}$ is randomly disturbing factors.

As we have seen in the previous sections, year 2004 is an important transition time point. Since 2004, the labor input has been declining more rapidly and capital input for rice has been increasing. So in the model we have added a year dummy variable year2004 (year2004 = 1 if year is between 2005 and 2008; year2004 = 0 if year is between 1980 and 2004) to capture the time effect. The specification is as follows:

$$\ln Y_{i,t}/L_{i,t} = \ln A + \alpha \ln K_{i,t}/L_{i,t} + \theta year2004 + prov_i + u_{i,t}. \qquad (5)$$

Furthermore, we expect that the output elasticity of capital and labor will have a significant difference before and after 2004. So we have also added the interaction term of capital input and year dummy variable. The specification is as follows:

$$\ln Y_{i,t}/L_{i,t} = \ln A + \alpha \ln K_{i,t}/L_{i,t} + \theta year2004 + \lambda \ln K_{i,t}/L_{i,t} year2004 + prov_i + u_{i,t}. \qquad (6)$$

Table 1 illustrates the production function result of japonica rice – Model 1 and Model 2, which are based on specification (5) and specification (6). Adjusted R^2 for the two models are 0.8313 and 0.8337, respectively, which indicates that the independent variables explain the dependent variable very well. In Model 1, year2004 significantly and negatively affects the dependent variable. However, in Model 2, when we add the interaction term of capital input and year dummy variable, year2004 becomes insignificant and interaction term is negative and significant, which indicates that the output elasticity of capital input for the period after 2004 is smaller than that for the period prior to 2004.

We can then calculate the output elasticity of labor for the period before 2004 and the period after 2004, respectively (output elasticity of labor input = 1-output elasticity of capital input). From Table 1, the output elasticity of capital input is 0.817 for the period before 2004 and the output elasticity of capital input is 0.663 for the period after 2004. Then the output elasticity of labor input increased from 0.183 for the period before 2004 to 0.337 for the period after 2004 (Table 2).

Table 1.   Production function result of japonica rice.

Dependent variable: ln Y/L	Model 1		Model 2	
	Coefficient	t value	Coefficient	t value
ln K/L	0.801***	33.83	0.817***	33.55
Year2004	−0.202***	−5.29	0.069	0.61
Interaction of ln K/L and year2004	–	–	−0.154**	−2.54
Provincial dummy variables	Omitted	Omitted	Omitted	Omitted
Constant term	3.028	65.41	3.014***	65.10
Observations	393		393	
Adjusted R^2	0.8313		0.8337	

Note: (1) t statistics in parentheses.
      (2) ***Significant at 1%, **significant at 5%.

Table 2.   Marginal labor productivity of japonica rice.

Period	Output elasticity of labor	Average labor productivity (kg/day)	Marginal labor productivity (kg/day)
Period before 2004 (1980–2004)	0.183	21.22	3.88
Period after 2004 (2005–2008)	0.337	32.21	10.86

According to the property of Cobb-Douglas production function, we can get marginal labor productivity by multiplying the output elasticity of labor by the average labor productivity. We do see a big increase of marginal labor productivity in agriculture, from 3.88 kg/day during the 1980–2004 period to 10.86 kg/day during 2005–2008. Precisely, the output elasticity of labor and the marginal labor productivity of japonica rice have risen to a large extent between the period 1980–2004 and 2005–2008.

6.   Conclusions

With the emergence and expansion of shortage of migrant workers, people are debating whether China has reached LTP. This paper uses China's national farm product cost-benefit survey data in order to analyze the changes in labor cost, labor input, capital input and marginal labor productivity in the agricultural sector.

The major findings of this paper are: (1) there has been a substantial and rapid decrease in both number and proportion of agricultural employment since 2004; (2) there has been a rapid rise of labor cost in the agricultural sector since 2004, accompanied by a rapid and significant wage increase for unskilled workers; (3) the total labor input and labor input per unit of the three major grain crops have been falling since the mid-1990s; (4) the capital-labor ratio has risen rapidly for the three major grain crops since the mid-1990s; (5) the output elasticity of labor and marginal labor productivity of japonica rice have risen to a large extent between the period 1980–2004 and 2005–2008.

The findings in this paper provide evidence to reject the null hypothesis that China has not reached LTP, which could help people clarify the debates linked to this point. Although this paper does not give an exact time point for the arrival of LTP, however, as Minami has mentioned (1968), LTP is more a time period than a time point. For China at this developmental stage, policy implications of LTP should be paid more attention than the timing of LTP. China needs to fully understand the opportunities and challenges under this context and figure out how making full use of the opportunities it can deal with the challenges.

Acknowledgment

The author is indebted to Fang Cai, Yan Shen, Yiping Huang, Yang Du, Ross Garnaut, Miaojie Yu and Ligang Song for their valuable comments and suggestions.

Notes

1. Daily wage for hired workers refers to remuneration (including wage, reasonable fee for food and so on) of a hired worker for a standard working day (8 hours).
2. Daily wage for family workers refers to theoretical remuneration of a family worker for a standard working day, which is used to measure the opportunity cost of family workers' work. Family workers' work refers to work of agricultural producers and their family members, exchanged work with others and free work provided by others.
3. Capital input refers to expense on various kinds of agricultural means of production consumed during the process of direct production, expense on various kinds of service, and other physical and cash expense related to production. Capital input can be divided into direct expense and indirect expense. Direct expense includes expense on seeds, fertilizer, pesticide, machinery, irrigation and so on. Indirect expense includes expense on depreciation of fixed asset, tax and sale and so on.
4. Price index of some categories of capital input is available in *China Statistical Yearbook*.
5. Calculated according to data from *Compilation of National Farm Product Cost-Benefit Data*.

References

Cai, Fang. 2008. *Lewis turning point: A coming new stage of China economic development*. Beijing: Social Sciences Academic Press.

Cai, Fang. 2010. Demographic transition, demographic dividend, and Lewis turning point in China. *Economic Research Journal*, no. 3: 4–13.

Cai, Fang, and Meiyan Wang. 2005. An economic analysis on shortage of migrant workers. *Guangdong Social Sciences*, no. 2: 5–10.

Chen, Jingmin, Ming Lu, and Zhao Chen. 2008. Has era of labor shortage reached? *Economic Information*, no. 4: 40–44.

Hayami, Yujiro, and Vernon Ruttan. 1980. *Agricultural development: An international perspective*. Baltimore and London: The John Hopkins University Press.

Jiang, Huadong. 2007. Shortage of migrant workers does not indicate the coming of Lewis turning point in China. *China Opening Held*, no. 3: 57–59.

Lewis, Arthur. 1954. Economic development with unlimited supplies of labor. *The Manchester School of Economic and Social Studies* 22: 139–191.

Lewis, Arthur. 1972. Reflections on unlimited labour. In *International economics and development*, ed. L. Di Marco, 75–96. New York: Academic Press.

Liu, Hongyin. 2009. Lewisian turning point: From Chinese farming development aspect. *Northwest Population Journal*, no. 4: 15–18.

Liu, Zuanshi. 2008. An empirical study of Mingong shortage. *China Opening Herald*, no. 4: 84–86.

Minami, Ryoshin. 1968. The turning point in the Japanese economy. *The Quarterly Journal of Economics* 82, no. 3: 380–402.

Minami, Ryoshin. 2008. *The turning point in economic development: Japan's experience*. Beijing: Social Sciences Academic Press.

Minami, Ryoshin, and Xinxin Ma. 2009. The turning point of Chinese economy: Compared with Japanese experience. *China Labor Economics*, forthcoming.

Ranis, Gustav, and John C.H. Fei. 1961. A theory of economic development. *American Economic Review* 51, no. 4: 533–565.

Song, Shifang. 2009. Lewis turning point: Theory and test. *Economist*, no. 2: 69–75.

Wang, Cheng. 2005. Lewis turning point and Chinese transition in dual economy. *Population Science of China*, no. 6: 2–10.

Wang, Taosheng. 2006. An empirical analysis on migrant workers' shortage in China and its projected trends. *China Rural Economy*, no. 7: 11–20.

Zhang, Xiaobo, Jin Yang, and Shenglin Wang. 2010. Has China reached the Lewis turning point: Evidence from poor regions. *Journal of Zhejiang University* (Humanities and Social Sciences), no. 1: 1–18.

Zhang, Zheng. 2008. Shortage of migrant workers: The present and the future. *Population and Development*, no. 3: 19.

Has China passed the Lewis turning point? A structural estimation based on provincial data

Yang Yao[a] and Ke Zhang[b]

[a] China Center for Economic Research & National School of Development, Peking University, Beijing, China; [b] Cornell University, New York City, USA

(Final version received 19 July 2010)

Using provincial data for the period 1998–2007, this paper estimates the supply and demand functions of migrant workers in each year for a typical Chinese province in a structural framework that explicitly takes into account the Lewis turning point (LTP) in the supply function. The results are extrapolated to the national level and the turning point and the equilibrium level of migrant employment are both estimated for each year. The comparison of those two estimates shows that China has not passed the Lewis turning point.

With agriculture contributing to 11% of the national economy but employing 45% of the country's labor force, China has long been characterized as a labor surplus economy. However, recent developments in China's demographic transition and labor markets have led to the speculation that China has passed or at least is approaching the Lewis turning point, namely, the point beyond which unlimited supply of labor to industry no longer exists (Cai 2008; Cai and Wang 2008; and the papers by Fang Cai and Ross Garnaut in this symposium). The evidence often cited to support this speculation is that wages of migrant workers are rising in coastal provinces.

However, other studies suggest that China has not passed the LTP. For example, Knight, Deng, and Li (2010), using the China Household Income Project (CHIP) data, find that there were 80 million rural people who would qualify for migration but did not migrate in 2007. Since the year 2007 was the highest point of the recent business cycle in China, it is thus doubtful that the pool of migrants was depleted in other years. Meng (2010) has reached similar conclusions using a multi-year survey of rural households, urban households, and migrants.

Indeed, rising wages are not a necessary result of an economy's passing the LTP– rising income in agriculture can lead to the same result. As shown in Figure 1, rural income grew slowly before 2004, but has accelerated since that year. It seemed not an accident that 2004 was the year when labor shortage began to emerge.

This paper offers an empirical study to directly measure whether China has passed the LTP. We use provincial data of 1998–2007 to estimate the supply and demand curves for migrant workers in the industry of a typical province. The demand curve takes the conventional form, but the supply curve is estimated to accommodate Lewis' theory of unlimited supply of labor, namely, it consists of a flat part of an infinite supply elasticity

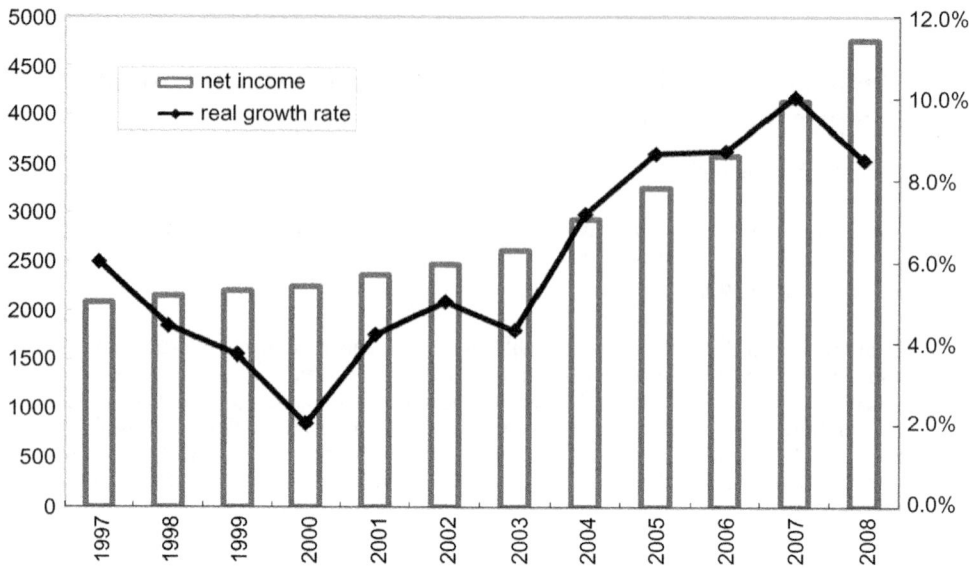

Figure 1.   Rural per-capita income and its growth: 1997–2008.
Source: NBS official website at www.stats.gov.cn.

and a curve of a finite supply elasticity. The LTP is endogenously estimated in a switching regression. Then the demand and supply curves are extrapolated to the national level and used to determine whether the country has passed the LTP. The answer reached by our study, however, is 'no'. In fact, the equilibrium levels of employment of migrant workers have fallen far below the levels implied by the LTP in recent years.

The rest of the paper is organized as the follows. Section 1 derives our econometric model. Section 2 introduces our data and presents the main results. Section 3 concludes the paper.

1.   The econometric model

When Lewis first proposed the concept of unlimited supply of labor, he relied on another concept, namely, surplus labor in agriculture. By surplus labor, he meant labor whose marginal product is zero. It has long been detected that there are inconsistencies in Lewis' theory. The first is that people would not spend labor hours that do not produce any output so the marginal product of labor hours cannot reach zero. This inconsistency was resolved by Sen (1966) who used the family as the unit of analysis. In a family, labor sharing is possible, and as a result, family output may not decrease when a member leaves agriculture. The second inconsistency is more substantial. Lewis allowed surplus labor to be paid by an institutional wage, but did not say anything about how this wage came about. In Sen's formulation, people are paid by the family average income. However, there would not be unlimited supply of labor to industry because average family income would increase as people left agriculture.

To resolve this new inconsistency, we introduce the following modifications. First, we assume that there is real unemployment in agriculture. That is, some people cannot get a job even if job-sharing of Sen's type exists. Second, we change Sen's formulation by allowing a farmer to ask for the average labor income, not average family income, when he chooses to work in industry. Third, we introduce imperfections in the labor market. When there is surplus labor in agriculture, the industrial wage is equal to average labor income in agriculture, which is unrelated to the number of people hired in industry. Because there is real unemployment in the countryside, this wage is unrelated to the number of workers left in agriculture either. Figure 2 below illustrates our idea.

In the figure, the upper part shows industrial labor supply and demand, and the lower part shows agricultural production. $O_u O_r$ represents the total amount of labor in the countryside. For any point, L, say, on $O_u O_r$, $O_u L$ represents the amount of labor working in industry, and $O_r L$ represents the amount of labor working in agriculture. L_0 is the shortage point. Before the economy reaches this point, the marginal product of an agricultural labor is zero because there exists real unemployment. As a result, industry can get unlimited supply of labor as long as it pays the average labor income in agriculture. After the economy passes the shortage point, the marginal product of labor becomes positive and increases in agriculture, but remains smaller than the average labor income at the shortage point, w^* in the figure. The industry continues to pay w^* until the economy passes the turning point beyond which the marginal product of labor in agriculture is larger than w^*. In summary, we define the LTP as the follows:

Definition. The LTP is the point beyond which the marginal product of labor in agriculture is larger than its average output at the shortage point.

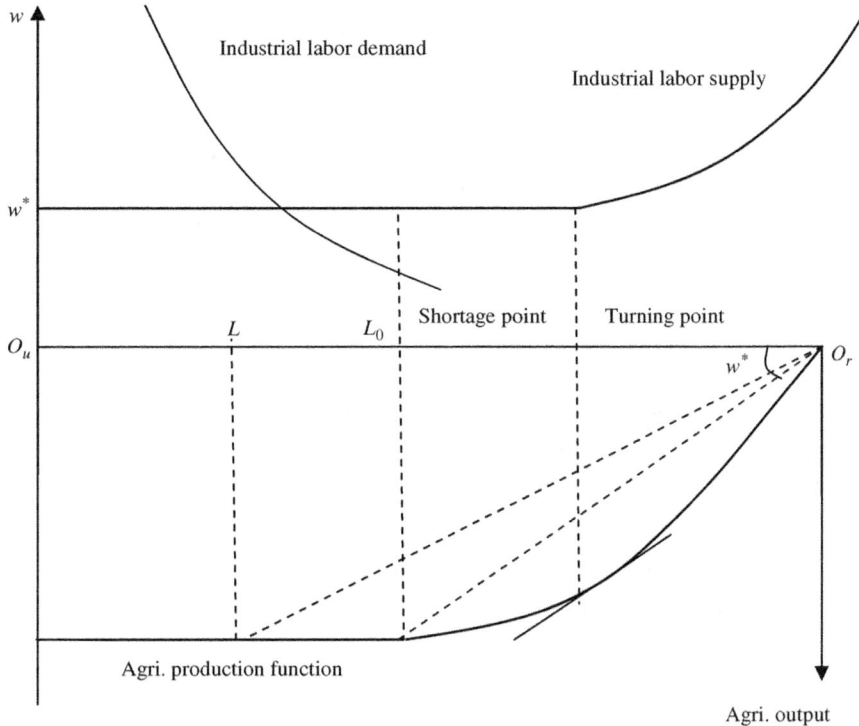

Figure 2.   Illustration of the Lewis turning point.

With the above setup, we can proceed to discuss the estimation of the institutional wage that sustains the unlimited supply of labor. The above discussion indicates that it is equal to the average labor income in agriculture. A_i be this income for province i, and w_i^* be its institutional wage. Then an equation to estimate is

$$w_i^* = \alpha_1 + \beta_1 * A_i + u_{1i}. \tag{1}$$

However, w_i^* itself is not observable, so equation (1) cannot be directly estimated. But with the industrial supply function beyond the turning point, we can estimate the equation in an endogenous switching model.

Let w_i denote the industrial wage rate in the ith province after it passes the turning point, that is, the wage rate paid on the upward-sloping part of the industrial labor supply curve in Figure 2. Further, let L_i^I denote the number of migrant workers working in industry, and P_i^R denote the size of the rural laborforce. Then its industrial wage rate can be characterized by the following the following labor supply function:

$$w_i = \alpha_2 + \beta_2 * \ln L_i^I + \beta_3 * \ln P_i^R + u_{2i} \tag{3}$$

where u_{2i} is the error term. The size of rural population is controlled because it defines the pool of labor supply. Notice that this labor supply function is observable only when w_i is larger than the province's subsistence wage, w_i^*. The whole industrial supply function thus can be defined as

$$w_i^* = \alpha_1 + \beta_1 * A_i + u_{1i} \quad \text{if } w_i < w_i^*, \text{and} \tag{4.1}$$

$$w_i = \alpha_2 + \beta_2 * \ln L_i^I + \beta_3 * \ln P_i^R + u_{2i} \quad \text{if } w_i \geq w_i^*, \tag{4.2}$$

which can be estimated by an endogenous switching model. It is reasonable to assume that the two error terms are uncorrelated because one is concerned with normal labor supply after the turning point and the other is concerned with the determination of the subsistence wage. Their correlation matrix thus is assumed to be

$$\Sigma = \begin{pmatrix} \sigma_1^2 & 0 \\ 0 & \sigma_2^2 \end{pmatrix}$$

We further assume that each error term follows a normal distribution, and then estimate the model by the maximum likelihood method.

Note that we can calculate the turning point using the estimated results of (4). We can first calculate the subsistence wage using equation (4.1). Then equating it to the right-hand side of equation (4.2), we can get the number of workers who are willing to work in industry given the size of rural population. This number of workers indicates the turning point.

For industrial labor demand, we estimate the following demand function:

$$\ln L_i^I = c + \gamma_1 w_i + \gamma_2 GDP_i + \gamma_3 P_i + e_i, \tag{5}$$

where GDP_i is the per-capita GDP in province i, and P_i is its population. We add per-capita GDP to control the level of income, which could raise the industrial wage; and we add the size of population to control the market size in a province that may raise the demand for industrial labor. If the demand curve estimated from (5) crosses the supply curve estimated by (4) on its flat portion, then the economy has not passed the turning point.

2. Empirical results

2.1. Data

We estimate the supply curve in (4) and demand curve in (5) for each year between 1998 and 2007 using the 31 provinces as the unit of analysis. The data come from *China Statistical Yearbook* (NBS 1999–2008a) and *China Regional Statistical Yearbook* (NBS 1999–2008b). The key variables are defined below.

For the supply curve, we obtain A_i by dividing a province's total income from agriculture by the size of its rural labor force. Then L^I_i is the number of rural non-farm workers in a province. Finally, we obtain w_i by dividing a province's total wage income of its rural population by the number of rural non-farm workers in that province. The supply curve measures the marginal cost of labor supply. For a migrant from the countryside, his opportunity cost of leaving the countryside is what he can earn in local non-farm activities. Therefore, it is sensible to use the average non-farm income for the wage rate in the supply function.

For the demand curve, however, the wage rate should be what firms pay for migrants. The problem is that there are no systematic data for migrant wages. As a substitute, the average wage of urban workers is used. But then γ_1 is not the true parameter for migrant workers. Assuming that the migrant wage rate is a fraction, k, say, of the urban wage rate, then γ_1/k should be the true parameter for migrant workers.

2.2. The supply curve

The results of the supply curve for each year between 1998 and 2007 are reported in Table 1. The unit of wages is yuan, and the unit of population and labor is 10,000 people.

The subsistence wage is not significantly linked with agricultural income before 2006, but is in 2006 and 2007. That is, the subsistence wage is roughly the same across provinces before 2006, but differs by agricultural labor income in 2006 and 2007. The parameters for the regular supply curve all make sense. As shown by the results for β_2, the wage rate is significantly positively linked with the number of workers hired, or conversely, the number of workers hired is a significantly positive function of the wage offered by industrial jobs. Then, by the results for β_3, we see that the wage rate is significantly negatively linked with the size of the rural labor force. That is, a larger reserve of labor suppresses the ask price of migrants. Last, the estimates for the two standard deviations are both significant.

Fitting the national data to equations (4.1) and (4.2), we can then obtain the subsistence wage and industrial supply curve after the turning point for the whole country in each year. The results are listed in the first and second columns of Table 2. Notice that the supply curve for each year is obtained conditional on the size of the country's rural population in that year.

The subsistence wage increases over time and is higher than the per-capita rural net income in the respective year (for example, the per-capita rural net income was 4140 yuan in 2007). However, our estimates of the subsistence wage are substantially lower than the migrant wages that are observed by Cai and Wang (2008) and listed in the second to the last column of Table 2. Nevertheless, the gaps between the two series are stable, with the observed migrant wage being 2.3 to 2.7 times of the subsistence wage. This means that

Table 1. Estimation results for the supply curves.

Year	α_1	β_1	α_2	β_2	β_3	σ_1	σ_2
2007	2491.49***	0.42***	29229.79***	9618.10***	−11474.59***	211.93***	2667.22***
	140.26	0.00	4333.79	1474.89	1467.88	73.46	484.56
2006	2328.03***	0.46***	18193.66***	10589.61***	−11402.29***	219.84	2402.85***
	485.27	0.05	6328.33	2695.67	2536.18	211.23	708.01
2005	2195.21***	0.41	17912.90***	10649.34***	−11443.92***	393.72**	2102.12***
	516.21	0.41	5186.79	3636.91	2852.35	150.37	568.62
2004	2241.75***	0.29	14173.25***	12078.75***	−12166.26***	375.71***	2252.62***
	854.57	0.24	2315.70	2277.35	2174.96	119.35	457.58
2003	3822.24***	−0.17	18344.20***	10843.34***	−11505.82***	378.83***	1705.61***
	767.18	0.20	2047.29	2183.39	1919.69	116.71	313.14
2002	3621.38***	−0.07	15696.77***	11675.03***	−11807.40***	412.30***	1707.26***
	777.27	0.25	5015.53	3493.90	2932.01	95.26	378.40
2001	3697.01***	−0.11	15323.47***	9443.29***	−9796.99***	491.12***	1653.84***
	940.20	0.33	3224.42	2762.48	2782.45	107.17	354.13
2000	3329.38**	−0.09	17652.60***	9954.50***	−10768.71***	555.69***	2359.23***
	1541.58	0.61	2768.37	2759.01	2576.18	184.07	599.33
1999	3763.86***	−0.16	13511.43***	10414.35***	−10397.59***	442.16***	1569.26***
	685.13	0.25	1860.55	1951.96	1805.19	89.27	265.28
1998	2818.55***	0.05	14990.85***	11038.65***	−11425.08***	447.97***	2142.64***
	1142.80	0.41	3386.85	9257.87	8124.59	132.73	892.71

Note: The supply functions in (4) are estimated for each year using the 31 provinces as the observations. The first row for each year is for the estimates, and the second row is for the standard errors. *, **, and *** indicate, respectively, significance levels of 10%, 5%, and 1%.

Table 2. Subsistence wages, turning points, and supply curves at the national level.

Year	Sub. wage	Supply curve After turning point	Turning point (10,000)	Observed migrant wage	Urban wage
2007	4817.15	$w = -95274.8 + 9618.1*\ln L_i^I$	33,078	12,180	24,932
2006	4489.18	$w = -105390.0 + 10589.6* \ln L_i^I$	32,085	11,352	21,001
2005	4034.87	$w = -105996.0 + 10649.3* \ln L_i^I$	30,705	10,332	18,364
2004	3420.88	$w = -117389.0 + 12078.8* \ln L_i^I$	22,067	9360	16,024
2003	3222.23	$w = -105907.0 + 10843.3* \ln L_i^I$	23,486	8424	14,040
2002	3400.74	$w = -111704.0 + 11675.0* \ln L_i^I$	19,130	7908	12,422
2001	3338.66	$w = -90324.4 + 9443.3* \ln L_i^I$	20,302	7728	10,870
2000	3037.75	$w = -98414.3 + 9954.5* \ln L_i^I$	26,678	n.a.	n.a.
1999	3266.99	$w = -98321.9 + 10414.4* \ln L_i^I$	17,235	n.a.	n.a.
1998	2972.30	$w = -107780.0 + 11038.6* \ln L_i^I$	22,769	n.a.	n.a.

Note: The unit of wages is yuan. Observed migrant wages and urban wages are from Cai and Wang (2008).

the subsistence wages have matched the growth rates of the observed migrant wages. We can then interpret the gaps between our estimates of the subsistence wage and the wages actually earned by migrants as the premiums that enterprises have to pay migrants to forgo their utilities staying home and to compensate for their higher living costs in the city.

The third column of Table 2 shows the turning points for the years. They indicate the amounts of surplus labor in the countryside. Before 2004, the number of surplus labor fluctuates, but after 2004, it has actually increased. This may have something to do with the spread of mechanization in agriculture. As income increases and labor becomes more expensive, as shown by the increases in the subsistence wage, it is natural to find that farmers substitute labor by machinery.

The surprising result is that China still has a large reserve of surplus labor. Out of the 476 million labor force in 2007, 331 million, or 69%, is shown to be redundant in agriculture. The question then is whether industrial demand is sufficiently high to absorb those redundant workers. The next subsection will answer this question.

2.3.   The demand curve

The results of the demand functions are reported in Table 3. The unit of wages and income is 1000 yuan, and the unit of labor and population is 10,000 people. Not enough data are collected for the years 2000 and 2001, and the demand curve is not estimated for those 2 years. The first five columns report the R^2 and the estimates of the parameters, and the last column reports the demand curves for the whole country conditional on the per-capita GDP and size of the population in each year. The parameter for the wage rate has the expected negative sign for all the years although it is statistically insignificant for some years. The parameters for per-capita GDP and size of the population both have the expected positive sign and are statistically significant.

Combining the supply and demand curves, we can calculate the equilibrium number of migrant workers working in industry in each year. None of them is larger than the number of surplus labor (at the turning point) except in 2004 when the equilibrium number is slightly larger (226.4 million versus 220.7 million). Figure 3 visually shows the case for 3 years, 1998, 2005, and 2007. The equilibrium numbers of migrant workers for these 3 years, respectively, are 70.7 million, 126.4 million, and 141.5 million, much smaller than the numbers of surplus labor in the respective years. On the other hand, they are close to the numbers of migrant workers reported by Cai (2008), which are 50.9 million, 125.8 million, and 137.0 million, respectively. This gives us some confidence in our estimation. We then conclude that China has not passed the LTP.

Table 3.   Results for the demand curves.

Year	R^2	c	γ_1	γ_2	γ_3	The national demand curve
2007	0.88	−1.29	−0.14	0.07	0.86	$\ln L_i^I = 10.23 - 0.14^*w$
		(1.1)	(−3.65)***	(7.33)***	(7.29)***	
2006	0.87	−2.11	−0.10	0.07	0.95	$\ln L_i^I = 10.12 - 0.10^*w$
		(1.81)*	(−1.98)**	(4.83)***	(8.43)***	
2005	0.91	−2.02	−0.051	0.06	0.92	$\ln L_i^I = 9.65 - 0.05^*w$
		(2.45)***	(−1.29)	(5.24)***	(11.54)***	
2004	0.87	−3.01	−0.11	0.06	1.07	$\ln L_i^I = 10.41 - 0.11^*w$
		(2.66)***	(−2.42)***	(5.06)***	(9.38)***	
2003	0.85	−2.19	−0.28	0.11	1.09	$\ln L_i^I = 11.76 - 0.28^*w$
		(1.55)	(4.33)***	(5.70)***	(7.55)***	
2002	0.86	−2.4	−0.06	0.07	0.96	$\ln L_i^I = 9.56 - 0.06^*w$
		(−2.52)***	(−1.34)	(4.65)***	(9.83)***	
1999	0.90	−2.8	−0.35	0.17	1.07	$\ln L_i^I = 10.98 - 0.35^*w$
		(−2.60)*	(3.79)***	(6.23)***	(10.42)***	
1998	0.90	−2.87	−0.09	0.10	0.96	$\ln L_i^I = 9.14 - 0.09^*w$
		(−3.40)**	(−1.16)	(4.24)***	(12.02)***	

Note: The demand function in (5) is estimated for each year using the 31 provinces as the observations. Figures in parentheses are t-statistic values. *, **, and *** indicate, respectively, significance levels of 10%, 5%, and 1%.

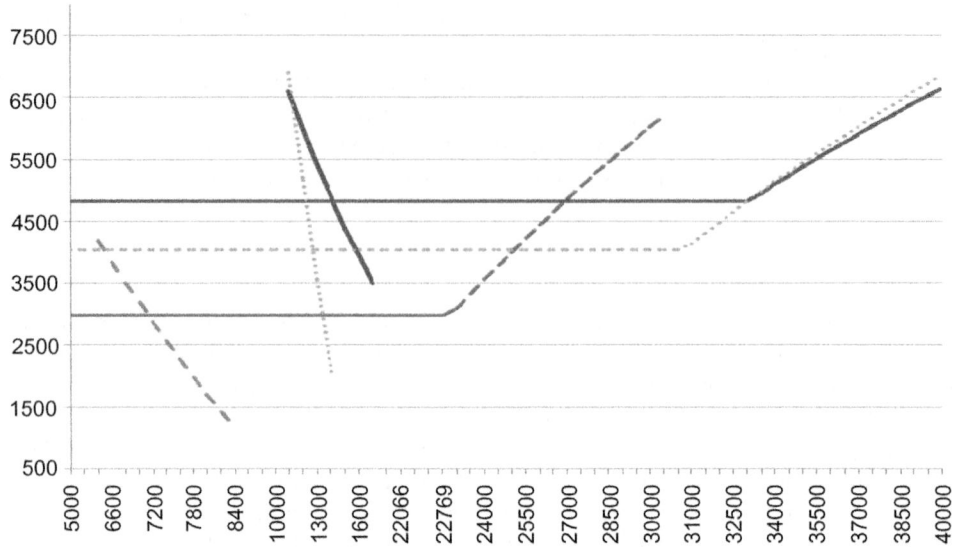

Figure 3.   The supply and demand curves: 1998, 2005, and 2007.

Note: The long dashed lines are for 1998; the short dashed lines are for 2005, and the filled lines are for 2007.

3.   Conclusions

This paper adopts a structural approach to estimate the supply function of migrant workers in China using provincial data. We are able to estimate the turning point for the whole country for each year. With the estimation results for the demand function, we are able to obtain the equilibrium level of migrant workers in each year. The comparison between these two estimates shows that China has not passed the LTP.

Our provincial data provide a limited number of observations for each year. Therefore, our results are more indicative than definitive conclusions. More reliable results can be obtained by using sub-provincial (e.g., city-level) data.

References

Cai, Fang. 2008. *The Lewisian turning point — the new stage of China's economic development.* (liuyisi zhuanzhedian — zhongguo jingji fazhan xin jieduan) Beijing: China Academic Press.

Cai, Fang, and Wang, Meiyuan. 2008. *Report on the Chinese population and labor issues no. 9.* (zhongguo renkou yu laodongli wenti baogao No. 9) Beijing: China Academic Press.

Knight, John, Deng, Quheng, and Li, Shi. 2010. The puzzle of migrant labour shortage and the rural labour surplus in China. The University of Oxford, DoE Working Paper Series No. 494.

Meng, Xin. 2010. "Migration and labor supply." *The China Update,* the Australian National University, July 13, 2010.

Sen, Amartya. 1966. Peasants and dualism with or without surplus labor. *Journal of Political Economy* 74: 425–450.

The Lewis turning point of Chinese economy: Comparison with Japanese experience

Ryoshin Minami[a] and Xinxin Ma[b]

[a]*Department of Economics, Toyo University, Tokyo, Japan;* [b]*Keio Economic Observatory University, Tokyo, Japan*

(*Final version received 12 July 2010*)

In this article, we estimate production function and calculate surplus labor in agriculture. The estimation results revealed that the Lewis turning point (LTP) was not yet passed in China. This study is also made in comparison with Japanese historical experience. The main contents are as follows. First, we survey the recent change in the urban labor market by using unemployment rate as an index to express the balance of labor demand and labor supply, and wage differentials between agriculture and urban industries with high productivity and high wages. Second, we estimate agricultural production function and calculate the marginal productivity of labor and surplus labor in order to demarcate LTP. Third, we reveal factors for the change in agricultural labor by referring to a growth in urban industry and argue on the role of rural industries in absorbing surplus labor. Finally, we refer to several important issues which are left for future studies.

I. Introduction

In 2004, it was reported in media that migrant workers became scarce to push up their wages considerably in coastal urban areas. They were anxious about its negative impacts to the economic growth, which has been dependent greatly on export and foreign investment: wage increase would deteriorate international competitiveness of Chinese export industries and would discourage foreign-owned enterprises to stay in China. This event, which is called as *Mingong Huang* (shortage of migrant workers), caused a debate among economists in and out of this country on whether the Chinese economy has passed the Lewis turning point (LTP) or not[1](Cai 2007, 2008; Cai and Wang 2006; Du 2008; Garnaut and Huang 2006; Meng and Bai 2007; Otsuka 2008; Tajima 2008; Wang 2008; Wu 2007; Yan 2005, 2008). Passing LTP in China, if it is not a misconception, is the fourth event in East Asia following Japan in around 1960 (Minami 1968, 1973, 2002, Chap.9),[2] Taiwan at the end of 1960s (Asamoto 2004; Chen 1983; Fei and Ranis 1975), and Korea at the beginning of 1970s (Kim 1983; Fei and Ranis 1975).

However, it would be a puzzle if China already passed LTP or not, the shortage of migrant workers has not been verified and there are no exact studies which show that it was the LTP. As LTP is a point in time when surplus labor in agriculture which is an index for 'subsistence sector', disappears completely, demarcation of LTP cannot be made without an empirical analysis about employment status in agriculture. In this article, we examine a change in the urban labor market by using appropriate statistics, and estimate surplus labor in agriculture by production function approach. In these discussions, contemporary China is compared with Japanese historical experience in order to promote this study exactly and deeply.

In Section II, we will survey the recent change in urban labor market by using unemployment rate as an index to express the balance of labor demand and labor supply, and wage differentials between agriculture and urban industries with high productivity and high wages. In Section III, we will estimate agricultural production function and based on these results, estimate the marginal productivity of labor (MPL) and the surplus labor in order to demarcate LTP. In Section IV, we will reveal factors for a change in agricultural labor by referring to a growth in urban industry and argue on the role of rural industries in absorbing surplus labor. In the final section, we summarize discussions and conclusions in the previous sections and refer to several important issues, which are left for future studies.

II.   Recent change of the urban labor market

1.   Unemployment rate

The most appropriate index to express the balance of labor demand and labor supply should be the unemployment rate. It is well known that there are some problems in the unemployment statistics compiled by the Bureau of Statistics: it does not include unemployment of migrant workers and laid-off urban workers, who are in fact in unemployment status. Considering these problems, we estimate a more appropriate series of the unemployment rate.[3] Figures from censuses in 1990 and 2000 and 1% sample surveys in 1995 and 2005 are used as benchmarks and we estimate annual series by linking with the annual rate of the Bureau of Statistics.

The unemployment rate, defined as a ratio of unemployed urban labors to the total numbers of urban labor force, increased considerably from 2.8% of 1985 to 12% of the first half of 2000s. The existence of large unemployed labors in urban China[4] should be one of the counter evidences to the phenomenon of *Mingong Huang*.

On the contrary, Japanese unemployment rate (based on census figures) decreased from 2% in the 1950s to 1% in 1960 (Bureau of Statistics, Prime Minister's Office 1987, 365). As is shown later, labor demand increased considerably and labor market became tight by the rapid growth of urban industries or the high-pitched economic growth in the 1950s and 1960s. Large number of labors graduated from junior high schools in the rural moved to the urban areas in groups organized by the urban industries. They were called as 'golden eggs' and contributed to the unprecedented economic growth.

2.   Real wages and wage differentials

Here we are arguing on the wage changes in agriculture, considered as a pool of surplus labor. According to the Lewis theory, agricultural wages are determined by the subsistence level (SL) before the turning point (LTP) and by the MPL after LTP. If SL is constant over time and MPL increases, therefore, agricultural wages should demonstrate a change from a constant to an increase, which demarcates the turning point.

Demarcation of the turning point in Japan by one of the present authors was dependent on the wages of annual contract workers in agriculture. As such statistics in China is not available, we had to use the substitution indices. They are per capita net income of rural households and per capita consumption expenditure of rural households. These

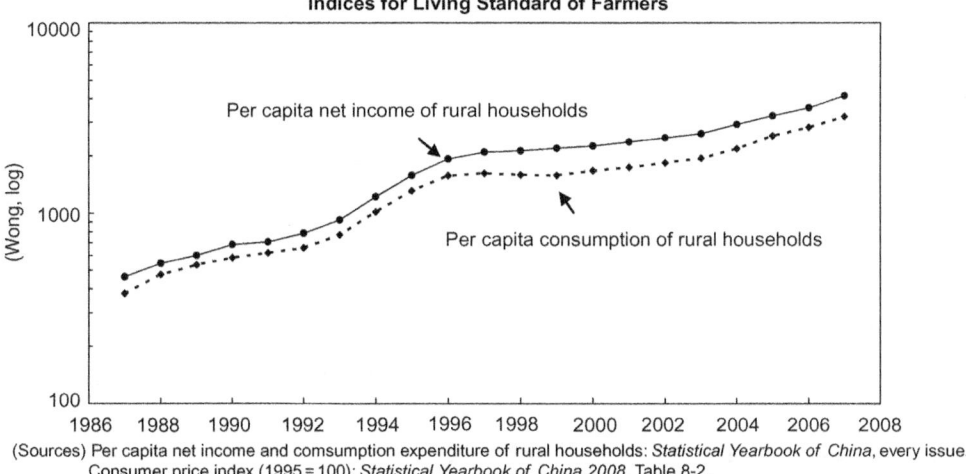

Figure 1.   Indices for living standard of farmers.

indices deflated by consumer price index in Figure 1 show a steady increase since the 1980s. Growth rates for 1988–2007 are respectively 5.3% and 4.9%.

It should be noted that a steady increase in SL does not necessarily demonstrate that the economy has passed the turning point; because SL itself tends to increase due to a development of culture and society even before LTP. Therefore, we are concerned here about an 'acceleration' in the increasing trend of real wages (or the increase of the growth rate), the growth rates of these indices do not show any increase in around 2004, the year of *Mingong Huang*.

Another point which should be studied is a change in the wage differentials between unskilled and skilled workers. Unlimited supplies of labor are only applicable to unskilled workers (supplied mainly from agriculture) and skilled workers in urban industries are limited in supply even in a labor surplus society. As unskilled worker wages tend to increase only after LTP, it can be supposed that wage differentials between the two groups of workers may be decrease after LTP.

Figure 2B depicts the ratios of SL (here per capita net income of rural households) to the three groups of urban industries, manufacturing, financial and infra industries (electric, gas and water supply). Manufacturing is the most typical urban industry, which employs a large number of migrant workers, while the other two industries[5] employ white color and skilled workers with high wages, but not many migrant workers. Such difference among these industry groups in employing migrant workers causes a difference in the pattern of change in wage differentials; the ratio to manufacturing decreased only slowly, while the ratios to the other industries demonstrated a rapid decrease since the 1990s even after 2004. They show that there was not a decrease in the wage differentials between skilled and unskilled workers.

The change of real wages of Japanese agriculture (annual contract workers) shows quite a different pattern compared with China. They did not show a significantly increasing trend for the prewar period. The growth rate was only 1.2% for 1898–1938. For the postwar period, it was 4.4% before LTP (1954–61), and 7.1% after LTP (1961–69) (Minami 1973, 147–54). In Figure 2A, the ratio of agricultural wages to machinery industry (male only), which is an index for wage differential between unskilled and skilled workers, was almost

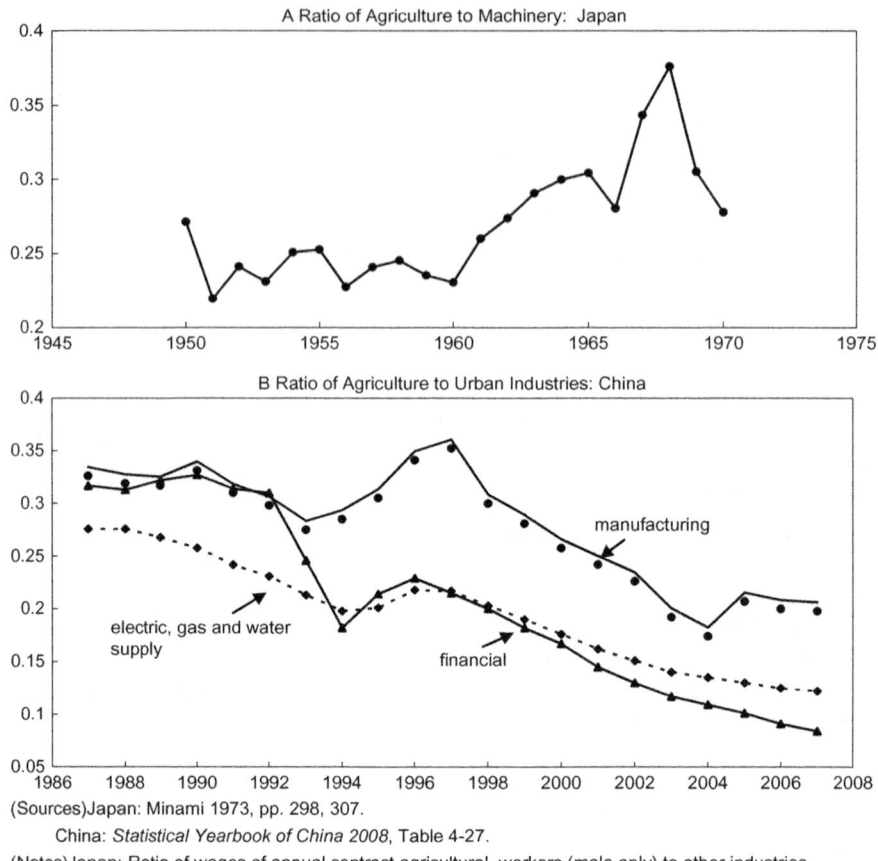

Figure 2.   Wage differentials of agriculture to other industries: Japan and China.

constant in the 1950s and decreased considerably in the 1960s.[6] This signifies unskilled workers that were supplied mainly from agriculture, became scarce to push up their wages considerably. This is one of the evidences for demarcating LTP in around 1960.[7] Such changes in the labor market are not seen in China.

III.   Estimation of agricultural production function and surplus labor

1.   Agricultural production function

Production function is estimated for primary industry, because forestry and fishery are included inseparably in the *Yearbook of Chinese Agriculture*. Because composition of agricultural products and technologies in producing these products are not constant over time and considerably different among regions, the estimation of production functions should be made by sub-periods and by regions. In this paper, however, the estimation by sub-periods (1990–95, 1996–2000 and 2001–05) is made only for a whole country and that by three regions, Eastern (11 provinces), Central (10 provinces) and Western (10 provinces),[8] is only for the whole period. Time-series (annual) data and cross-sectional statistics (by 31 provinces) are combined together in all estimation.

Agricultural production function to be estimated is as follows:

$$LnY_{it}/L_{it} = A + \alpha LnN_{it}/L_{it} + \beta LnK_{it}/L_{it} + \sum \delta_j D_{ijt} + \lambda t + u_{it}. \tag{1}$$

Here Y, N, K and L signify gross value added (1995 prices), labor force, gross capital stock (1995 prices) and land area. A is a constant. Suffix i and j denote 31 provinces and three districts, respectively. Parameters α and β are production elasticity of labor and capital, and the elasticity of land γ is calculated as 1 - α - β. D_{ij} is a dummy variable for regions. They are Eastern district dummy (1 for Eastern district and 0 for other districts, Central district dummy (1 for Middle district and 0 for other districts) and Western district dummy (1 for Western district and 0 for other districts).[9] In the case of estimation by districts, we set forth one dummy variable for each district: Eastern district dummy (1 for Beijin, Tianjin, Shanghai, Jiangsu, Zhejiang and Guangdong and 0 for other provinces), Central district dummy (1 for Shanxi, Inner Mongolia, Jilin and Heilongiang and 0 for other provinces), and Western district dummy (1 for Chongqing, Sichuan, Guizhou and Yunnan and 0 for other provinces). Suffix t denotes year. 't' denotes a time trend (assumed as 1 for 1990) and λ is its parameter. 'u' is an error term.

Table 1 is the result of estimation by three sub-periods for a whole country. Our estimates of α, β and γ for the first sub-period are not so different from previous estimates by other authors for 1993–95; they are 0.337, 0.225 and 0.408, respectively in Shintani's estimates (1998, 121) and 0.352, 0.458, 0.190, respectively in Hondai and Luo's estimates (1999, 66).

An interesting finding in our estimates is the increasing trend in α, 0.215, 0.259 and 0.379 in the three sub-periods, respectively. This fact is similar to the case of Japan.

Table 1. Estimation of agricultural production function: Japan and China.

	Production elasticity of labor α	Production elasticity of capital β	Production elasticity of land γ	Dummy variable of east district D1	Dummy variable of middle district D2	Trend λ	Coefficient of determination
Japan							
1916 ~ 1930	0.125	0.112	0.763				
1931 ~ 1940	0.254	0.143	0.603				
1953 ~ 1966	0.562	0.221	0.217				
China							
1990 ~ 1995	0.215	0.148	0.637	−0.494	−0.555	−0.052	0.604
	(4.34)	(4.99)		(−9.25)	(−10.86)	(−2.46)	
1996 ~ 2000	0.259	0.140	0.601	−0.515	−0.671	0.017	0.621
	(4.03)	(2.64)		(−9.22)	(−12.82)	(1.11)	
2001 ~ 2005	0.379	0.098	0.523	−0.622	−0.746	0.067	0.649
	(5.37)	(2.00)		(−9.75)	(−12.91)	(3.86)	

(Sources) Japan: Figure for 1916 ~ 30 is a simple average of 1916 ~ 20, 1921 ~ 25, and 1926 ~ 30. Figure for 1931 ~ 40 is a simple average of 1931 ~ 35 and 1936 ~ 40. Prewar estimates are from Minami 1981, p.359.
Figure of the postwar period (1953 ~ 66 is a simple average of the estimates by five classes of farm-size [Minami 1973, p.194].
China: See text.
(Notes) Figure in ( ) is t-value. Coefficient of determination is adjusted by the degree of freedom.

In Japan, α increased from 0.125 for 1916–30, to 0.254 for 1931–40, and to 0.562 for 1953–66 (Minami 1981). These results may signify that the same type of technological change of agriculture (labor-using type) was dominant both in prewar Japan and contemporary China. Also it should be noticed that α is almost equivalent between the two countries.[10]

Dummy variables of Central and Western districts are all statistically significant for all periods, which demonstrate that Eastern district has rather higher production efficiency compared with other districts.

Table 2 is the result of estimation by three districts for the whole period (1990–2007). Production elasticity of labor α is almost equal between Eastern and Western districts (0.259 and 0.328, respectively), and it is very small in Central district (0.097). This result is similar to the previous study by Anxia Li, who estimated production functions for the years 1982–2002 by three regions. Production elasticity of labor is 0.363, 0.019 and 0.440, respectively for Eastern, Central and Western districts (Li 2005, Table 3–3).[11] As will be stated in the next section, that α is smaller in Central district is one of the factors for smaller MPL in this district (another factor is lower average productivity of labor).

2. Agricultural surplus labor

In Table 3, MPL, which is obtained as a product of α with average labor productivity (APL), is compared with the two indices for the subsistence level of agricultural population (SL). They are per capita net income of rural households and per capita consumption expenditure of rural households, respectively in Estimations (1) and (2).

The ratio MPL/SL demonstrates an increasing trend in all estimations, which shows a change in agricultural labor market. For instance in Estimation (1), the ratio increased among three sub-periods, they are 35.6% (1990–95), 39.1% (1996–2000) and 56.6% (2001–05).

In Table 4, surplus labor is estimated as a difference between the total labor force and 'equilibrium labor', which makes MPL = SL. In the last column, the 'rate of surplus labor' (a ratio of surplus labors to total labor force) is shown. For instance in Estimation (1), they are 75.7%, 71.5% and 64.8%, respectively in the three sub-periods. This demonstrates an

Table 2. Estimation of agricultural production function by regions for 1990 ~ 2007.

	Production elasticity of labor α	Production elasticity of capital β	Production elasticity of land γ	Dummy variable of east district D1	Dummy variable of central district D2	Trend λ	Coefficient of determination
Total	0.307 (8.97)	0.055 (3.36)	0.638	−0.573 (−17.20)	−0.675 (−21.50)	0.028 (7.40)	0.645
Eastern District	0.259 (3.63)	0.022 (0.74)	0.719	0.218 (5.15)		0.040 (6.86)	0.603
Middle District	0.097 (1.54)	0.024 (1.04)	0.879	−0.330 (−5.85)		0.028 (5.13)	0.593
Western District	0.328 (4.25)	0.074 (2.48)	0.598	−0.071 (−1.13)		0.019 (2.55)	0.506

(Sources) See text.
(Notes) See text for definition of three districts.

Table 3. Comparison of marginal productivity of labor and wages in agriculture: Japan and China.

	Average productivity of labor APL	Production elasticity of labor α	Marginal productivity of labor MPL=α APL	(Wong) Estimation (1)		Estimation (2)	
				Subsistence level SL	MPL/SL (%)	Subsistence level SL	MPL/SL (%)
Japan							
1920 ~ 1937	184	0.245	45	139	32.4		
1955 ~ 1968	342	0.562	192	183	104.9		
China							
1990 ~ 1995	2,380	0.215	512	1,438	35.6	1,213	42.2
1996 ~ 2000	2,979	0.259	772	1,974	39.1	1,497	51.6
2001 ~ 2005	3,486	0.379	1,321	2,333	56.6	1,749	75.5
Eastern District	4,596	0.259	1,190	4,114	28.9	2,390	49.8
Central District	3,225	0.097	313	2,519	12.4	1,849	16.9
Western District	2,399	0.328	974	1,920	50.7	1,534	63.5

(Sources) Japan: Minami 1973, p.200. α is from Table 1. SL is wages for annual contract agricultural workers.
China: APL is calculated as a ratio of GDP to employment of primary industry. GDP is from Statsitical Yearbook of China 2008, Table 2–1, Table 2–5.
Employment is our estimates based on census figures (See Table 5).
α is from Table 1 and Table 2.
SL(Estimation 1: per capita net income of rural households, Estimation 2: per capita comsumption expenditure of rural households) is same to Figure 1.
Deflator is obtained as a ratio of nominal GDP to real GDP of primary industry. GDP is from *Statistical Yearbook of China 2008*, Table 2–1, Table 2–5.
(Notes) Japan: 1934 ~ 36 prices. China: 1995 prices.

Table 4.   Estimation of surplus labor in agriculture: Japan and China.

	Total labor force	Estimation (1)			Estimation (2)		
		Equilibrium labor force	Surplus labor	Ratio of surplus labor (%)	Equilibrium labor force	Surplus labor	Ratio of surplus labor (%)
Japan							
1906 ~ 1940	2,133	917	1,216	57.2			
China							
1990 ~ 1995	45,907	11,129	34,778	75.7	19,316	26,591	57.9
1996 ~ 2000	45,671	13,077	32,761	71.5	24,585	21,253	46.4
2001 ~ 2005	45,803	16,112	29,691	64.8	29,913	15,890	34.6
Eastern District	15,925	6,960	8,965	56.3	13,829	2,096	13.2
Central District	17,154	2,733	14,421	84.1	5,120	12,034	70.2
Western District	12,724	6,419	6,305	49.6	10,964	1,760	13.8

(Sources) Japan: Minami and Ono 1977, p.159.
China: Calculated from Table 3.
(Notes) Equilibirium labor force is the size of employment with MPL = SL.
Surplus labor is a difference between total labor force and equilibrium labor force.

existence of a large number of surplus labors in cotemporary China and a decreasing trend of the surplus labors which signifies that the Chinese economy is approaching to LTP.

We compare our estimates of the rate of surplus labor for the first sub-period (75.7% and 57.9%, respectively in Estimations (1) and (2)) with previous estimates by other authors.[12] Estimates by Shintani for 1990–95 is 50–55% (1998, 128) and that by Hondai and Luo for 1993–95 is 60–68% (1999, 73). Both of them are between Estimation (1) and (2). Furthermore the estimate for prewar Japan by one of the present authors is 57% for 1906–40 (Minami and Ono 1977, 159) that is also between the two estimates in China.

In this table, the rate of surplus labor is shown by three districts for 2001–05. It is the smallest in Eastern and it is the largest in Central districts. This result shows that the rate of surplus labor tends to be larger in less-developed areas. Also, it should be noticed that the rate is negative in some provinces. In case of Estimation (2), for instance, two provinces (Hainan and Xinjiang) show negative rate.[13] However, these areas are rather exceptions and China as a total has not passed LTP.

IV.   Factors for a change in agricultural labor force and employment absorption by rural industries

1.   Outflow of agricultural labor force

It is MPL (therefore APL) of agricultural labor force that decides the level and its change in surplus labor. APL depends on the level of agricultural technology and the size of employment. This is the reason why we are arguing on the change of agricultural labor force. In China, according to Table 5, primary industry labor force increased significantly in the 1970s and 1980s, and has been decreasing since the 1990s. For all periods (1981–2007), it shows an increase in trend. There was an increase of 1310 thousand persons per year.[14] In Japan, on the contrary, it showed a slightly decreasing trend in the prewar period (since the early 1900s up to the end of 1930s) and a rapid decrease in the postwar period, the decrease was 465 thousands persons per year since 1951 through 1960, the year of LTP.

Table 5. Factors for the changes in primary labor force: Japan and China.

	(10 thousands persons)					
	Increase in primary labor force				Increase in non-primary labor force	
	Total increase	Natural increase	Net outflow	Rate of net outflow (%)	Total increase	Ratio of net inflow in total increase (%)
Japan						
1901 ~ 1940	−4.3	10.4	14.7	0.96	24.2	60.7
1951 ~ 1970	−46.0	24.7	70.7	4.93	123.4	56.8
China						
1981 ~ 1990	1,019	1,112	93	0.27	531	17.5
1991 ~ 2000	−77	435	512	1.13	734	69.8
2001 ~ 2007	−840	418	1,258	2.83	1,282	98.1
(1981 ~ 2007)	131	682	551	1.25	801	68.8

(Sources) Japan: Minami 1973, p.106.
China: Estimated from the number of labor force by industry groups. The number of labor force up to 2000 is from [Minami and Xue 2010]. Figures from 2001 is extrapolated by linking with the figures in *Statistical Yearbook of China* 2008, Tale 4–3.
(Notes) Annual figures.

Such a difference in the pattern of changes in agricultural labor force between the two countries is the main reason for a difference in the change of surplus labor between the two countries.

An increase of agricultural labor force is a difference between natural increase and net outflow to non-agriculture. Table 5 shows that smaller net outflow than natural increase was a reason for an increase in agricultural labor force in China. In the total period, net outflow per year was 5510 thousands, which was smaller than the natural increase that was 6820 thousands. In Japan, to the contrast, net outflow (807 thousands per year) was much larger than natural increase (342 thousands per year). A difference of the speed of outflow in two countries becomes clearly for the net outflow rate, it was 5.16% per year in the 1950s in Japan, while it was only 1.25% in China for 1981–2007.

The main reason for the comparatively small outflow of agricultural labor force in contemporary China is a rather moderate increase of the labor demand in urban industries compared with Japan.[15] Figure 3 shows the close correlation between the rate of net outflow of agricultural labor force and the growth rate of real GDP of non-primary industries, which signifies that the former is dependent basically on the growth of urban industries.[16] In the same diagram, the growth rate of migrant workers is drawn. The data which are the survey result of the Office for the Observation of Rural Areas and the Bureau of Statistics, show a close correlation to the net outflow of agriculture, which is in our estimates.[17]

2. Evaluation of demographic factors

In China, employment absorption capacity of urban industries was smaller than in Japan. This should be the main reason for a delay in approaching to LTP in China. Percentage of non-primary industries in total employment in Figure 4 decreased since the 1970s, but this change was not significant compared with Japan in the 1950s and 1960s.

Here, we are arguing on the view which emphasizes a role of demographic factor in changing labor market. Cai and others emphasize the fact that a decrease in the growth rate

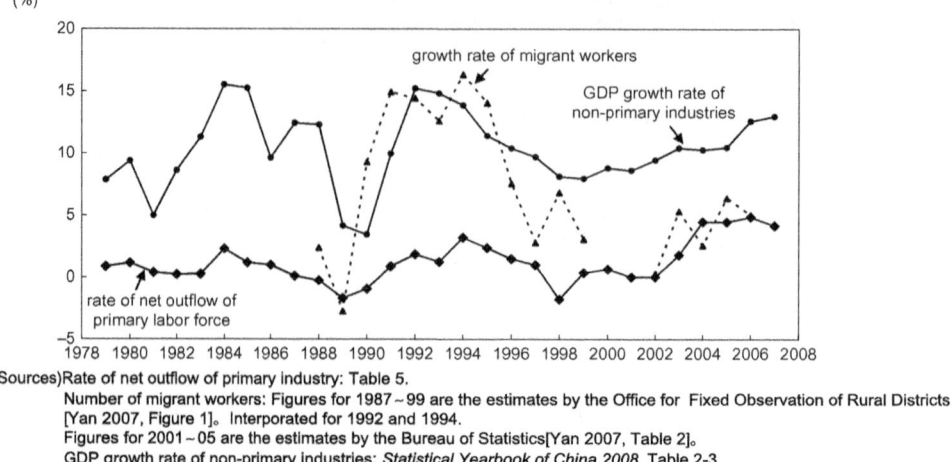

(Sources)Rate of net outflow of primary industry: Table 5.
Number of migrant workers: Figures for 1987~99 are the estimates by the Office for Fixed Observation of Rural Districts [Yan 2007, Figure 1]。 Interporated for 1992 and 1994.
Figures for 2001~05 are the estimates by the Bureau of Statistics[Yan 2007, Table 2]。
GDP growth rate of non-primary industries: *Statistical Yearbook of China 2008*, Table 2-3.

Figure 3. GDP growth rate of non-primary industries, the rate of net outflow of primary labor force and the growth rate of the number of migrant workers.

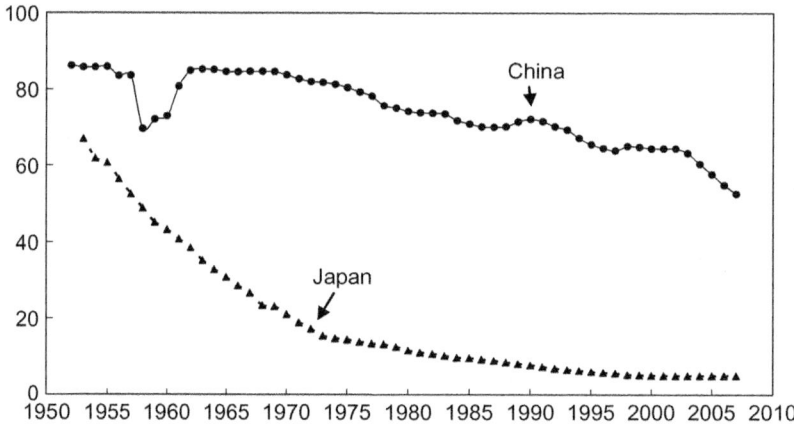

(Sources) China: Figures up to 2000 are from [Minami and Xue 2010]. Figures from 2001 are extrapolated by linking with the figures from *Statistical Yearbook of China 2008*, Table 4-3.
Japan: Figures up to 1970 are from [Minami 1973, p.91]. Figures from 2001 are from *Annual Survey of Labor Force*.

Figure 4. Percentage of primary industries in the total number of labor force: Japan and China.

of labor supply coming from a decrease in the population natural increase is contributing to the change of labor market from surplus to shortage in the first half of 2000s or in the near future (Cai and Wang 2006). In Table 6, we use the growth rates of population above 15 years old and labor force as indices of labor supply. In fact, the growth rate in China since the 1990s is smaller than in Japan. For instance, the growth rate of labor force was only 1.2% for 1991–2000 and 0.9% for 2001–07, almost half of what it was in Japan in the 1950s and 1960s. However, in prewar Japan it was not high, it was 1.3% for 1921–40, which was equivalent to China in the 1990s. It was due to such a rapid increase in labor demand caused by the rapid economic growth that surplus labor disappeared in Japan in around 1960, although the growth rate of labor force increased to 2% in this period. Although it cannot be denied that the slow increase in labor supply is a favorable factor in approaching

Table 6. Changes in labor supply: Japan and China.

	(%)	
	Annual rate of increase	
	Population 15 years old and over	Labor force
Japan		
1921 ~ 1940	1.39	1.26
1956 ~ 1960	1.97	2.00
1961 ~ 1970	1.94	1.90
China		
1981 ~ 1990	2.47	2.73
1991 ~ 2000	1.65	1.21
2001 ~ 2007	1.69	0.88
(1981 ~ 2007)	1.96	1.69

(Sources) Japan: Minami 1973, p.239.
China: Figures up to 2000 are the estimates based on censuses [Minami and Xue 2010].
Figures from 2001 are extrapolated by linking with *Population Change Survey* in 2004 and 2007 (*Statistical Yearbook of China*, every issue) in case of population and *Statistical Yearbook of China 2008*, Table 4–3 in case of labor force.

to and passing LTP, Japanese experience shows that we should pay more attention to the labor demand than the labor supply when we argue about the change of the labor market in China, such as whether it is approaching to or passing LTP in China.

3. Labor absorption of township and village enterprises

A part of outflow of agricultural labor force is absorbed in township and village enterprises. Following the Lewis theory, there is a part of 'capitalist sector' (or modern sector), although located in rural districts. This is one of the points to be noticed in applying the Lewis theory to the Chinese economy.

Production function to be estimated is as follows:

$$LnY_i/K_i = A + \alpha LnL_i/K_i + \sum \delta_j D_{ij} + u_i. \qquad (2)$$

Y, N and K (1995 prices for Y and K) are value added, labor force and capital stock respectively. Suffix i and j denote 31 provinces and three districts, respectively. D_j denotes regional dummy variables (same to agricultural production function). A is a constant. 'u' is an error term. α is production elasticity of labor. Estimation is made by combining cross-sectional and time series statistics. Due to data availability, however, estimation is made for two sub-periods, 1990–92 and 1996–2000.

Results of the estimation are shown in Table 7. Estimates of α are statistically significant in all periods and show an increasing trend. This is the same to agricultural production function. In Table 8, MPL is calculated and compared with wages. We find that they are almost equivalent and surplus labor is not existent in this group of industries. This is the same finding as the study by Hondai and Luo (1999, 65).

In China, rural industries developed rapidly during the early phase of modernization, because of less-developed industrialization in rural areas before the economic reform period. However, they are rather stagnant since the latter half of 1990s due to their being

Table 7. Estimation of production function of rural industries.

	Production elasticity of labor α	Production elasticity of capital β	Dummy variable of east district D1	Dummy variable of central district D2	Coefficient of determination
1990 ~ 1992	0.615 (6.24)	0.385	−0.146 (1.71)	−0.352 (4.07)	0.643
1996 ~ 2000	0.552 (2.99)	0.448	0.114 (0.65)	−0.297 (−1.63)	0.471

(Sources) *Statistical Yearbook of Rural Indsutries*, every issue.

Table 8. Comparison of marginal productivity of labor and wages in rural industries.

	(Wong)				
	Average productivity of labor APL	Production elasticity of labor α	Marginal productivity of labor MPL $= \alpha$APL	Wages W	Ratio MPL/SL (%)
1990 ~ 1992	5,077	0.615	3,122	2,646	118.0
1996 ~ 2000	8,754	0.552	4,832	4,481	107.8

(Sources) APL: Output divided by the number of labor force of rural industries.
Data is from *Statistical Yearbook of Rural Indsutries*, every issue.
α: Table 7.
W: See Table 3.
Deflator: Nominal GDP divided by real GDP of non-primary industries. Data is from *Statistical Yearbook of China 2008*, Table 2–1 and Table 2–5.
(Notes) 1995 prices.

at a disadvantage competing with modern industries in urban areas. Annual increase of the employment in rural industries is 1856 thousands persons for 1995–2007.[18]

V. Conclusions and future prospects

1. Summary and conclusions

Our research based on macro-data did not find any evidences for labor shortage in China, although the phenomenon of *Mingong Huang appeared* in the first half of 2000s, which was reported that was meaning that migrant workers became scarce in China. That is, unemployment rate, the most representative index for the balance of demand and supply of labor force, did not show any decline and wage differentials of agriculture to urban industries were increasing even in the 2000s.

More important conclusion of our research is that China has not yet passed the turning point. We estimated agricultural production functions and calculated MPL for three periods: 1990–95, 1996–2000 and 2001–05. Main findings are as follows: First, even in the most recent sub-period, MPL is only 56.6% of per capita net income and 75.5% of per capita consumption expenditure of rural household. The rate of surplus labor (labor force whose MPL is smaller than SL in total employment) was 64.8% (Estimation (1)) and 34.6% (Estimation (2)). Second, the rate of surplus labor demonstrates a declining trend among three periods. This result may suggests that MPL of agriculture has been increasing and China is approaching to LTP. Third, in two provinces (Hainan and Xinjiang) we find negative rate of surplus labor, which shows that LTP was already passed. In summary, we can say that the significant number of surplus labor is still existent in Chinese agriculture and that LTP has not yet been passed, but it cannot be denied that China is on a process to LTP.

The most important reason for delaying an approach to LTP was that the outflow of labor force from the rural to the urban was not enough, which disturbed an increase in MPL in agriculture. On the contrary, in Japan for the 1950s, with the rapidly growing labor demand in the urban industries, a large number of agricultural labors were absorbed in these industries, which caused a drastic decline in agricultural labor force. As a result surplus labor disappeared around 1960.

There are two reasons for insufficient outflow of agricultural labor in China. The first is a labor market segmentation between urban and rural by the registration system (Cai, Du, and Wang 2005; Ma 2008). For example, discriminations to migrant workers in urban in employment status, wages, education for their children, social security and others that tend to increase opportunity costs to migrate from rural to urban. As a result of this, there is a possibility that labor supply becomes scarce in the urban, even though a large number of surplus labors still exist in rural. This shows that the policies to decrease the opportunity cost of migration and to promote labor mobility from rural to urban are necessary. Policies to integrate urban and rural labor markets by abolishing registration system should be considered in future.

The second is a deficiency of the demand for labor in urban industries. This is evident from the fact that the unemployment rate has increased and remained at a high level for the recent period. The labor-intensive industries, especially in the less-developed areas, should be developed more to promote employment expansion.

2. Future prospects for study

Here we are referring to five important questions, which should be studied in future.

The first comes from the fact that there are differences in the balance of demand and supply among different groups of labors. A typical case is a difference in age group; for instance, young female migrants are employed in assembling process of machinery industry. This may cause an earlier LTP for young workers.[19] Viewed from long-term perspective, however, unbalance in demand and supply of a certain group of workers can be adjusted by using other groups of workers. In this sense, demarcation of LTP may tend to coincide with each other among different groups of labors.

The second is an impact of the regional difference to the timing of LTP. In such a wide country like China, regional differences tend to be large. It is a reason why we estimated agricultural production functions by the three districts (Eastern, Central and Western Districts). There are also regional differences in non-agricultural industries, which tend to cause differences in labor demand and consequently in demarcation of LTP. Careful studies on the regional differences are important.

The third is an analysis on the 'informal sector' in urban China. The Lewis theory of dual economy assumes a coexistence of capitalist and subsistence sectors, and in general, the urban (non-agricultural) industries and the rural (agricultural) industries are considered to represent the former and the latter, respectively. However, adjustment or modification should be needed in applying this theory to study the Chinese economy. 'Rural industries' should belong to the capitalist sector and 'urban small firms' (such as small family firms, self-employed firms and so on) should be a part of subsistence sector. Although the contribution of rural industries to absorb surplus labor was argued in Section 3 of this paper, but the role of urban small firms (Marukawa 2002, 94–108; Ma 2008) is not considered here. It is widely known that urban small firms in prewar Japan absorbed a lot of unskilled workers moving from rural, and as was mentioned in footnote 7 of this paper, relative wages of these workers showed a decline compared to the wages in large-scale enterprises. Elaborate research about informal sector in urban China is needed.

The fourth is about a study on the relation between surplus labor and the relative income share of labor. Surplus labor in the rural areas tends to disturb wage increase in the urban industries and to cause a decline in the relative income share of labor. One of the present authors, who estimated the relative income share of labor in non-primary industries in Japan, found that it decreased from 70% in 1896 to 46% in 1940 and explained this phenomenon by referring to the availability of agricultural surplus labor. In the postwar period, the relative share of labor continued a declining trend for some years, but turned to be stable since the beginning of 1960s (Minami and Ono 1978, 1981). A study on China, on the other hand, revealed a declining trend in the relative share of labor in the urban industries (Marukawa 2002, 173–180), which may signify that China has not yet passed LTP. Much more elaborate study is needed.

The fifth is a study on the relation between surplus labor and income distribution. It is supposed that total income distribution becomes more unequal when surplus labor is existent, because, as was pointed out in the above, wage increase of unskilled workers in low productivity sector with surplus labor tends to lag behind the wage increase of skilled workers in other sectors. This signifies a possibility of a coincidence of two turning points: the LTP and the Kuznets LTP (the point when inequality of income distribution turns from increasing to decreasing trend).[20] The coincidence was observed typically in Japan. During the prewar and the early postwar periods various income differentials widened and consequently income distribution became more unequal. Since around 1960 we can observe both the narrowing of income differentials and the equalization of income distribution, which means that the two LTPs were passed in the same time (Minami 1998, 2008).[21] In China, on the contrary, we observe both the increasing income differentials between the rural and the urban, and the worsening income distribution (Li, Sicular, and Gustaffson 2008; Minami, Makino, and Luo 2008, Chap.10; Sato 2003; Xue, Arayama, and Sonoda 2008). This signifies that China is still in the period before these two LTPs. But we should be careful in this issue, because there is a possibility that the income inequality problem does not disappear even if the economy passes the LTP. In many developed countries including Japan, income distribution turned to a worsening trend since the 1980s. This new phenomenon necessitates developing a different theoretical framework.

Notes

1. Lewis dual economy model assumes a coexistence of 'capitalist sector' and 'subsistence sector'. The former is characterized with profit maximizing behavior of capitalists, while in the latter, the marginal productivity of labor (MPL) is smaller than wages, which are determined by the subsistence level (SL) dominant in the society. In general, they are represented by urban industries and agriculture, respectively. Labor force of subsistence sector is supplied to capitalist sector at constant SL (unlimited supplies of labor). When MPL increases and reaches to SL, profit maximizing behavior starts to operate and labor force of subsistence sector is now available only with increasing wages (limited supplies of labor). This point in time is the 'turning point' (Lewis 1954). It is referred to as Lewis turning point (LTP) in this article.
2. For the other demarcation see Minami 2002, 213–214.
3. As for a detailed explanation of the estimation procedure, see (Minami and Xue 2010). However, the estimation in this article is limited to the years up to 2000. The estimation between 2001 and 2005 was made in a similar procedure to the former period.
4. For a detailed discussion of the unemployment see (Marukawa 2002, Chap. 3).
5. They are the industries with the highest wages among 19 industry groups in *Statistical Yearbook of China 2008*, Tables 4–27.

6. The most representative wage differential is that by the scale of enterprises. Ratio of small and medium-size to large-scale enterprises decreased in the 1950s and turned to increase in 1959 (Minami 1973, 175–177).

7. In demarcating LTP wages for unskilled workers in the urban industries are also important. One of the authors, in a study on Japan, used not only wages of annual-contract workers in agriculture but also wages of female workers in textile (Minami 1973, 133–178).

   Meng and Bai (2007), based on wage statistics in seven factories in Guangdong Province, revealed that there was not a significant increase in the real wages of unskilled workers and criticized the view that China passed LTP. However, we should be modest in arguing about the whole country based on such micro-statistics.

8. Eastern district includes Liaoning, Beijing, Hebei, Tianjin, Shandong, Jiangsu, Shanghai, Zhejiang, Fujian, Guangdong and Hainan. Central district includes Heilongjiang, Inner Mongolia, Jilin, Shanxi, Henan, Hubei, Hunan, Anhui, Jiangxi, and Guangxi. Western district includes Xinjiang, Ningxia, Gansu, Shanxi, Tibet, Sichuan, Chongqing (since 1997), Qinghai, Guizhou and Yunnan. Chongqing City, which was a part of Sichuan Province in 1996, was estimated from the data in 1997 and separated from Sichuan.

9. In estimation, Eastern district is a reference in these three districts dummy variables.

10. Production elasticity of labor showed a decline after the 1960s in Japan (Shintani 1983, 174).

11. Estimated production functions include four variables of labor, capital, land and intermediate inputs. If we exclude intermediate inputs in order to make a comparison with our study the production elasticity of labor becomes 0.628, 0.032 and 0.506, respectively for the three districts. The estimate for the Central district is too small, which needs careful examinations.

12. There is a various kind of estimation of surplus labor different from Lewis's definition (for instance, the number of labors who have smaller productivity than other industries). They are not considered here.

13. A development of fishery industry and a production of specific melons may be responsible to the higher labor productivity of primary industry in Hainan and Xinjiang Provinces, respectively.

14. Annual statistics of the number of employment by industry groups in the postwar period is published by the Bureau of Statistics in every issue of *Statistical Yearbook of China*. Bureau of Statistics also publishes more reliable figures from the population censuses in 1982, 1990 and 2000. One of the present authors estimate and will publish annual series, which is based on census figures and estimated for other years by linking with the annual statistics in the above (Minami and Xue 2010). These figures are utilized in this paper.

15. For 1981–2007, according to Table 5, 69% of an increase in non-primary industries employment comes from primary industry.

16. Adjusted coefficient of determination for 1979–2007 is 0.358.

17. Figures used here are 68,720 and 94,730 thousands in 1999 and 2001, respectively (no data for 2000). As it is evident that there is a discontinuity between the two years, a diagram of the growth rate of the number for migrant workers is discontinuous in Figure 3.

18. Statistical Yearbook of China 2008, Table 4–2.

19. Same thing can be found for a difference in the degree of education. According to surveys on migrants they are biased to junior high school graduate, which shows that urban industries demand these types of workers (Yan 2005, Chap.7). If so, LTP should be different among education levels of employment.

20. Impacts of passing Lewis LTP to income distribution are not simple, because income distribution in the total economy is composed of three components: income distribution within rural areas, income distribution in urban areas, and rural-urban income differentials. Careful studies should be needed for the impacts of LTP on these components.

21. Asamoto found the same thing in Taiwan (2004, 11–13).

References

Asamoto, Teruo. 2004. *Development economics and experience of Taiwan: Mechanism of Asian economies*, Tokyo, Keiso Shobo (in Japanese).

Cai, Fang, ed. 2007. *Reports on China's population and labor no.8: The Lewisian turning point and the challenge of policies*. Social Sciences Academic Press, Beijing (in Chinese).

Cai, Fang, ed. 2008. *Reports on China's population and labor no. 9: Linking up Lewis and Kuznets turning points*. Social Sciences Academic Press, Beijing (in Chinese).

Cai, Fang, and Deweng Wang. 2006. Employment growth, labor scarcity and the nature of China's trade expansion. In *The turning point in China's economic development*, eds. Ross Garnaut and Ligang Song, 143–171. Asia Pacific Press at the Australian National University, Canberra.

Cai, Fang, Yang Du, and Meiyan Wang. 2005. The segmentation of labor market. In *Transition and development of the labor market China*, eds. Fang Cai, Yang Du, and Meiyan Wang, 181–204. Commercial Press, Beijing (in Chinese).

Chen, Chun-shun. 1983. Economic development and labor market in Taiwan. *Asian Economies* 24, no. 5 (May): 30–41 (in Japanese).

Du, Yang. 2008. Wage level, wage differentials and labor structure. In *Reports on China's population and labor no.9, linking up Lewis and Kuznets turning points*, ed. Fang Cai, 122–137. Social Sciences Academic Press, Beijing (in Chinese).

Fei, J.C.H., and Gustav Ranis. 1975. A model of growth and employment in the open dualistic economy: The case of Korea and Taiwan. *Journal of Development Studies* 11, no. 2 (January): 32–63.

Garnaut, Ross, and Yiping Huang. 2006. Continued rapid growth and the turning point in China's development. In *The turning point in China's economic development*, eds. Ross Garnaut and Ligang Song, 12–34. Asia Pacific Press: Australian National University, Canberra.

Hondai, Susumu, and Huangzhen Luo. 1999. Transformation of rural economy and labor market. In *The flowing big river: Labor mobility in rural China*, eds. Ryoshin Minami and Fumio Makino, 57–79. Nihon Hyoronsha, Tokyo (in Japanese).

Kim, Chang-Nam. 1983. Economic development and labor market in the Republic of Korea. *Asian Studies* 30, no. 2: 1–42 (in Japanese).

Lewis, W.A. 1954. Economic development with unlimited supplies of labor. *Manchester School of Economic and Social Studies* 22, no. 2: 139–191.

Li, Anxia. 2005. An empirical analysis of the sources of regional differences in agricultural productivity in China: 1982–2002. Dissertation to Master Degree of Tsukuba University, 1–39 (in Japanese).

Li, Shi, Terry Sicular, and Bijorn Gustaffson. 2008. Introduction. In *Study on income distribution in China*, eds. Sicular Li and Gustaffson, 1–33. Beijing Normal University Publishing Groups, Beijing (in Chinese).

Ma, Xin Xin. 2008. Rural to urban migration and wage differentials in urban China(1) and (2). *Journal of OHARA Institute for Social Research*, no. 591 (February): 39–51, no. 592 (May): 62–72 (in Japanese).

Marukawa, Tomoo. 2002. *Crustal movement of the labor market in China, Modern China economy 7*. Nagoya University Press, Nagoya (in Japanese).

Meng, Xing, and Nansheng Bai. 2007. How much have the wages of unskilled workers in China increased? In *China: Linking markets for growth*, eds. Ross Garnaut and Ligang Song, 151–175. Asia Pacific Press at the Australian National University.

Minami, Ryoshin. 1968. The turning point in the Japanese economy. *Quarterly Journal of Economics* 82, no. 3: 380–402.

Minami Ryoshin. 1973. *The turning point in economic development: Japan's experience*. Kinokuniya, Tokyo.

Minami Ryoshin. 1981. Long-term changes in the output elasticity of labor in agriculture: Estimation and analysis. *Economic Review* 32, no. 4 (October): 358–366.

Minami Ryoshin. 1998. Economic development and income distribution in Japan: An assessment of the Kuznets hypothesis. *Cambridge Journal of Economics* 22, no. 1 (January): 39–58.

Minami Ryoshin, cooperation by Fumio Makino. 2002. *Economic development in Japan*. 3rd ed. Toyo Keizai Shinposha, Tokyo (in Japanese).

Minami Ryoshin 2008. Income distribution of Japan: Historical perspective and its implications. *Japan Labor Review* 5, no. 4: 5–20.

Minami, Ryoshin, Fumio Makino, and Huangzheng Luo 2008. *Education and Economic development in China*, Toyo Keizai Shinposha (in Japanese).

Minami, Ryoshin, and Akira Ono. 1981. Behavior of income shares in a labor surplus economy: Japan's experience. *Economic Development and Cultural Change* 29, no. 2: 309–324.

Minami, Ryoshin, and Akira Ono. 1977. Surplus labor of Japan in the prewar period. *Economic Review* 28, no. 2: 156–166 (in Japanese).

Minami, Ryoshin, and Akira Ono. 1978. Estimation of factor income and factor shares: Non-primary industry. *Economic Review* 29, no. 2: 143–169 (in Japanese).

Minami, Ryoshin, and Jinjun Xue. 2010 (forthcoming). Labor force in postwar period. In *Long-term economic statistics in China – Long-term economic statistics in Eastern Asia*, eds. Ryoshin Minami and Fumio Makino. Toyo Keizai Shinposha (in Japanese).

Otsuka, Keijiro. 2008. Shortage of rural labor force in China: Already passed the turning point. *Nippon Keizai Newspaper*, October 9 (in Japanese).

Prime Minister's Office, Statistics Bureau. 1987. *Historical statistics of Japan, Vol. 1*. Japan Statistical Association, Beijing.

Sato, Hiroshi. 2003. *Inequality and poverty, modern China economy 7*. Nagoya University Press, Nagoya (in Japanese).

Shintani, Masahiko. 1983. *Production function analysis of the Japanese agriculture*. Taimeido, Tokyo (in Japanese).

Shintani, Masahiko. 1998. Under-employment of labor in agricultural sector under economic development in China. *Economic Review of Seinan Gakuin University* 32, no. 4: 111–136 (in Japanese).

Tajima, Toshio. 2008. Unlimited labor supply and the Lewisian turning point. *Monthly Journal of Chinese Affairs* 62, no. 2: 40–45 (in Japanese).

Wang, Dewen. 2008. Lewisian turning point: Chinese experience. In Reports on China's population and labor no.9: Linking up Lewis and Kuzuets, ed. Fang Cai, 88–103, Social Sciences Academic Press, Beijing (in Chinese).

Wu, Yaowu. 2007. The coming of the Lewisian turning point: The chance of the adjustment in our country. *China Opening Herald*, no. 3: 50–56 (in Chinese).

Xue, Jinjun, Hiroyuki Arayama, and Tadashi Sonoda, eds. 2008. *Inequality in China*. Nihon Hyoronsha, Tokyo (in Japanese).

Yan, Sanping. 2005. *Population mobility and migrants in China: Quantitative analysis based on micro-data and macro-data*. Keiso Shobo, Tokyo (in Japanese).

Yan, Sanping. 2007. Migrants and the change of migration policy. *China 21* 26: 67–88 (in Japanese).

Yan, Sanping. 2008. Has China passed the Lewisian turning point: Around the social and economic. *EAST ASIA*, December, 30–42 (in Japanese).

Macro-economic implications of the turning point

Ross Garnaut

Institute of Applied Economic and Social Research, University of Melbourne, Melbourne, Australia

(*Final version received 27 July 2010*)

China's rapid growth in the reform era has been built around the availability of large amounts of migration from the countryside to the industrial cities, associated with only small increases in real wages. This pattern of growth has generated high savings, investment, rates of output growth, external payments imbalances, and high and growing inequality in the distribution of income. Slow and soon negative population and work force growth, rapid increase in modern sector demand for labor from an ever-higher base, and rapidly increasing investment in education per school-age person have absorbed most or all of the 'surplus' labor from the countryside, and rapid urban demand for labor is now associated with large increases in real wages in town and village. This paper explores analytically the effects of the exhaustion of underemployed labor in the countryside on these economic variables, and on the structure of trade and industry. It suggests some approaches to policy that can make this a favorable time for growth with equity in China.

It is now 4 years since Yiping Huang and I introduced into the discussion of China's economic development, the idea that China 'in the period ahead' would move into a Lewis 'turning point'. At this point, the national labor market would tighten. Beyond the turning point, real wages would rise rapidly, forcing change in the structure of the economy (Garnaut 2006; Garnaut and Huang 2006; Chapters 1 and 2 in Garnaut and Song 2006). That idea became part of a larger discussion of labor market changes in the course of Chinese economic growth, involving many of the contributors to this special issue of The China Economic Journal, most importantly Cai Fang and his colleagues at the Chinese Academy of Social Sciences.

The notion that labor shortages would play a role in early future Chinese development was pushed from most minds when the recessionary impact of the Great Crash of 2008 came to China through the sudden dramatic reduction in demand for Chinese exports, and the associated collapse of demand for labor in China's coastal cities (Garnaut and Llewellyn-Smith 2009, especially Chapter 9). It has been brought back to mind by the extraordinary strength of the Chinese economy's response to the expansionary monetary and fiscal policies that were introduced in late 2008 in response to the global recession. The dramatic fall in urban demand for labor in the export-oriented industrial cities turned out to be brief; and the growth in real wages of low-skilled workers soon resumed a rapid upward movement.

This paper examines the implications of the 'turning point' for macro-economic dimensions of Chinese economic development and its interaction with the global economy. This paper is conceptual, focusing on the main economic ideas. Other papers in this issue of the journal have rich empirical content, broadly consistent with the theory presented here.

The surplus labor economy

The idea of the 'turning point' comes from a highly stylized model of economic development in a labor surplus economy. The model was first developed by West Indian economist Arthur Lewis (Lewis 1954). The model was elaborated and applied in an East Asian context by Fei and Ranis (1964a, 1964b, 1966; Ranis and Fei 1961, 1963). It was embedded in Minami's influential books on Japanese postwar economic development (Minami 1973, 1986).

The labor surplus economy of the model is dualistic, with a highly productive and dynamic 'modern' or 'urban' or 'industrial' sector, and a relatively unproductive and stagnant 'traditional' or 'rural' or 'village' sector. In the stylized labor surplus economy of the model, the marginal product of labor in rural areas is well below the living standards that poor residents of rural areas enjoy. (In some versions of the model, the marginal product of rural labor is zero or even negative in the early stages of modern economic growth).

Living standards in rural areas can remain above the marginal product of labor because they are supported by village institutions, which lead to some sharing of incomes and employment. There are risks and costs of moving from the rural to the urban sector for employment. Assessments of these costs and risks, on top of the customary rural standard of living, establish the 'reserve price' of labor, or the urban wage at which migrants are prepared to migrate. It follows that the marginal product of labor in urban areas (sometimes called the 'modern' or 'capitalist' sector) is strongly positive.

When a worker moves from rural-to-urban employment, the total output of the economy rises: there is an increase in urban output, but no or little reduction in rural production. Rural-urban migration is a main source of growth in average productivity and total output. As a matter of arithmetic, average output rises in rural areas (with the same output and less people). However, in the early stages of expansion of the modern economy, and perhaps for a considerable while, there is still redundant rural labor, and marginal product of labor in rural areas remains low or zero. The reserve price of rural labor remains low, and for a while is unresponsive to increased urban demand for labor and emigration.

The availability of an 'infinitely elastic' supply of labor from rural areas has important implications for the structure of growth in both the urban and the rural economies.

Rapid expansion can proceed in the urban sector without increases in real wages. The improvements in infrastructure, labor culture, and management practices that raise productivity with the passing of time are reflected in a rising rate of return on investment and an increasing profit share of modern sector income. The rising modern sector share of the economy contributes to a rising profit share in the economy as a whole.

Savings are a much higher share of profits than of wages, so that a rising profit share of income is associated with a higher savings share. The higher savings, in turn, support higher levels of investment in the usual situation of home-country bias in investment, encouraged by the high and rising rates of return on investment.

A falling consumption share is the other side of the coin to a rising savings share. Also as a matter of arithmetic, although not mentioned in the early theoretical treatments of the subject, and highly relevant to the Chinese reality of rapid growth through the reform period, the share of investment in output must rise as rapidly as the consumption share falls if the maximum possible employment of resources and the maximum possible rate of growth are to be maintained – unless the public sector expands its claims on resources.

To extrapolate further in a direction that is also highly relevant to understanding the Chinese reality, if the share of investment does not rise as rapidly as the share of savings, an excess of rising savings over investment causes the rate of growth of output to be unnecessarily low. In the labor surplus economy, this does not lead to increasing unemployment of domestic resources. Rather, it leads to unnecessarily slow absorption of underemployed labor in the village economy into the modern sector.

On the other hand, if the high and rising returns to investment in the modern sector cause the investment share to rise more rapidly than the savings share, there will be a tendency toward deficits in external trade and current payments. The same outcome will follow if the public sector's claims on resources expand more rapidly than is necessary to absorb any surplus private sector savings. Such external current payments deficits are only sustainable if the country has ample access to international markets for capital on favorable terms. Where they are sustainable, their presence is likely to raise the sustainable rate of growth, and also the rate at which underemployed labor in the countryside is absorbed into modern and economically productive activity.

With rising returns on investment and a rising profit and therefore savings share of income, it can be expected that the rate of investment will rise over time. The combination of rising investment rates and the likelihood, discussed above, that marginal returns to capital rise, are likely to cause the rate of growth in output to accelerate over time.

In the rural sector, the marginal product of labor remains well below the customary minimum income level. Expansion of the modern sector and migration from the village introduce no pressure to economize on the use of labor in production. Average standards of living rise in the village, without noticeably affecting the customary income level of the low-income workers who are available for emigration to the modern sector.

In the labor surplus economy, comparative advantage in international trade is initially in small volumes of commodity exports, prior to the emergence of a dynamic modern sector. Modern economic growth and the development of the urban economy see comparative advantage shift to labor-intensive manufactured products: these contribute most of the growth in exports as the modern sector expands, and the proportion of exports from the modern sector rises over time. The rapid accumulation of capital in the modern sector and the increase in productivity associated with this and the labor force's learning of industrial disciplines and techniques makes production of a wider range of traded goods and services profitable in the modern sector. This causes comparative advantage to emerge in some more sophisticated manufactured products, without any weakening of competitiveness in the production of labor-intensive traded goods. At this stage, there is no pressure for absolute contraction of labor-intensive industries in the traded goods sector.

In the labor surplus economy, the fall over time in the wage share of income is associated with a widening of inequality in the distribution of income. The faster the rate of growth in investment and output, the faster the rate of increase in inequality. But the faster the rate of growth, the greater the rate of emigration from rural to urban areas, the quicker the absorption of the surplus rural labor into productive modern sector employment, and the earlier the turning point from an economy in which labor is in surplus to one in which labor is scarce.

The turning point

If the rate of economic expansion in the modern sector is fast enough for the rate of emigration from the villages to exceed the natural increase of the rural population that is of working age, sooner or later there will be no surplus of labor in the rural economy that makes itself available for urban employment at the established wage of the labor surplus economy. At this point, any further emigration raises the marginal productivity of labor in rural employment above the rural wage. The real wage rate increases in both the rural and the urban sectors. This is the 'turning point in economic development'.

From the turning point, the wage share of income rises and the profit share falls. The rate of consumption can be expected to rise with the wages share. The rate of consumption in the whole economy rises, and the rate of savings falls.

The increase in urban wages is likely to cause the rate of return on investment in labor-intensive investment in the modern sector to fall. The combination of lower profitability of investment, and of lower savings accompanied by the usual home bias in investment, is likely to reduce the share of investment.

All other things being equal, one would expect the rate of growth of output to fall with share of investment in expenditure. This is not, however, an inevitable accompaniment of the turning point in economic development. There are two circumstances in which there will be no fall in the rate of growth in output. One of these circumstances may arise if, prior to the turning point, savings exceed investment, giving rise to a surplus in external trade and current payments. This would be a case in which the rate of growth prior to the turning point was unnecessarily low, and therefore the turning point of economic development unnecessarily delayed. In this case, some rebalancing of expenditure from investment demand to consumption associated with the rising wage share of income could be accompanied by an increase in expenditure relative to incomes, so that there is no reduction in the ratio of investment to GDP.

The second circumstance in which there may be no reduction in the rate of growth after the turning point is present if the rate of total factor productivity growth increases to balance a reduced rate of investment and reduced rate of increase in the capital stock. There are reasons to expect some increase in productivity growth beyond the turning point. First, higher wages are likely to force economization in the use of labor, and to raise productivity growth in both rural and urban sectors. Higher productivity growth offsets the tendency to lower growth in output associated with a lower rate of investment.

It follows that the rate of economic growth may be faster, similar to, or slower after the turning point than in the labor surplus economy.

Whatever the impact of the turning point on the rate of economic growth, the tendencies toward decline in the savings rate are likely to be more powerful than the tendencies for decline in the investment rate, leading to a tendency toward smaller surpluses or larger deficits in foreign trade.

Beyond the turning point, there is a reversal of the tendency for economic growth to exacerbate the widening of income inequalities. At last, rural communities and low-skilled urban workers come to share in the fruits of modern economic growth. The faster the rate of growth in investment, productivity, and output after the turning point, the more rapid the rise in rural standards of living and of workers' income levels everywhere. The faster the rate of growth after the turning point, the more rapid the reduction in the inequalities of income distribution that were of increasing importance through the years of growth of the labor surplus economy.

The critical contribution of rapid growth before the turning point to reduction in inequality is its bringing forward in time the point at which labor becomes scarce and labor incomes rise. The critical contribution of rapid growth to reduction of inequality after the turning point is to accelerate the increase in real wages and rural living standards relatively to incomes from ownership of capital.

The changes in labor's share of income before and after the turning point is one explanation of the 'Kuznets curve': the observed tendency for modern economic growth at first to exacerbate and later to reduce inequality in the distribution of income, at least for some time beyond the turning point in economic development.

There is no inevitability about the labor surplus economy reaching the turning point. It will only reach this point if growth in modern sector growth is sufficiently rapid and sufficiently labor-intensive to absorb labor from the countryside substantially more rapidly than it is augmented by natural increase. If the modern sector of the labor surplus economy grows too slowly relative to population increase, or policy distortions cause growth to be associated with low increases in demand for labor, modern economic growth can be associated with ever-increasing dispersion in the distribution of income.

Real wages rise rapidly with continuing economic growth beyond the turning point in economic development. Whether or not this is inflationary depends on the stance of monetary policy. So long as economic growth continues reasonably strongly, the increase in real wages increases domestic costs relative to the prices of internationally traded goods – that is, it increases the real exchange rate. The increase in the real exchange rate occurs no matter how the nominal exchange rate is managed. The conduct of monetary policy in a way that leads to an increase in the foreign exchange value of domestic currency – that is, to nominal exchange rate of appreciation – allows the increase in the real exchange rate to occur with lower inflation than would otherwise occur. The avoidance of inflation as economic growth continues beyond the turning point requires firm monetary policy alongside appreciation of the nominal exchange rate.

Here, there are risks of errors in economic policy that may unnecessarily diminish the rate of economic growth and the rates of increase in real wages and living standards in rural and urban areas. If the authorities become worried about inflation while wanting to avoid an appreciation of the nominal exchange rate (perhaps in an attempt to protect the labor-intensive industries whose competitiveness is declining), they may seek to tighten expenditure policy in an attempt to hold inflation to low levels. This generates a tendency to surplus in external trade and payments. For a while this reduces the rate of growth below sustainable levels. The payments surplus generates tendencies to monetary expansion and to the re-emergence of inflationary pressure. In the end, it is likely that the rate of growth will tend toward sustainable levels, with the real appreciation emerging after a lag through inflationary processes.

Any protection of old, labor-intensive industries that comes with the avoidance of appreciation in the foreign exchange value of domestic currency turns out to be temporary. The temporary respite comes with potentially large costs: the economy will experience unnecessary inflation, and needlessly forego some increase in economic output, real wages, and living standards. In the worst case, the inflation will destabilize aspects of political as well as economic life, and indirectly lead to larger losses in economic growth and potential increases in living standards.

Comparative advantage in foreign trade after the turning point shifts out of labor-intensive products, into more capital-intensive and technologically more sophisticated goods and services. In the nature of things, these more technologically complex products require higher-quality inputs of human resources (education and training), infrastructure including for communications, finance and regulatory arrangements. These requirements make heavy demands on the quality of various services provided by government. Weaknesses in these areas are more likely to emerge as bottlenecks to the continuation of rapid economic growth after than before the turning point in economic development.

Real-world variations on the stylized surplus labor model

Like any model, the Lewis model of the labor surplus economy embodies simplifications of reality. Some of these simplifications materially affect its application to analysis of contemporary Chinese economic development. This section of the paper examines some of the most important departures of the real from the stylized economy when the model is applied to China's economic development.

The most important departure of reality from the model is in the geographically differentiated nature of the labor market in the huge Chinese economy. Within China, there is imperfect mobility of labor among provinces and regions, and between differentiated barriers between various rural areas and various cities. Imperfect mobility and differentiated barriers are reflected in differing wage levels and material standards of living across the various parts of the rural economy, and across cities. As a consequence, as urban demand for labor grows, labor may be drawn disproportionately for a while from one source while being drawn less intensively from others. One part of the rural economy may find that its surplus labor has been absorbed fully into the modern economy and that the real wages demanded by potential immigrants from that rural region begin to rise strongly, when the surplus labor and availability of labor at 'traditional' wages persist elsewhere. Relatively low-skilled labor may become relatively scarce and real wages rise in some cities, when it is available at lower costs in others.

The main consequence of the geographically differentiated labor market is that there is a 'turning period' over which real wages begin to rise strongly, rather than a 'turning point'. Real wages rise rapidly in some cities, forcing reduction in the profit share of income, increases in consumption, and structural change out of simple, labor-intensive production, while lower wages persist and labor-intensive production continues to prosper and expand elsewhere. Similarly, in the rural economy, labor becomes relatively scarce, living standards rise rapidly, and production shifts out of labor-intensive activities in some villages when labor remains abundant in others.

The surplus labor model's second major departure from reality is the assumption that there is a stable conventional standard of living for rural residents. Even in the early stages of emigration from part of the rural economy, higher average material living standards and consumption are likely to be reflected in some enhancement of the living conditions of potential emigrants, so that the reserve price of rural labor, and therefore wages of urban workers, rise to some extent from an early stage in modern economic development. Entry into the turning period will be marked by an acceleration of wage increases, rather than a sharp movement from stable to rapidly increasing real wages.

The third major departure is that in reality, but not in the model, labor is highly differentiated by skills, resulting from differences in education, training, and experience in the modern economy. The model focuses on relatively unskilled labor, the availability of which is diminished by increases in education and training and experience. Changes in these factors affecting the quality of human resources influence the turning period during which relatively unskilled labor becomes scarce and its wages rise. In particular, the high and on average rapidly rising investment in education per student, and the accumulation of skills through experience in the modern sector of the economy, are reducing the stocks of low-skilled labor available to the urban economy. This has been bringing forward the turning period in economic development. In combination with the demographic crunch following the sharp decline in fertility in the 1970s and 1980s, these factors will cause the rate of increase in real wages during and beyond the turning period to be much sharper than in other labor surplus economies which have moved through and beyond the turning point.

The fourth major departure is that the real economy does not contain only 'traditional' and 'modern' sectors. There is also a government sector that provides services and modifies demand and supply for various types of labor, and affects living standards in rural and urban areas, and supplies inputs that are critical to economic growth. The government sector's command over resources and also its role in providing essential inputs for development is likely to be relatively small in the early stages of development of a labor surplus economy. Government's potential command over resources expands with the modern sector, and its role in continued rapid growth becomes more important over time.

The main effect of the first two departures of reality from the model is to turn the turning point into a turning period.

The main effect of the third departure is to bring forward in time the turning period and to shorten its length.

The effect of the fourth departure is wide and complex. Provision of various rural services can raise the reserve price of emigrant labor and therefore the urban wage for unskilled labor. Provision of education services can reduce the pool of surplus labor and bring forward the turning point. Public sector demand for labor augments demand from the modern industrial sector and brings forward the turning point.

Government policy can affect population growth and over time the amount of unskilled labor in the countryside. It can affect the labor-intensity of modern sector economic growth. The effectiveness of government provision of various inputs into the development process affects the rate of growth before the turning point, and especially after, as growth comes to make larger demands on infrastructure, education and skills, financial services, and sound regulation of private economic activity.

Evidence on China entering the turning period?

Huang and I (2006) went through a number of factors influencing the turning point in China's economic development and concluded in a preliminary way that it was not far away if indeed it had not yet been reached. The anecdotal evidence of shortages of labor in some areas and large recent increases in real wages started to make the point. The looming demographic transition deriving from the large and sudden decline in fertility a generation ago; the strength of modern sector economic growth; the improvement in rural education including for girls; and the evidence of labor shortage in some rural as well as urban areas all pointed to the imminent arrival of the turning point.

It appears that Huang and I were observing the early part of the turning period in 2006 (Garnaut and Huang 2006). Evidence presented in other papers in this issue of the China Economic Journal suggests that the Chinese economy entered the turning period in about 2004 (Du and Wang 2010, Cai 2010, Yao and Zhang 2010). The rate of increase in real wages has been tending to rise through the intervening years, confirming the presence of a turning period rather than a single turning point.

The second departure of the surplus labor model economy from reality is also evident in data presented in this volume. Real wages in rural and urban areas have both been rising throughout the country for a number of years. Contemporary China, as the economy has entered the turning period, has seen an acceleration of the rate of increase in real wages.

Since 2006, two contradictory tendencies have intervened to make the story of the turning period more complex. First, the global financial crisis led to sharp reduction in demand for labor in the export-oriented coastal cities in late 2008 and early 2009. For a while, the greatest migration in human history went into reverse, as redundant workers returned to the countryside. Second, the Chinese Government responded to the recessionary impact of the global financial crisis by launching the world's greatest ever exercise in Keynesian expansionary policy, to counteract the effects of global recession (Garnaut and Llewellyn-Smith 2009). The success of the expansionary policies meant that by the middle of 2009, the flow of migrants from rural to urban areas had been restored and then increased beyond the pre-crisis norm, hastening movement into and through the turning period in China's economic development.

Chinese Government policy over recent years has emphasized more strongly the provision of infrastructure and services away from the old centers of modern economic dynamism in the coastal cities. This has enhanced growth in demand for labor. To the extent that it has been successful in raising living standards in rural areas, it would have been an additional source of downward pressure on labor supply to urban areas and of upward pressure on wages.

The turning period and Chinese development

What are the implications of the turning period for China's continuing economic development, for China's interaction with the global economy, and for economic policy? I will focus on four of the most important consequences, and then mention a consequence which is widely anticipated and feared, but which need not eventuate.

As China enters deeply into the turning period, there will be large and continuing increases in real wages and in the wage share of income. The powerful tendency since the 1980s toward increased inequality in income distribution is likely to be reversed. This is one important consequence. The rise in the wage share of income is likely to be reflected in an increase in the consumption share of expenditure. There will be a reduction in the savings rate.

It is likely that China's savings rate will fall more than its investment rate. (It is possible that, at least for a while, the investment rate will actually rise, which increases the strength of the point). This will reduce the external surplus in trade and current payments. This will ease current international pressures over payments imbalances and exchange rates. It would be wise for China to ensure that total domestic demand – the sum of demand from private and public investment and private consumption – expands enough to ensure that this is the case.

The reduction in Chinese current external payments surpluses is therefore a second important consequence of moving through the turning period. This may ease tensions with other countries, especially the United States, which have identified Chinese surpluses as a principal cause of their own economic problems. Regrettably, the reduction of Chinese surpluses will not help the reality of other countries' economic problems as much as perceptions of them. Indeed, a large fall in Chinese current payments savings relative to investment would put upward pressure on global long-term interest rates, and increase the requirement to reduce domestic expenditure in the countries facing large challenges in the management of external and public debt, including the United States. This will make economic management problems in those countries more difficult and not easier.

The third important consequence of China moving through and beyond the turning period is that the center of China's comparative advantage in international trade will shift rapidly from a fairly narrow range of labor-intensive products to a wider range of more capital-intensive and technologically sophisticated products. This will ease some dimensions of China's trade problems with the rest of the world (perceptions of competitive pressure on other developing countries, and heavily concentrated pressures for adjustment on particular sectors in developed countries), and complicate others (competitive pressures will be felt across a much wider range of industries in developed countries). The diversification of China's comparative advantage will probably halt the decline in Chinese export prices that had been associated with heavy concentration of export expansion in a small number of products.

The fourth important consequence of entering the turning period involves a policy risk to economic stability and growth in the period ahead. Rising real wages and the pressure of strong increases in demand for other non-traded goods and services will be inflationary unless accompanied by a combination of firm monetary policy and an appreciating renminbi. Nevertheless, the Chinese authorities may be tempted to maintain the fixed exchange rate to avoid adjustment pressures on export-oriented labor-intensive industries, which have played such an important part in Chinese economic growth since the mid 1980s.

To seek to maintain a fixed exchange rate against the US dollar through and beyond the turning period, would only postpone and not avoid the structural adjustments that are a necessary accompaniment of the current stage of Chinese economic growth. Payments surpluses would eventually overwhelm the efforts to sterilize their monetary effects. The adjustments would occur through inflation.

It is likely that the authorities would respond to higher inflation by tightening fiscal and monetary policies. This would unnecessarily reduce the rate of economic growth below sustainable levels, and postpone the increase in Chinese living standards that can come through and beyond the turning period. The inflation and the delays in reduction in inequality may be destabilizing to domestic political stability. The delays in reduction in the external payments surplus would certainly be destabilizing for China's productive interaction with the international economy and society.

I conclude by pointing to one consequence of moving through and beyond the turning period that is often feared but which is unlikely to be important unless there are mistakes in economic policy: a reduction in the rate of growth in output per worker. The rise in real wages as China moves through the turning period is likely to lead to an increase in the rate of total factor productivity growth. In the nature of things, this will be concentrated in industries producing relatively sophisticated products. It is possible that the increase in Chinese domestic demand that is necessary to reduce external current payments surpluses will require an increase in the investment rate for a while. Together with the expected acceleration of productivity growth, this would support an increase in the growth rate in total output, above the high rates of the early twenty-first century. That will surprise the world and also the Chinese authorities, but it may be necessary to maintain internal and external balance in the period ahead.

How successful China is economically in this period of rapidly rising real wages will depend on the flexibility of the economy; its openness to foreign trade and investment, and the world's most productive ideas about managing enterprises; the quality of the human resources created by the rapid expansion of the education system over the past couple of decades; and the quality of the regulatory systems applied to the more complex economy that is emerging. If China does well in these areas, it is possible that an acceleration of growth in total factor productivity growth will fully offset the effects on growth of a lower rate of capital accumulation. And for a while, the rate of increase in the capital stock may not need to fall much, if at all.

It is possible that the rate of growth in total output can be maintained at something like the average rates of the decades of reform, until the approach of the developed countries' frontiers of productivity and living standards reduces the scope of rapid productivity growth through 'catching up' with the developed countries.

References

Cai, F. 2010. Demographic transition, demographic dividend, and Lewis turning point in China. *China Economic Journal* 3, no. 2: 107–120.

Du, Y., and M. Wang. 2010. Discussions on potential bias and implications of Lewis turning point. *China Economic Journal* 3, no. 2: 121–136.

Fei, J.C.H., and G. Ranis. 1964a. *Development of the labor surplus economy: Theory and policy.* Homewood, IL: Richard D. Irwin,.

Fei, J.C.H., and G. Ranis. 1964b. Development of the labor surplus economy: Theory and policy. *Economic Development and Cultural Change* 41: 147–174.

Fei, J.C.H., and G. Ranis. 1966. Agrarianism, dualism and economic development. In *Theory and design of economic development*, eds. I. Adelman and E. Thorbecke. Baltimore, MD: Johns Hopkins University Press.

Garnaut, R. 2006. The turning point in China's economic development. In *The turning point in China's economic development*, eds. R. Garnaut and L. Song, 1–11. Canberra: Asia Pacific Press.

Garnaut, R., and Y. Huang. 2006. Continued rapid growth and the turning point in China's economic development. In *The turning point in China's economic development*, eds. R. Garnaut and L. Song. Canberra: Asia Pacific Press, The Australian National University.

Garnaut, R., and D. Llewellyn-Smith. 2009. *The great crash of 2008.* Melbourne: Melbourne University Publishing. Also published in Chinese by Social Sciences Academic Press, Chinese Academy of Social Sciences (Beijing, 2010).

Garnaut, R., and L. Song., eds. 2006. *The turning point in China's economic development.* Canberra: Asia Pacific Press, The Australian National University.

Lewis, W.A. 1954. Economic development with unlimited supplies of labour. *Manchester School of Economic and Social Studies* XXII (May): 139–191.

Minami, R. 1973. *The turning point in economic development: Japan's experience.* Tokyo: Kinokuniya Bookstore.

Minami, R. 1986. *The economic development of Japan: A quantitative study.* London: MacMillan.

Ranis, G., and J.C.H. Fei. 1961. A theory of economic development. *The American Economic Review* 51, no. 4: 533–565.

Ranis, G., and J.C.H. Fei. 1963. The Ranis-Fei model of economic development: Reply. *The American Economic Review* 53, no. 3: 452–454.

Yao, Y., and K. Zhang. 2010. Has China passed the Lewis turning point? A structural estimation based on provincial data. *China Economic Journal* 3, no. 2: 155–162.

What does the Lewis turning point mean for China? A computable general equilibrium analysis

Yiping Huang[a] and Tingsong Jiang[b]

[a]China Center for Economic Research, National School of Development, Peking University, Beijing, China; [b]Center for International Economics, Canberra, Australia

(Final version received 16 March 2010)

We apply a computable general equilibrium framework to assess likely impacts of the Lewis turning point (LTP) on China and the rest of the world. Modeling results suggest that China will probably transition from an abnormal economy to a normal economy with somewhat lower growth but higher inflation, which requires significant revision to the macroeconomic policy framework. China would lose competitiveness in labor-intensive activities, its current account surplus should fall but overinvestment risk could rise. These changes in China should help improve other countries' current accounts and boost low-cost countries' production. The LTP, however, does not provide automatic solutions to some of the key challenges, such as service sector development and innovation capability. China will need to make serious policy efforts to avoid the so-called 'middle-income trap'.

Introduction

With 1.3 billion people, China is known for abundant labor, especially rural surplus labor. And 'unlimited labor supply' has been one of the key factors contributing to China's unusual economic performance during the reform period (Sachs and Woo 2001). By shifting large number of farmers into non-agricultural jobs every year, China is able to achieve extraordinary productivity growth and at the same time keep inflation stable. Low labor cost is a cornerstone of China's global manufacturing center.

But the history of economic development suggests that no country can rely on cheap labor forever. Arthur Lewis pointed out that, as the modern sector of a low-income country continued to expand, rural surplus labor would eventually disappear (Lewis 1958). This transition from a labor surplus economy to a labor shortage economy is now popularly known as the Lewis turning point (Minami 1968). The LTP often signals the beginning of more rapid wage increase and, therefore, has important implications for economic growth and economic structure.

China saw the first waves of labor shortage in 2004, when employers in very dynamic Pearl River Delta and Yangtze River Delta experienced difficulties in recruiting enough migrant worker shortage (Yiping 2004). But labor shortage situation eased later as faster rises in wage rates increased supply from inland provinces. In 2009, however, shortage of migrant workers again hit the country, although the economy was still suffering from damages of the global financial crisis (Kroebor 2010).

These dramatic changes in labor market conditions made some economists reckon if China is already approaching the LTP (Garnaut and Yiping 2006; Cai 2007). However, the exact timing when this turning point will occur remains a controversial subject. One common counter-argument is based on the fact that the country still has about 350 million agricultural workers. More rigorous analyses compared productivity and real wages in agricultural and non-agricultural sectors to judge the extent of surplus labor in the agricultural sector (Minami and Xin Xin 2008; Yao et al. 2010).

For non-labor economists, perhaps a more critical question is potential implications of the LTP for the broad economy, including macroeconomic conditions and international economic relations. Leaving aside the interesting debate about the exact timing, the LTP will arrive sooner or later. And transitioning into a labor shortage economy can bring about profound transformation to the economy. A good understanding of these likely changes is critical for better preparing both the government and the corporate sector adapting to new economic conditions.

Earlier studies about the Japanese experience reveal important structural changes around its LTP. Existence of 'unlimited labor supply' may boost growth through high household savings, large corporate profits and low labor cost. Growth could decelerate after surplus labor disappears. Meanwhile, the LTP may improve income distribution due to faster increases in wages, especially wages for unskilled workers (Minami and Ma 2010).

A more fundamental question driving our interest in the LTP issue is if China is able to avoid what the World Bank called 'middle-income trap' (Gill and Kharas 2007). Many countries, primarily those in Latin America and Middle East, were able to raise their income initially but were then stuck in the middle-income range. When China hits the LTP, whenever that might be, it will be a middle-income country. Its past growth model relying on cheap labor input will no longer work. Can China find a new growth model and continue its rapid growth? We may not be able to provide a complete set of answers in this study. But we hope to at least shed some lights on what new challenges China will face.

In this paper, we apply a general equilibrium framework, the Global Trade Analysis Project (GTAP) model, to assess economy-wide effects of the LTP for China. To simulate the labor market transition, we implement a styled shock of 5% reduction to unskilled labor supply. We are aware that the LTP is not necessarily equivalent to reduction in labor supply. However, in a static model, this is the best we could implement to simulate tighter labor market conditions. We may think of the shock as 'slower increases' instead of 'outright declines' in labor supply. This is true in the sense that we implement the shock to and report simulation results as percentage deviation from a 'baseline' where the labor supply and the economy are in equilibrium with existing tendency.

Like any quantitative tools, this model has a number of limitations. The model is static and financial aspects of the economy are not well represented. We should, therefore, interpret modeling results with caution. But it is a global model with detailed sector disaggregation. It enables us to gauge not only the economy-wide impacts of the shocks for China but also the likely economic consequences for the rest of the world.

Despite possible deficiencies of the framework, quantitative analyses in this study reveal some interesting findings. The LTP or emergence of labor shortage will most likely lower China's GDP growth but lift its inflation. Growth of wage rates, especially those for unskilled workers, may accelerate. This should impact competitiveness of Chinese manufacturing sectors and trigger significant structural changes. These, in turn, may cast shadow over China's position as the global manufacturing center. Surprisingly, modeling results suggest that China's external imbalances might improve but internal imbalance could worsen.

Labor shortage in China should also have important implications for the rest of the world, although magnitudes of the impacts are sometimes tiny. GDP growth may also slow in other countries but their inflation may fall as a result of lower aggregate demand. India represents a special case compared with other countries, probably because of its similarities with China. World economic structure, especially structure of manufacturing production and trade, could experience significant adjustments. As China graduates from labor-intensive industries, other low-cost countries may benefit.

All these findings have very important policy implications for China and the world. The central message from this paper, however, is that China may transition from an abnormal economy during the first 30 years of economic reform, with unusually high growth and unusually stable inflation, to a normal dynamic emerging economy. This means China may have to learn to live with slightly lower growth and slightly higher inflation. And this calls for significant reconfiguration of China's current policy frameworks.

The remainder of the paper is organized as follows. In the next section we introduce the GTAP model and explain the simulations conducted for this study, including the model closure and the shocks. The third section discusses the economy-wide consequences of the LTP for the Chinese economy. The fourth section looks at the likely impacts on the rest of the world. The fifth section discusses some of the qualifications for the results, summarizes the key findings and draws some policy implications. And the final section concludes the paper by shedding some lights on the question if China will be able to avoid the so-called 'middle-income trap'.

The GTAP model and experiments

The GTAP is a multiregional, multispectral, computable general equilibrium model of the global economy, with perfect competition and constant return to scale (Hertel 1997). It is widely used in analyses of economic and policy issues such as trade liberalization and environmental protection. The GTAP framework consists of a system of multi-sector economy-wide models linked at the sector level through trade flows between commodities and factors of production.

GTAP is a comparative static equilibrium model. In the GTAP model the activities of economic agents – consumers, producers and government – are modeled according to the neoclassical economic theory. Consumers are assumed to maximize utility and producers to maximize profits. Markets are assumed to be perfectly competitive. Production exhibits constant returns to scale. Different regions and economies are linked through trade.

Being a static model, however, GTAP is unable to model the transition process how a new equilibrium is reached after a shock. Rather, it provides the results of the new equilibrium. This may be an important deficiency. However, our focus in this study is primarily the new equilibrium after the LTP occurs.

The latest database (version 7) of the model has a detailed treatment of the world economy – 113 countries and 57 sectors (Narayanan and Walmsley 2008). For the purpose of this study, we aggregate the countries and sectors into 10 country/country groups and 10 broad sectors (see Table 1).

For regional disaggregation, we separate out a list of Asian country groups, Japan, India, ASEAN, newly industrialized economies (NIEs) and rest of Asia, in addition to United States and EU. Our rationale is that these country groups are different from one

Table 1.   Country and sector aggregation of GTAP model.

Country/country group	Sector
China	Grains
Australia	Meat and livestock
Japan	Mining
Newly industrialized economies (NIEs)	Food processing
India	Textile and wearing apparel
ASEAN excluding Singapore	Light manufacturing
Rest of Asia	Heavy manufacturing
United States	Utility and construction
EU-25	Transport and communication
Rest of the world	Other services

Note: NIEs include Hong Kong, Korea, Singapore and Taiwan.
Source: GTAP Database 7 (Narayanan and Walmsley 2008).

another in terms of income levels and comparative advantages. And they might react to China's labor market transition differently. For instance, as China moves up the industrial ladder, India and rest of Asia could see more opportunities, while Japan and NIEs may feel more competition pressure.

The sector disaggregation is standard in GTAP application. Our focus will primarily be placed on the three manufacturing sectors. Most importantly, changes in the textile and wearing apparel sector are of particular interest. But we are also interested in seeing potential impacts on service sectors, which are now the new policy focus for the next stage of economic development.

It is useful to first look at different labor-capital ratios across sectors in China (see Figure 1). The labor-capital ratio is defined as the ratio between total wages and total capital returns. It is an indicator on how intensively labor is used relative to capital. In principle, the higher the labor-capital ratio, the more significant the impacts of the LTP.

It turns out that the agricultural sectors have the highest labor-capital ratio. The mining industry (resource extraction) also has relatively high labor-capital ratio. This is certainly

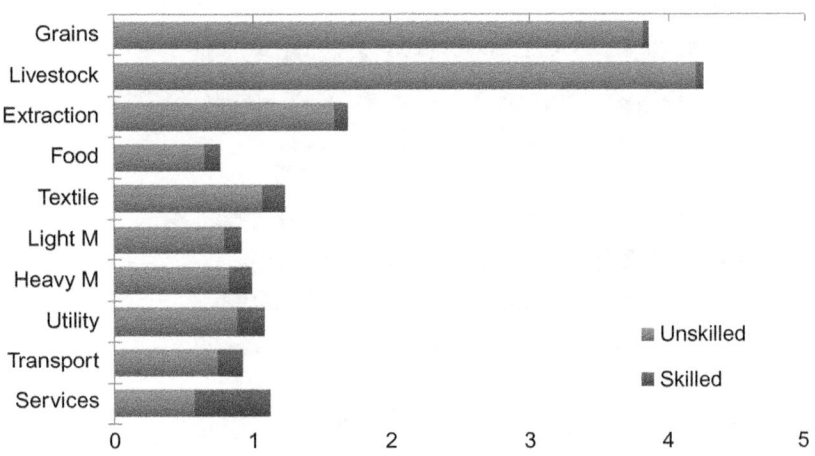

Figure 1.   Labor-capital ratios of Chinese sectors.
Note: Labor-capital ratio is the ratio of total wage to total capital return.
Source: GTAP Database 7 (Narayanan and Walmsley 2008).

at odds with general impression, as normally we think the mining industry is quite capital-intensive. But these three primary industries also require land and natural resources for production, in addition to labor and capital.

Therefore, it should be useful to look at the share of labor in total value-added for each sector, which may present a pattern conforming to conventional perception. In fact, the labor share of the mining industry is the lowest among the 10 sectors, and that of agricultural sectors is only slightly higher than that of the textile industry (see Figure 2).

Of the three manufacturing sectors, textile has the highest labor-capital ratio. So it will be interesting to see changes in this sector following labor market transition. Other services also have quite high labor-capital ratio, but almost half of the labor input is skilled labor.

In order to understand different sectors' responses to the labor shortage shock, it is also useful to look at the substitution elasticity among primary factors in Chinese sectors, in addition to labor-capital ratio and labor share of total value-added (see Figure 3). We notice that the elasticity is much smaller for the primary industries than for the other sectors. A small elasticity of substitution means input mix has to be relatively stable. As a result, the adverse effect of the labor supply shortage would be smaller, even if it is a labor-intensive sector.

In this analysis, the standard closure of the GTAP model is used. The amount of endowments, that is, labor, capital, land and natural resources, is fixed, and the price of them adjusts to ensure the factor market is in equilibrium. Labor and capital are perfectly mobile across sectors within an economy. In other words, wage rate and rate of return to capital are identical for each of the sectors. Meanwhile, land and natural resources are sluggish, and their prices or returns are different across sectors.

Design of experiments is somehow complicated. The LTP means increasing demand in the modern sector of the economy eventually exhausting surplus labor in the traditional sector and therefore pushing up labor costs. This, however, is difficult to implement in a static model. One possible way of simulation is to reduce labor productivity, which would increase demand for labor for fixed level of economic activity. However, decline in productivity may generate other undesirable consequences for the economy.

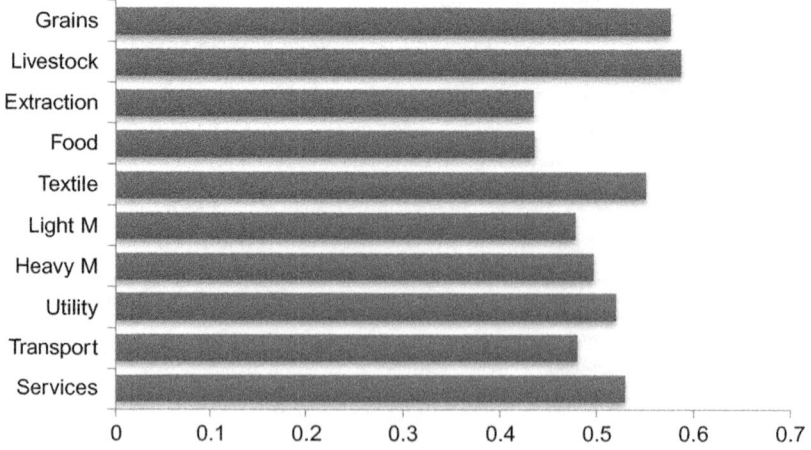

Figure 2.   Labor share in total value-added of Chinese sectors.
Source: GTAP Database 7 (Narayanan and Walmsley 2008).

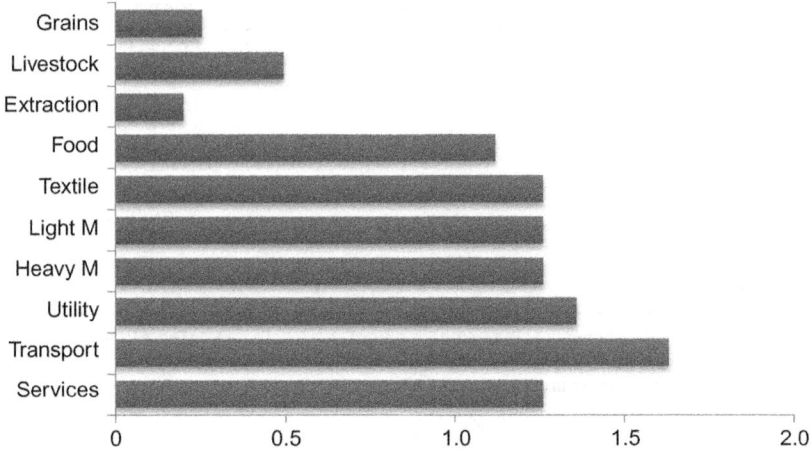

Figure 3.   Elasticity of substitution among primary factors in Chinese sectors.
Source: GTAP Database 7 (Narayanan and Walmsley 2008).

An alternative is to reduce labor supply, which would create labor shortage in the economy. Again this is not perfect, as it shrinks the size of the economy. We should think of the simulations as slowdown in growth of labor supply, not outright decline in labor supply. The nature of the LTP implies that labor shortage would occur primarily in market for unskilled labor, at least initially.

One possible justification for this supply decline designation is that, due to the family planning policy, China's total labor supply is likely to take a downturn in the coming years. But, again, this is not LTP in original definition. We should interpret the modeling results with caution.

For the purpose of this study, we devised a styled shock of 5% reduction in unskilled labor supply in China. Simulation results are presented as percentage changes to the baseline represented by the GTAP model. For example, a 2% reduction in GDP does not necessarily mean such a reduction from the current GDP level, rather it means a 2% reduction from what otherwise would have been without labor supply shortage.[1]

Consequences of labor shortage for the Chinese economy

Increases in wage rates are probably the most apparent responses to the labor shortage shock (see Table 2). This is understandable as declining supply leads to rising prices. Wage of unskilled workers rises by 3.7%. But wage for skilled workers actually declines by 1.1%. Similarly, prices of land, capital and natural resource fall, respectively, by 4.6%, 1% and 7.6%.

Declines in prices of other factors are probably associated with lowering of these factors' marginal returns, as a result of labor shortage. We may think of a Cobb-Douglas production function in which unskilled labor, skilled labor, capital, land and natural resources are production inputs. Taking partial derivatives can confirm that the marginal products of other factors are positively correlated with levels of unskilled labor inputs. Another way of understanding this result is through lower GDP and, therefore, less aggregate demand, as a result of unskilled labor shortage.

A more general price consequence, however, is higher inflation following emergence of labor shortage. According to modeling results, the 5% reduction in unskilled labor supply,

Table 2.   Changes in GDP deflator, CPI, terms of trade and factor prices (%).

	Unskilled labor shock (−5%)
GDP deflator	0.48
CPI	0.35
Terms of trade	0.42
Unskilled labor	3.66
Skilled labor	−1.13
Land	−4.90
Capital	−1.00
Natural resources	−7.58

Note: The shock implemented is reduction of unskilled labor by 5%. All numbers are percentage changes relative to the baseline scenario.
Source: Author's simulation applying the GTAP model.

pushes up CPI inflation by 0.4 percentage point. Product prices rise in almost all sectors, by an average of 0.3%. The only exception is resource extraction, presumably because this is the least labor-intensive sector. Change in GDP deflator is even greater, at 0.5 percentage points.

Terms of trade improves as a result of labor shortage. Reduction of unskilled labor by 5% leads to terms of trade improvement by 0.4%. This implies that while Chinese exports worth more in the international markets, their competitiveness could be under pressure. But this may not be an undesirable development given the policymakers' concern about too much reliance on export markets.

These results suggest that the LTP may signal the beginning of a period of relatively high inflation. This will be very different from what China has become used to for the past decade or so. It may also raise questions about China's monetary policymaking, especially the appropriate levels of inflation.

Labor shortage leads to lower levels or, at least, slower growth of GDP (see Table 3). Apparently this is the expected result of a static and short-run model. In short, the -5% shock to unskilled labor supply leads to fall of GDP by 2%.

We should note that, GDP per capita actually increases by 2% assuming population changes along with total labor supply. This means that while the aggregate GDP activity shifts to lower level, the population becomes richer. It is mainly because there are less people to share the production resources.

The model also confirms that labor shortage in China would lower its current account surplus by increase investment ratio. This is consistent with the argument that perhaps China's current account surpluses in the early twenty-first century were a result of population dividends. This could be reversed once the dividends disappear (Cai 2010).

Table 3.   Changes in real GDP, saving, investment and current account (%).

	Unskilled labor shock (−5%)
GDP (%)	−2.01
Saving ratio (% GDP)	−0.03
Investment ratio (% GDP)	0.34
Current account (% GDP)	−0.28

Note: The shock implemented is reduction of unskilled labor by 5%. All numbers are percentage changes relative to the baseline scenario.
Source: Author's simulation applying the GTAP model.

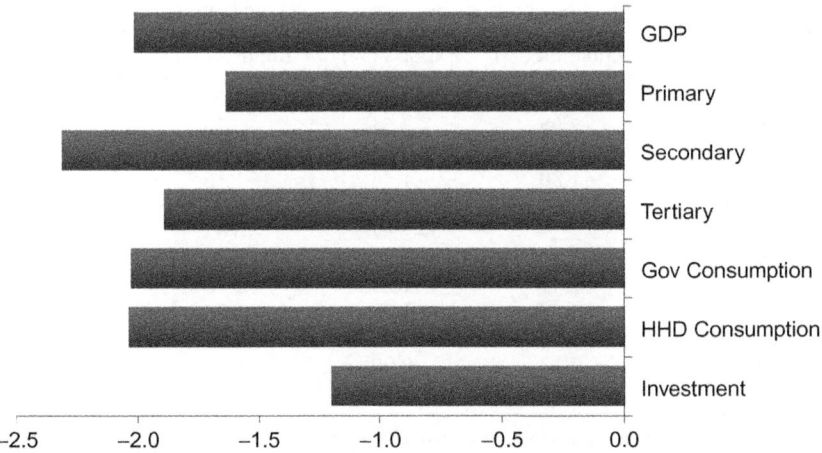

Figure 4.   Responses of macroeconomic indicators to unskilled labor shocks (%).

Note: The shock implemented is reduction of unskilled labor by 5%. All numbers are percentage changes relative to the base line scenario. Source: Author's simulation applying the GTAP model.

The unskilled labor supply shock reduces China's current account surplus by 0.3% of GDP. However, the fall comes mainly from increase in investment ratio. Actually, investment also declined in absolute terms. But investment falls less than GDP and, therefore, investment ratio increases. Saving falls slightly more than GDP, leading to a small decline of saving ratio by 0.03% of GDP.

Macroeconomic structure may experience sea changes once labor shortage hits China (see Figure 4). On the production side, the secondary and tertiary industries are hit hardest. Meanwhile, relatively the importance of the primary industry rises. These results may appear to be odd given that these primary industries have the highest labor-capital ratios. The reason why they respond much less to labor shortage than any other industries was because of much lower elasticity of substitution between labor and other factors, such as land, capital and natural resource (substitution elasticity of 0.2–0.5 for the primary industries versus over 1 for other industries in the GTAP model, see Figure 3). Therefore, even when labor cost rise, the primary industries have limited room to lower labor demand, and thus have the lowest change in production.

On the expenditure side, consumption falls almost in proportion to GDP. Shrink of current account surplus relative to GDP should be a positive development, given current concerns about China's external surpluses and the global imbalance. The fact that exports fall faster than GDP also imply relatively lower export share of GDP. But investment falls less than GDP, which means investment share of GDP rises. So implications of labor shortage for structural imbalances of the Chinese economy are mixed.

These findings also have important policy implications. While emergence of labor shortage may help ease the external imbalance problem, it cannot effectively deal with the internal imbalance problem. To certain extent, population transition actually makes the consumption-investment disproportion problem even worse. However, if labor shortage really begins to raise shares of labor compensation and household income, then it could support consumption. Bottom line is that the government still needs to find ways for curing the overinvestment risk and boosting domestic consumption.

Table 4.   Responses of production and trade by sectors to unskilled labor shocks (%).

	Production (%)	Exports (%)	Imports (%)	Trade balance (US$m)
Grain crops	−1.69	−1.69	−1.04	65
Meat & livestock	−2.05	−3.54	−0.70	−75
Resource extractions	−1.33	3.81	−3.63	2,201
Processed food	−1.80	−1.46	−1.16	−45
Textile & clothing	−2.69	−2.74	−0.83	−2,037
Light manufacturing	−2.29	−2.57	−0.63	−2,627
Heavy manufacturing	−2.30	−2.23	−1.16	−2,348
Utility & construction	−1.41	−1.83	−1.30	−4
Transport & communication	−2.09	−1.50	−1.25	41
Other services	−2.12	−0.99	−1.65	243
Total	−2.07	−2.21	−1.33	−4,586

Note: The shock implemented is reduction of unskilled labor by 5%. All numbers are percentage changes relative to the baseline scenario.
Source: Author's simulation applying the GTAP model.

Changes at the sector level reveal more structural adjustment of the economy (see Table 4). By decomposing changes in trade balance, we find that shrink in external surplus concentrate mainly in the manufacturing sectors: textile and clothing, light manufacturing and heavy manufacturing. Textile and clothing is by far the hardest hit industry, consistent with the expectation that China will lose competitiveness in labor-intensive activities quickly. Declines in trade surpluses of three manufacturing sectors account for 150% of fall in total trade surplus. Meanwhile, grains, resource extraction, transport and communication, and other services actually improve their trade balance.

Changing trade of the manufacturing sector is basically reflected in greater-than-average falls in their exports but smaller-than-average declines in their imports. Similarly, production of manufacturing activities also falls most drastically, as a result of labor shortage. However, services decline even more, confirming that these activities are also labor-intensive.

Potential changes in production structure are probably best illustrated by comparing individual sectors' percentage changes with the economy-wide average (see Figure 5). A positive number indicates the sector shrinks less than the economy and, therefore, its share in the economy expands. Of the 10 broad sectors included in the model, five sectors, including utility and construction, processed food, resource extraction, livestock and grain crops, all expanded in relative terms. The other five sectors, including textile and clothing, light and heavy manufacturing, transport and communications and other services, all shrink.

Lessons from these simple findings are apparent. The arrival of the LTP could signal difficulties for China's massive manufacturing expansion. Industrial upgrading will be the key for China to sustain rapid growth. But the model does not tell where Chinese industries should move to. The policymakers hope to boost the service sectors. But labor market transition does not automatically support service sector development. The government will need to look for effective measures to overcome the existing barriers.

The modeling results also do not reveal possible impact on industrial upgrading within the manufacturing sector. This can be partly attributed to the aggregate levels of sector groups. A 5% reduction in unskilled labor implies rising share of skilled labor in total workforce. And thus comparative advantage should shift toward more skill-intensive industries.

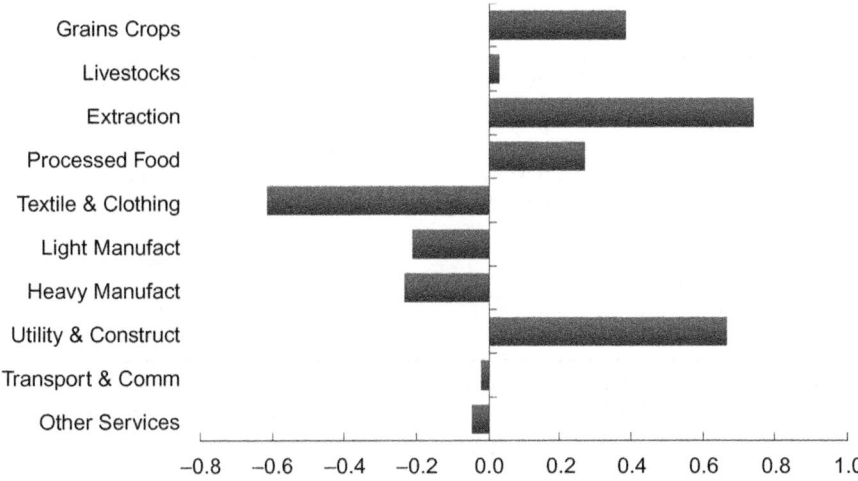

Figure 5.   Individual sector production change relative to the economy's average production change (percentage points).

Note: The shock implemented is reduction of unskilled labor by 5%. All numbers are percentage changes relative to the baseline scenario minus the average change rate.
Source: Author's simulation applying the GTAP model.

And faster development of high-technology, high skill and high value-added manufacturing should be a natural result of labor market transition, if relevant obstacles can be overcome.

But this is not the whole story. Industrial upgrading is not automatically guaranteed by emergence of labor scarcity. In fact, many developing countries were captured by the so-called 'middle-income trap'. They were dynamic and rapidly growing when cheap labor was abundant. Once this resource runs out, their growth also unraveled. Whether or not China can avoid the middle-income trap will eventually determine if China will really overtake the United States to become the world's largest economy in the coming decades.

Implications for the world economy

Given China's importance in today's global economy and markets, it's likely that the expected labor market transition in China should have important implications for other countries, especially China's close economic partners. But individual countries' economic relations with China are different. From trade point of view, for some, such as India, China is probably more of a competitor since both are labor-abundant countries. For others, such as Australia, China is probably more complementary. These relations, however, are becoming increasingly more complex given China's rapidly diversifying economic structure.

The first issue we want to explore is if relatively higher inflation rate in China means higher inflation for the world. This is an important question since many attribute stable global inflation during the past decade to cheap Chinese exports. If Chinese prices are going to rise, would it lead to high inflation in the world as well?

The modeling results, however, do not support that hypothesis. In fact, CPI inflation fall in all countries/country groups except India (see Table 5). Magnitudes of such negative impacts are small, ranging between 0.01% and 0.4%. The greatest effects are seen in Australia and NIEs, while the smallest impacts are observed in the USA, EU and Rest

Table 5.   How does China's Lewis turning point affect other countries' inflation? (%).

	GDP deflator	CPI	Terms of trade
Australia	−0.05	−0.03	−0.09
India	0.02	0.02	0.04
Japan	−0.04	−0.03	−0.06
NIEs	−0.07	−0.04	−0.05
ASEAN	−0.04	−0.02	−0.04
RoAsia	−0.07	−0.02	−0.10
USA	−0.01	−0.01	−0.03
EU_25	−0.01	−0.01	−0.01
RoWorld	−0.02	−0.01	−0.04

Note: Results reported in this and the following tables are for 5% reduction of Chinese unskilled labor. All numbers are percentage changes relative to the base case scenario.
Source: Author's simulation applying the GTAP model.

of the World. India's CPI rises by 0.02%, compared with 0.35% increase in Chinese CPI. Movements in GDP deflators generally follow the same pattern.

We should not take the results as evidence that Chinese inflation would not lead to global inflation. In fact, two changes are happening simultaneously in China in the model: one is higher price and the other is slower growth. *Ceteris paribus*, higher Chinese prices should lead to higher global prices, although the elasticity may be small. But slower Chinese growth helps ease pressure on global inflation. Clearly, this second effect dominates the modeling results. But the conclusion of the study is still valid: emergence of labor shortage in China does not necessarily lead to higher inflation in the world.

Changes in India provide a unique case study. At highly aggregated level, India shares a lot of commonalities with China, especially abundant unskilled labor and low labor cost. In fact, India's wages for both unskilled and skilled labor increase, just like what happen in China, an evidence of substitutability between Chinese and Indian labor-intensive products in international markets, although labor is not mobile in the GTAP model. For this reason, India's other factor prices except natural resources all experience positive changes, even though the net impacts on India's GDP and current account remain small.

Given relative changes in price levels in China and the rest of the world, it is easy to understand why current accounts improve for all other countries, including India. This should be a positive change for important deficit countries like USA, Australia and India. And, therefore, labor market transition in China may help these countries take one step forward in reducing their external imbalances. Whether or not this would help resolving the global imbalance is unclear, since other surplus countries also experience deterioration of their terms of trade.

Except India, all other countries suffer from falls in factor prices; although magnitudes of these changes are small (see Table 6). Again, this is probably because of lower economic activities as a result of changes in Chinese labor market. The largest falls occur in natural resource prices. This confirms the popular perception that if Chinese investment weakens, global commodity prices are likely to soften.

Changes in economic activities in the rest of the world are somewhat less uniform albeit magnitudes of impacts are all very small (see Table 7). Both India and Rest of Asia benefit from China's lower activities, an indirect evidence of competitive relations between China and these countries. The saving ratios increase slightly in India, Japan, USA and EU but

Table 6. Likely changes in factor prices in other countries (%).

	Unskilled labor	Skilled labor	Land	Capital	Natural resources
Australia	−0.03	−0.04	0.10	−0.04	−0.93
India	0.05	0.04	0.06	0.04	−1.05
Japan	−0.04	−0.04	0.07	−0.04	−0.75
NIEs	−0.07	−0.07	0.09	−0.07	−0.68
ASEAN	−0.01	−0.03	0.00	−0.03	−0.75
RoAsia	−0.01	−0.04	0.02	−0.03	−0.54
USA	−0.01	−0.01	−0.01	−0.01	−0.49
EU_25	−0.01	−0.01	0.03	−0.01	−0.74
RoWorld	0.00	−0.01	−0.01	−0.01	−0.62

Note: The shock implemented is reduction of unskilled labor by 5%. All numbers are percentage changes relative to the baseline scenario.
Source: Author's simulation applying the GTAP model.

Table 7. Effects on macroeconomic indicators of other countries (%).

	Real GDP (%)	Consumption (%)	Saving ratio (% GDP)	Investment ratio (% GDP)	Current account (% GDP)
Australia	−0.003	−0.02	−0.001	−0.01	0.01
India	0.001	0.01	0.004	0.00	0.00
Japan	−0.001	−0.01	0.000	−0.02	0.02
NIEs	−0.002	−0.03	−0.007	−0.02	0.01
ASEAN	−0.003	−0.03	−0.005	−0.02	0.01
RoAsia	0.001	−0.05	−0.007	−0.01	0.00
USA	−0.001	−0.01	0.000	−0.01	0.01
EU_25	−0.002	0.00	0.000	−0.01	0.01
RoWorld	−0.002	−0.02	−0.001	−0.01	0.01

Note: The shock implemented is reduction of unskilled labor by 5%. All numbers are percentage changes relative to the baseline scenario.
Source: Author's simulation applying the GTAP model.

decrease in all other countries. The investment ratios decline slightly everywhere except India. As a result, all countries experience improvement in the current account.

Unfortunately, this model does not capture the dynamic nature of international economic relations. Therefore, the negative correlations discovered in this study between China, on the one hand, and India and Rest of Asia, on the other, may be problematic. But at least from a static point of view, China's rapid rise in the technological ladder should make some room for other low-income countries with abundant labor.

Finally, what are the implications of Chinese labor market transition for sector structure of the rest of the world? The first to note is that almost all countries or country groups experience visible expansion in their manufacturing activities, especially in the textile and clothing industry (see Table 8). While this result sounds reasonable in terms of direction of change, the magnitudes of some of changes look problematic. For instance, it is probably easy to understand why the textile and clothing industries in ASEAN and Rest of Asia expand, but how much Australia, Japan and USA can gain from this market vacuum left by China remains a question given the relatively small share of the industries in these countries in the baseline scenario.

The sharp rise in exports of resource extraction sector in China and the widespread fall of resource exports in other countries warrant some detailed explanation. This is primarily

Table 8.   Changes in production by sectors in other countries (%).

	Australia	India	Japan	NIEs	ASEAN	RoAsia	USA	EU_25	ROW
Grains	0.03	0.00	0.02	0.02	0.00	0.03	0.00	0.01	0.00
Livestock	0.05	0.00	0.05	0.02	0.00	−0.02	0.00	0.01	0.00
Extraction	−0.13	−0.17	−0.10	−0.09	−0.10	−0.07	−0.07	−0.11	−0.08
Food	0.02	−0.01	0.01	0.02	−0.01	−0.01	0.00	0.00	−0.01
Textile	0.43	0.22	0.37	0.45	0.44	0.50	0.25	0.23	0.32
Light M	0.06	0.01	0.08	0.15	0.08	0.13	0.04	0.03	0.08
Heavy M	0.13	0.04	0.02	−0.03	0.02	0.30	0.04	0.02	0.10
Utility	−0.04	0.01	−0.06	−0.06	−0.06	−0.01	−0.03	−0.03	−0.02
Transport	0.00	0.01	−0.01	−0.03	−0.01	0.00	0.00	0.00	−0.01
Services	−0.01	−0.01	0.00	0.00	−0.02	−0.03	0.00	−0.01	−0.02

Note: The shock implemented is reduction of unskilled labor by 5%. All numbers are percentage changes relative to the baseline scenario.
Source: Author's simulation applying the GTAP model.

driven by the fact that the extraction sector is the most capital and resource-intensive industry – capital and natural resources account for 53% of value added of the sector.

The LTP significantly increases China's endowments in capital and natural resources, relative to labor, and decreases their prices. With lower prices of capital and natural resources, competitiveness of Chinese resource exports improve sharply, leading to higher exports and lower imports, and thus lower production elsewhere. But because the overall economic activity in China falls, the demand for mining products falls, leading to fall in the mining production in China.

The broad conclusion about structural change is clear. If the first decade of the twenty-first century saw China rapidly rising as a global manufacturing center, then the post-LTP time could see the opposite. In other words, global manufacturing activities concentrate in China today may find their ways elsewhere. Of course this is likely to happen gradually.

Toward a normal dynamic economy

Before summarizing the findings, we like to reiterate important limitations of the framework applied in this study. Like any models, GTAP has its own advantages and disadvantages. One most important advantage of the GTAP model is its detailed structure with 10 country groups and 10 industries. The model is widely used and well respected among some applied international economists. It enables us to look at not only the macroeconomic impacts but also changes at sector level. It also enables us to pick up likely important changes in the rest of the world.

Initially, however, GTAP was designed primarily for trade policy analysis. So it is more sophisticated on trade linkages across countries. But it is light on financial aspects, especially capital markets. This is an important deficiency for analyzing important international economic issues in today's world. The most important setback, however, is its static nature. To analyze a long-term issue like labor market transition, a dynamic CGE model is much preferred. GTAP is the second best that we have access. We plan to revisit the question in the future by applying a dynamic computable general equilibrium framework.

We also like to caution on drawing too much implications from the simulation results. Like any models, simulation results from GTAP are to certain extent driven by the model structure and elasticities chosen. We take the results more as references for verifying our economic analysis, not hard evidences for predicting future events.

And, finally, by implement the shock described above in GTAP framework essentially means we simulate a multi-year process in an annual framework. Decline of labor supply of the order of 5% only occurs gradually, not within a single year. The simulating results may be over- or under-estimated. Short-term elasticity is often smaller than long-term one. Meanwhile, productivity gains may also grow with time, which may be able to offset the negative impacts of labor supply shocks.

With these qualifications in mind, we still find the modeling results revealing and exciting. First, emergence of labor shortage in China could see the beginning of a period of higher inflation. Wages will probably rise quickly for understandable reasons, although in the near term other factor prices may fall. But the overall impact is likely to be inflationary. Product prices of all sectors, except one, increase.

Second, decline in labor supply should have negative impact on economic activities, especially real GDP growth. This holds as long as marginal product of labor remains positive. The falls are broad-based in the primary, secondary and tertiary industries, on production-based measures, and in investment, consumption and net exports, on expenditure-based measures.

Third, labor shortage would have mixed impacts on China's imbalance problems. According to the modeling results, it improves external imbalance, by lower current account surplus, but worsens internal imbalance, by higher investment share of GDP. GDP growth is also going to be less dependent on exports, which fall faster than GDP.

Fourth, labor-intensive manufacturing is likely to lose out quickly after the LTP. In fact, manufacturing as a whole could be adversely affected, raising questions about China's future as the global manufacturing center. In the short term, economic structure could be skewed toward capital-, land- and resource-intensive activities.

And, finally, the world economy may slow slightly alongside moderation of Chinese growth. Low-income countries should be able to grow more rapidly in labor-intensive industries. Almost all other countries should experience improvement in their current accounts. Their prices may rise or fall, depending on which mechanism dominates: price transmission or demand connection.

We have not discussed the impacts on exchange rates. This is because exchange rate is treated as the monetary numéraire in the model. So unfortunately, simulation results do not reveal explicit changes in renminbi nominal exchange rate. However, rising inflation in China, especially against the background of lowering inflation elsewhere, suggests that renminbi should appreciate in real effective terms. This is consistent with China's improving terms of trade and lowering current account surplus.

So what are the key takeaways? The most important conclusion is that China will transition from an abnormal economy to a normal dynamic emerging economy. The modeling results tell us the Chinese economy will probably see slower growth and higher inflation after the LTP.

It may be argued that if China can accelerate productivity growth, then its growth rate does not have to fall. This is certainly possible theoretically. But in reality it is difficult. Not only resource constraints become tighter, but China is also closer to the global technology frontier, which makes rapid growth more difficult. And experiences of other countries also confirm some slowdown in GDP growth with emergence of labor shortage.

But this transition needs not to be a worry. In a way, China's macroeconomic performance during the past three decades, with average GDP growth of 9.6 % and average CPI inflation of 1.3%, was unprecedented and abnormal. In comparison, the post-LTP Japan and Korea experienced periods of 8–9% GDP growth and 5–6% CPI inflation (see Table 9). So the expected changes will probably only move China back to the neighborhood of other dynamic emerging economies.

Table 9.   Real GDP growth and CPI inflation in Japan, Korea and China (%).

	Japan (1960–1972)	Korea (1982–1996)	China (1997–2009)
GDP: Average	8.9	8.5	9.6
CPI: Average	5.6	5.2	1.3
CPI: Maximum	13.1	11.1	4.8
CPI: Minimum	3.6	2.3	−1.5

Source: Arthur Kroebor (2010), page 45.

In fact, labor market transition is only one of the factors that will help convert China to a normal economy. A more fundamental cause is the expected elimination of cost distortions. During the past 30 years, the Chinese government adopted a unique asymmetric reform approach: complete liberalization of product markets but heavy distortions in factor markets. The estimated factor cost distortions amount to between 6% and 12% of GDP in 2000–2009 (Yiping 2010).

These distortions are like producer subsidies. They artificially raise profits from production, increase returns to investment and improve international competitiveness of Chinese products. These distortions are important reasons why Chinese growth is so strong but imbalance problems are so serious. They also naturally repress inflation rates. Liberalization of factor markets and elimination of cost distortions, which have already begun, are likely to lead to slightly lower GDP growth but slightly higher inflation.

And this transformation is very important for policymaking and investment decisions. The government may have to revise its current policy framework. For instance, the government should learn to live with somewhat higher inflation. The central bank normally sets inflation target at around 3% and tightens monetary policy aggressively when CPI hits 5%. These constraints should probably be relaxed. After all, slightly higher inflation is a natural result of correcting domestic price distortions.

The government should also get used to slightly slower growth. The 10% average growth was partly contributed by productivity gain from transforming farmers into industrial workers. But it was also a result of the government's over-emphasis of GDP growth, which came at the expenses of growth quality and other social problems. It is much for the government to focus on efficiency of the economy and social protection of the people. To achieve this, the government will have to modify its system for reviewing performance of the local officials.

Concluding remarks: Can China avoid the 'middle-income trap'?

The modeling results reveal that China is likely to transition toward a 'normal economy'. But they do not tell if China is able to avoid the so-called 'middle-income trap'. In this final section, we offer a few remarks on two subjects: one, resolution of the structural risks; and, two, new sources of growth.

China managed extraordinary economic growth during the reform period. In the meantime it also accumulated a long list of risks, which already threaten sustainability of growth. And these risks include overinvestment, large external surplus, income inequality among households, declining shares of household income and consumption in the economy and under-developed service sector. Whether or not China is able to avoid the 'middle-income trap', first of all, depends on its ability in defuse the existing risks.

Analyses in this study confirm that the LTP may be able to solve some of the existing problems. For instance, labor shortage may lead to decline in saving ratio and reduce current account surplus. Of course, complete resolution of external imbalance problem will likely require a more comprehensive policy package, including reforms of the exchange rate regime and domestic factor markets.

The LTP may also help increase wages and raise the share of household income in national income. Japan's experiences also confirm that the labor market transition can improve income distribution. Alongside the other reforms such as development of social welfare systems and redistribution of incomes, consumption growth may start to gather momentum. The modeling results, however, point to higher investment share of GDP following labor shortage. This may require more decisive policy actions such as financial liberalization to end financial repression.

The modeling analyses do not offer any insights on how to boost China's underdeveloped service sectors. In fact, simulation results point to relative shrink of the service sectors since they are generally more labor-intensive. But development of the service sector is critical for China to continue its rapid growth. Therefore, the government may need to find ways to overcome the existing obstacles for service sector development.

What really trapped many Latin America and Middle East middle-income countries was lack of innovation capability. They failed to move up the industrial ladder beyond resource-based activities. This will also be the real test for China. The government has set its eyes on high tech and high value-added industries to carry Chinese growth forward. But currently there are still huge gaps in China in areas of education, research and development, financial services, legal protection and lowering entry barriers.

To sum up, the LTP will likely transform China from an abnormal economy into a normal dynamic emerging economy, probably with lower GDP growth and higher inflation. Labor market transition should help deal with some of the existing risk factors but does not provide automatic solutions to all the problems.

The biggest post-LTP challenge is how to avoid the so-called 'middle-income trap'. And this depends on China's ability to resolve existing risks, maintain macroeconomic stability and, most importantly, build innovation capability that will continuously push China closer to the global technology frontier.

Acknowledgment

We want to thank Ross Garnaut and Fang Cai, among others, for sharing insights on this important issue during the past few years. Wang Xun provided helpful comments on the first draft.

Note

1. Suppose the 5% reduction in unskilled labor supply happen over a 10-year period. During this period, the Chinese economy would become 1.6 times bigger with a growth rate of 10% per annum without any labor shortage problem (the baseline scenario). The result of 2% reduction in GDP means that the economy would be 1.5 times bigger than current level, that is, it would grow at 9.8% per annum with the existence of labor shortage.

References

Cai, Fang, ed. 2007. *Reports on China's population and labor, no. 8: The Lewisian turning point and policy challenges* (in Chinese). Beijing: Social Sciences Literature Press.

Cai, Fang 2010. Demographic transition, demographic dividend and the Lewis turning point, in China. *China Economic Journal* 3, no. 2: 107–120.

Cai, Fang, and Dewen Wang. 2006. Employment growth, labor scarcity and the nature of China's trade expansion. In *The turning point in China's economic development*, eds. Ross Garnaut and Ligang Song, 143–171. Canberra: Asia Pacific Press.

Garnaut, Ross, and Yiping Huang. 2006. Continued rapid growth and the turning point in China's economic development. In *The turning point in China's economic development*, eds. Ross Garnaut and Ligang Song, 12–34. Canberra: Asia Pacific Press.

Gill, Indermit Singh, and Homi Kharas. 2007. *An East Asian Renaissance: Ideas for economic growth*. Washington, DC: The World Bank.

Huang, Yiping. 2004. A labor shortage in China. *Wall Street Journal*, A7, August 6–8, 2004.

Huang, Yiping. 2010. Dissecting the "China puzzle": Asymmetric liberalization and cost distortion. CCER Working Paper No. 2010003, China Center for Economic Research, Peking University, Beijing.

Kroebor, Arthur. 2010. Economic rebalancing: The end of surplus labor. *China Economic Quarterly*, March 2010.

Lewis, W. Arthur. 1958. Unlimited labour: Further notes. *Manchester School of Economic and Social Studies* 26, no.1: 1–32.

Minami, Ryoshin. 1968. The turning point in the Japanese economy. *Quarterly Journal of Economics* 82, no. 3: 380–402.

Minami, Ryoshin, and Xinxin Ma, 2008. The turning point of the Chinese economy: Compared with Japanese experience. Paper presented at the Study Meeting of the Chinese Labor Market, December 20, 2008, Tokyo University, Tokyo.

Minami, Ryoshin, and Xinxin Ma. 2010. The Lewisian turning point of Chinese economy: Comparison with Japanese experience. *China Economic Journal* 3, no. 2: 163–179.

Narayanan, G. Badri, and Terrie L. Walmsley. Global Trade, Assistance, and Production: The GTAP 7 Database, center for Global Trade Analysis, Purdue University.

Sachs, Jeffrey, and Wing Thye Woo. 2001. Structural factors in China's economic reform. In *Growth without miracles: Readings on the Chinese economy in the era of reform*, eds. Ross Garnaut and Yiping Huang, 474–488. Oxford: Oxford University Press.

Yao, Yang, and Ke Zhang. 2010. Has China passed the Lewis turning point: A structural estimation based on provincial data. *China Economic Journal* 3, no. 2: 155–162.

Will Chinese growth slow after the Lewis turning point?

Ligang Song[a] and Yongsheng Zhang[b]

[a]Australian National University, Canberra, Australia; [b]Development Research Centre of China, Beijing, China

(Received 28 May 2010; final version received 31 August 2010)

The paper argues that China's economic growth will not necessarily slow after China reaches the Lewis turning point (LTP) when wages and subsequently costs of production, as a result of the exhaustion of the unlimited supplies of labor from rural areas, are increasing. Reaching the turning point leads to significant structural change signifying that China enters a new phase of development in which those endogenously determined factors such as human capital, innovation, R&D expenditure and technological progress begin to play more important roles than contributions made simply by inputs of physical capital, labor and resources in enhancing economic growth. To achieve the continual growth, certain conditions are needed in the transition toward and beyond the turning point including among others the institutional reform which enables China to further transform itself in order to embrace a new mode of economic growth driven predominantly by efficient, sustainable and equitable considerations.

Introduction

The Chinese economy grew at an average rate of nearly 10% per annum over the period 1978–2008. It is often argued that the supply of abundant cheap labor from the rural areas to the industrial sector has long been a key source of China's rapid economic growth in the past 30 years (Chan 2009). To show the magnitude of this contribution to growth, the latest Population Census reports that the number of migrant workers in China has now reached 170 million (Song, Wu, and Zhang 2010) rising from 78.5 million in 2000 (Cai, Yang, and Zhao 2007). The contributions to economic growth resulting from the rapid pace of urbanization, which is unprecedented in human history in terms of its scale and speed,[1] are often termed in literature as 'resource shift' effect reflecting the gains in total output resulting from shifting resources from a country's low productivity areas such as agriculture to high productivity areas such as manufacturing.

In the course of economic development, however, a country with a dual economic structure will reach the LTP (Lewis 1954) when the pool of unlimited supplies of labor in the rural areas has been exhausted and started causing the general level of wages to increase as a consequence. While debates are going on with respect to whether China is approaching or will soon reach the turning point (Garnaut and Huang 2006, Cai and Wang 2009), one may wonder whether China's rapid economic growth will slow down after reaching this turning point as by then with the rising wages China will lose the advantage of low-cost labor in production and then the competitiveness of its exports on world markets which have been an engine for growth in the past. This impact of shifting labor structure on growth is even more pronounced when one considers that changes in China's demographic structure lead to a fast pace of moving the country into an aging society bringing about a fall not only in the growth of labor supply and saving, but also an increase in the financial burden in looking after the old. In other words, China 'demographic dividend' (output and other economic gains from having a large proportion of working-age group in the total population) will start disappearing (Cai and Wang 2009).

This paper argues that China's economic growth will not necessarily slow after China reaches the LTP when wages and subsequently costs of production are increasing resulting from the exhaustion of the unlimited supplies of labor in the rural areas. This is because that reaching the turning point leads to significant structural changes signifying that China enters a new phase of development in which those endogenously determined factors such as human capital, innovation, R&D expenditure and technological progress will play more important roles than contributions made simply by inputs of physical capital, labor and resources in enhancing economic growth.

This article argues further that to achieve continuing growth after reaching the turning point, certain conditions need to be put in place in the transition toward and beyond the turning point including among others the institutional reform which enables China to further transform itself in order to embrace a new mode of economic growth driven predominantly by efficient, sustainable and equitable considerations. The success of doing so will, to a great extent, offset the negative impact of falling labor supply resulting from the aging of China's population. This suggests that the long-run growth of China's economy at a more reasonable pace will continue until the country eventually reaches the world technological frontier with little room for deepening the scope of specialization further.

The turning point theory and its implications

To make the arguments tenable, it may be useful first of all to briefly clarify whether the theory of the turning point is universally applicable to all countries and all times or whether it is rather specific and applicable to certain kinds of countries and over certain periods of time in the process of development. If, for example, the theory is confined or applicable only to certain periods in the process of development, then the theory may not be relevant in explaining the phenomena including the growth prospects at a more advanced stage of development. In that case, new theories will have to be applied in order for one to be more accurately analyzing those forces which begin to work in determining the economic growth and development in the post-LTP period.

The applicability of the theory of the turning point has been summarized by Minami (1973, 72) in the following ways. First, the theory is applicable only to the unskilled labor force because skilled workers are limited in supply. This suggests that one cannot apply the theory in analyzing the role of human capital and human skill in enhancing growth which becomes important at a more advanced stage of economic development (to be discussed). Second, the theory is not applicable to the 'modern' sector as it depends on the existence of a dual structure in the economy. According to the theory, when a country reaches the turning point, the dual structure will disappear as wages will be equalized between the modern and traditional sectors. This suggests that once the turning point is reached, the theory itself is no longer applicable in analyzing those economic forces working at the new phase of development. Third, the turning point is not a specific point in time as it may extend over a number of years. Fourth, the turning point is a long-term and trend-related economic phenomenon as the transition from the stage of unlimited supplies of labor to that of limited supplies of labor is a structural change in the economy or a trend phenomenon.

This implies that the turning point theory foreshadows the economic structural change resulting from rising wages, but it does not directly answer the question as to whether or to what extent that economic growth will continue after the turning point. This is because shifting from the case of unlimited supplies of labor to the case of limited supplies of labor represents two stages of economic development and the basic mechanisms of economic development are different before and after the turning point (Minami 1973). The approach taken by Lewis (1954) in illustrating the different mechanisms at the different stage of development is to refer to the former as the case for the classical stage, and the latter as the case of neoclassical stage of development in which the marginal productivity theory of production and distribution are dominant. Thus 'a transition from the classical to the neoclassical stages is explained by the theory of the turning point' (Minami 1973, 10).

However, at the same time, some doubt with respect to applicability of the neoclassical theories has been raised because those theories do not explain 'the most urgent problem in the under-development economies, that of attaining the economic take-off or the break through' and 'they are concerned mainly with a proportional growth in the economy: in other words, they tend to overlook structural changes' (Minami 1973, 5). This means that to illustrate the growth prospect resulting from the structural change after a country has reached the turning point, we would need to go beyond the neoclassical growth theories for explanation.

New theories in explaining the growth potential after the turning point

The key in understanding the importance as well as the relevance of applying the new theories in explaining the growth potential at a more advanced stage of development, is first of all to elaborate on how structural changes induced by reaching the turning point will lead to the endogenously determined pattern of economic growth; and then to illustrate how those endogenously determined factors could offset the possible negative impact of the shortage of labor, rising costs of labor and further on the falling return to capital (because of the rising capital/labor ratio) on future growth.

Both capital accumulation and technological progress play important roles in a country's transition from the unlimited to limited supplies of labor in that both are needed in generating an increase in the demand for labor in the modern sector. In the transition from the labor surplus to the labor shortage economy, wages and then costs of production increase pushing firms to substitute labor with capital and thereby raising society's capital/ labor ratio. According to the neoclassical growth theories, this rising capital/labor ratio will lead to the diminishing return to capital and as a consequence to slower growth. However, it is well known that in reality those industrialized countries with higher capital/labor ratio experienced on average higher growth of per capita income than those less-developed countries.

The reason why the rising capital/labor ratio did not slow down growth is that there is something happening in the economy which raises the productivity of labor in the same proportion as capital/labor increases keeping the capital/output ratio constant (certainly not raising it). This is where the 'new' models of endogenous growth come to apply. In these theories, 'there are assumed to be positive externalities associated with human capital formation and research and development (R&D) that prevent the marginal product of capital from falling and the capital/output ratio from rising' (Thirlwall 2006, 154). Hence, the production of human capital may be an alternative to improvements in technology as a mechanism to generate long-term growth (Barro and Sala-i-Martin 2004). R&D may improve the productivity of labor or capital, or both leading to new inventions and then to innovation – either process innovation or product innovation (Thirlwall 2006, 211). These positive externalities can exist resulting from the accumulation of knowledge (Romer 1986); they resided in the effect of human capital on output (Lucas 1988); they can take the form of specialized human capital relating to learning by doing which could become an engine of growth making it possible that the economy grows in the long run even without technological change (Lucas 1988); they can be generated by innovation which becomes an important source of productivity growth (Romer 1990). All these make a country's long-run growth possible as shown by the experiences of the industrialized economies.

Studies are abounding in illustrating the validities of new growth theories. Some of them provided empirical evidence to show how these theories have been applied to illustrate the cases which resemble the post-LTP stage of development. For example, Helpman (2004) reports the case that during the twentieth century about a quarter of the US growth in income per worker was due to the rise in education. Young (1995) points out that the rise in years of schooling played a central role in the growth of the Asian newly industrialized economies (NIEs). Mohnen (1996) attributed between 10% and 50% of output growth in the major Organization for Economic Co-operation and Development (OECD) countries to R&D growth, 40% of US total factor productivity (TFP) growth to R&D spillovers, and 66% of TFP growth in Japan to US R&D growth (Helpman 2004).

The experience of Japan offers an example of how a country's economic growth continues after reaching the LTP. According to Minami (1973),[2] Japan reached the LTP in the 1950s. However, we know that the growth of the Japanese economy did not slow down afterward. To the contrary, it marked the beginning of Japan's period of nearly 30-year long high economic growth. Japan's average annual growth rate of GNP per capita over the period 1961–1968 is 9.9%, the highest among all the major economies (Table 2 in Meadows et al. 1972). Close to 50% of Japanese output growth during 1960–1995 (the highest among the top seven industrialized economies) is attributed to TFP growth (Helpman 2004).

There are several elements in illustrating the mechanisms through which these endogenously determined factors impact on growth. First, technological change is endogenously determined by the accumulation of human capital, the increase in R&D, the diffusion of knowledge and therefore plays a key role in enhancing growth. Second, technological change drives the pace and direction of the structural change which in turn is accompanied by further specialization. Third, specialization is enhanced by the enlarged domestic and world market. Fourth, specialization affects the return to capital and leads to economies of scale and technological progress which may be endogenous and therefore lead to growth-enhancing effects. Finally, in the new phase of development, the role of physical capital has also changed, namely the scope for capital to permit roundabout methods of production will be widened (Thirlwall 2006).

Applicability of the new growth theories to China

We have made the argument that the new endogenously determined growth theories are more applicable in explaining the growth prospects after a country has reached the LTP, and provided some empirical evidence to show how those endogenously determined factors work in the way that they offset the negative impact on growth resulting from the rising wages and costs of production as well as the diminishing return to capital in the industrialized countries. We have also pointed out that the key to understand the process of adjustment is the structural change derived in responding to changes in the relative prices, the rising wages, and the altered pattern of factor endowment such as capital/labor ratio.

This structural change has been dictated by two key factors: one is technological progress and the other is the scope of specialization. The questions we need to ask now are two: how relevant these theories and the arguments developed are to China now; and whether it is too early for China to consider adopting a strategy incorporating those endogenously determined factors in sustaining growth at this transition phase toward a more advanced stage of development. The questions can be addressed as follows.

First, it is true that China is still some distance away from reaching the tuning point. It is also true that China is far from reaching the technological frontier (Figure 1). Under these circumstances, it may sound too early for China to do as the new growth theories suggest. It is not. In an earlier work, Minami (1966) put forth three rather than two stages of development, namely the stage of unlimited supplies of labor, the stage of semi-limited supplies of labor and the stage of limited supplies of labor. The final stage is regarded as 'the purely conceptual third stage' with an infinite elasticity of labor supply which comes into existence after a disappearance of the subsistence sector.[3] This specification of stages of development seems more pertinent to the case of transition toward the turning point in that the second stage of semi-limited supplies of labor indicates the period in which the elasticity of the labor supply is positive and finite.[4]

This second stage resembles more closely the situation of China now in that with rising wages the labor supply curve has been positively sloping, shifting toward an infinite elasticity of labor supply defined as the turning point. Looking from the perspective that 'the turning point is a long-term and trend-related economic phenomenon' (Minami 1973), it does not matter much as to how long it will take for China to reach that turning point. What matters most is what China will or be compelled to do now in order to achieve the growth potential in the future. That is why it is not too early for China to adopt the strategy aimed

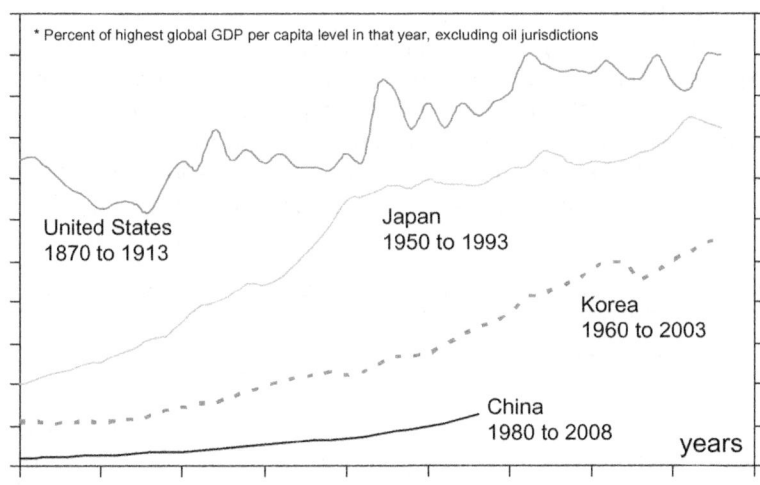

Figure 1. Income per capita relative to the frontier (Years from the start of modern industrial development).

Source: Figure 1 in McKay and Song (2010, 4).

at encouraging the endogenous growth because the mechanisms which determine growth have already started to change. Once again, the observation by Lewis illustrates the point.

> There is no doubt that one of the main deficiencies of under-developed countries is their failure to spend adequately upon research and upon the development of new processes and materials appropriate to their circumstances. Part of the reason for this is institutional. (Lewis 1955, 175)

Second, China has also been compelled to be more actively engaged in carrying out structural changes by readjusting its growth strategy. As pointed out by McKay and Song (2010), the cyclical re-emergence of excess capacity in Chinese heavy industry, serious questions about the medium term ability of other major regions to accommodate further large gains in Chinese market share, and the stark conflict between the contemporary style of industrial development and the health of the biosphere all indicate strongly that now is the time for China to catalyze the required adjustment and reform processes that will underpin sustainable long-run growth and prosperity.

Third, McKay and Song (2010) also argue that there are some advantages for China to do so, as there is huge potential for China to narrow its technological gap with mature industrialized economies. This statement holds particularly strongly in the areas of green technologies. If a wholesale effort is launched, China will catch up more quickly and could even rise to leadership in the application of green technologies, given the economies of scale that would be associated with their use in China's projected mega-market, its strong foundation of human capital and, more importantly, the administrative determination to adopt a new model for economic growth. This is because China basically satisfies those conditions that must hold if introduction of a new technology is to lead to a leapfrogging process (Brezis, Krugman, and Tsiddon 1991). In this respect, China is certainly making progress, for example, on R&D, but will need to do more (Table 1).

There are a few other factors which need to be dealt with by way of discussing China's potential for further growth toward and beyond reaching the turning point. They are contributions of labor, physical capital and TFP to economic growth, the rising income inequality and the process of demographic transition.

First, labor as an input of production plays an important role in production. However, labor is only one factor in contributing to economic growth, and that role becomes less important as compared with the role of physical capital, human capital and productivity (TFP) in contributing to growth. For example, the decomposition of contributions by factors of production and TFP during the reform period in China shows that labor contributes least to economic growth and the transition from an inputs-based growth pattern to a

Table 1.   Shares of R&D expenditure in total GDP (%): 1990, 2000 and 2007.

Country	1990	2000	2007
China	0.80	0.90	1.49
United States	2.65	2.74	2.67
Japan	2.79	2.99	3.45
United Kingdom	2.15	1.86	1.84
Germany	2.67	2.45	2.55
France	2.33	2.15	2.10
Canada	1.53	1.94	2.03
Italy	1.25	1.05	1.14

Source: OECD Factbook 2007 and the World Development Index, various years.

TFP-based one become ever urgent as the LTP approaches (Cai and Wang 2009). In developed countries, more than half of the variation in income per capita results from differences in TFP and the same applies to differences in growth rates of income per capita (Helpman 2004, 34).

In comparison with the role of labor, both physical capital and TFP will continue to play an important role in contributing to growth at the more advanced stage of development. More importantly, the function of physical capital has changed, for in the context of the new growth theory, increase in investment is the major determinant of technological change to the extent that the distinction between input-driven and technology-driven economic growth is blurred (Chen 1997).

Second, China's rapid economic growth in the past has been accompanied by rising income inequality. There are many factors which contribute to the rising inequality during the reform period and some of them are clearly due to the nature of economic transition such as privatization of state-owned enterprises or the imperfection of the labor market. While it is debatable as to whether inequality is an inevitable outcome of rapid growth especially at the early phase of development (Kuznets 1955), it is recognized in China that the rising inequality, which is socially undesirable, could hamper long-term economic growth.

With China approaching the turning point, the rising wages propelled by the increasingly limited supplies of labor, the general living standard with rising per capita income could be increased (see Garnaut in this edition). Kindleberger (1967) also observed by studying the turning point in European countries that the relative share of labor in total income would decline or remain constant before the turning point and rise after the turning point. However, there is no guarantee that income will be more equally distributed after a country reaches the LTP. Table 2 shows that a relatively high degree of income inequality is still associated with majority of those most developed countries. This is because that both capital input and technology will play more important roles for an economy at a more advanced stage of development and both of them could impact on the evolution of wage inequality (Helpman 2004). It is therefore important for China to face the challenge of income distribution in the transition toward the turning point in order to achieve more equitable growth in the long run.

Following the logic of the new growth theory, both private and public investment in education will generate higher return, higher income and therefore be more favorable to income distribution and equitable growth. China will need to increase further its share of education expenditure in total GDP (Table 3). The demand for funding education for migrant workers and their families is particularly pronounced. It is well documented that rural migrant workers have had fewer years of education than their urban counterparts and

Table 2. Gini coefficients: China and industrialized countries.

Country	Gini coefficient
China	41.5 (2007)
United States	45.0 (2007)
Japan	38.1 (2002)
United Kingdom	34.0 (2005)
Germany	27.0 (2006)
France	32.7 (2008)
Canada	32.1 (2005)
Italy	32.0 (2005)

Source: The World Factbook, various years.

Table 3. Shares of education expenditure in total GDP (%): 1990, 2000 and 2008.

Country	1990	2000	2008
China	1.79	1.78	1.81
United States	4.72	4.87	4.85
Japan	4.09	3.23	3.28
United Kingdom	4.52	5.24	5.10
Germany	4.38	4.27	4.33
France	5.07	5.17	5.10
Canada	6.63	5.48	4.43
Italy	3.07	4.21	4.42

Source: The World Bank Development Indicators Database, various years.

as a result there have been substantial gaps in educational attainment between migrant workers and urban workers. For example, Wang (2009) shows that only 23% of migrant workers graduated from a senior high school while 76% of urban workers attained the same level of education in 2005.

Finally, demographic transition is defined as 'a dynamic process of changes in fertility and mortality that causes corresponding changes in population quantity and structure' (Wang and Cai 2009, 68). The current demographic transition in China is characterized by its rapid move toward an aging society which is arguably causing the fall in labor supply and saving when the proportion of the economically active population begins to shrink which will have some negative impact on growth (Du 2009). The phenomenon happens in many parts of the world now such as Japan, but what is unique for China is that this kind of demographic transition coincides with the transition toward the turning point. Both have important implications for further growth.

It is difficult to predict whether and to what extent that those endogenously determined factors could offset the negative impact on growth by the transition toward the turning point on the one hand and the demographic transition toward aging on the other. In any case, there is need to offset those negative effects on growth through improvement in efficiency and widening the scope of specialization which can be done by deepening domestic market (especially factor markets) reform, enlarging the domestic and international markets, and deepening institutional reform including the social security system, the regulatory system reform and the governmental reform.

Just to take the size of the market as an example. It is true that a long-run rate of productivity growth is higher in economies with faster population growth (Howitt 1999), but a country's large size of population such as China's means a large market which matters in that there is an inherent link in the new growth theory between market size and the incentive to innovate meaning that larger markets encourage more R&D (Helpman 2004, 50).[5] One of the pressing issues for China now is to enlarge domestic market consumption in order to address the issue of global imbalances. Song, Wu, and Zhang (2010) show how to boost domestic demand through urbanizing migrant workers which could be accomplished by all the institutional reforms just discussed.

By relying on those endogenously determined factors with the reformed institutional framework which supports the generation of those endogenous factors, a reasonably high economic growth rate can be achieved in the long run until China reaches the international technological frontier, or exhausts the room for further specialization, or simply runs out of ideas for further innovation and technological breakthrough.

Conditions for further growth in China

Reaching the turning point in the sense that is described in this paper indicates that the changed economic circumstances require that the existing institutions must also change to accommodate the new development. As argued by Helpman (2004) that the ability of a country to grow depends on its ability to accommodate such changes in economic circumstances, and the ability to accommodate changes depends in turn on a country's economic and political institutions. This is because 'institutions affect the incentives to innovate and to develop new technologies, the incentives to reorganize production and distribution in order to exploit new opportunities, and the incentives to accumulate physical and human capital' (Helpman 2004, 139). Therefore, failure to reform and change the institutions in a timely fashion reflecting the rapid change in underlying economic structure, even in the process of the transition toward the turning point, will mean that growth will be compromised.

Key institutions, which need to be reformed to accommodate the rapid technological, structural and distributional changes, include the rule of law, protection of property rights, the market institution, the legal system, the social welfare system, the government system and the political system, as well as the value system including the social norms. Precisely because of the fact that the institutional changes have always been slow in keeping up with the rapid change in economic circumstances, we argue that China has made tremendous progress in reforming its institutions in the first 30 years of reform and transformation. What has been achieved in the past has laid the groundwork for China to deepen the institutional reform at the next stage of its development. In the sense the new institutional reform is more challenging than what has been achieved in the past because the new reform will prepare China to embrace a new mode of economic growth driven predominantly by not only efficient, but also sustainable and equitable considerations. One important lesson we have learned from the past experience of reform is that 'once institutions begin to change, they change in ways which are self-reinforcing' (Lewis 1955, 146). There is reason to be optimistic as far as the future change in institution is concerned as pointed out by Lewis in the same book (1955) that changes reinforces itself cumulatively. 'Once economic growth has begun, institutions change more and more in directions favourable to growth, and so strengthen the forces making for growth' (p. 143). China's economic growth experience in the past 30 years illustrates the point.

Conclusions

Reaching the LTP in economic development has important implications for the long-run economic growth in China. The rising wages with an aging population propels China to embrace a significant structural transformation leading to the altered mode of economic growth toward endogenously determined growth in which new sources for further growth have been generated. The big challenges that China faces now such as global imbalances, aging population and environmental degradation accelerate the pace of adjustment. In this new mode of growth, productivity gains through technological change, enhanced by education, innovation and R&D expenditure, and even the new way of organization of production will play a more important role than the inputs of physical capital and labor in contributing to economic growth. Furthermore, because of the endogenous nature of growth at this more advanced stage of development, an increase in physical capital itself would generate more technological progress in production than what it does in an extensive phase of growth and development.

It is therefore reasonable to expect that China's economic growth will continue after reaching the LTP and beyond. For a smooth transition toward the new and more advanced phase of development, China needs to deepen the reform of its various kinds of institutions including economic, social, legal and political institutions to make them more conducive to market integration, innovation, R&D, protection of intellectual property rights, respectful for knowledge and social justice. All these will increase China's capability of generating endogenous growth which, as demonstrated by the experience of those industrialized economies after reaching that advanced stage of development, can be sustained in the long run.

Acknowledgment

The authors thank Dr Miaojie Yu and other participants in the Workshop on the Lewis Turning Point held in Beijing on 6 April 2010 for their comments on the ideas presented, and Yixiao Zhou for her help with preparing the Tables used in the paper.

Notes

1. China's urbanization ratio, defined as the ratio of urban population to the total population, rose from less than 20% when reform started in the late 1970s to about 45% in 2009 with nearly 300 million people having been urbanized over this period.
2. Minami quoted Lewis (1958) in making this point.
3. See the footnote 30 on page 39 in Minami (1973).
4. In fact, Minami (1973) refers this second stage as the stage of limited supplies of labor in the definition in that volume.
5. China's total population is expected to rise from the current 1.3 billion to 1.5 billion in about 30 years from now.

References

Barro, Robert J., and Xavier Sala-i-Martin. 2004. *Economic growth*. Cambridge, MA: MIT Press.
Brezis, Elise S., Paul R. Krugman, and Daniel Tsiddon. 1991. "Leapfrogging: A theory of cycles in national technological leadership." NBER Working Paper No. 3886, National Bureau of Economic Research, Cambridge, Massachusetts.
Cai, Fang, Du Yang, and Changbao Zhao. 2007. "Regional labour market integration since China's entry into the World Trade Organisation: Evidence from household-level data." Chapter 8 in *China—linking markets for growth*, eds. Ross Garnaut and Ligang Song, 133–150. Canberra: The Australian National University E-Press.
Cai, Fang, and Meiyan Wang. 2009. "China's process of ageing before getting rich." Chapter 3 in *The China population and labour yearbook, volume 1: The approaching Lewis turning point and its polity implications*, eds. Cai Fang and Du Yang, 49–64. Leiden and Boston: Brill.
Chan, Kam Wing. 2009. "Introduction: Population, migration, and the Lewis turning point in China." Introduction in *The China population and labour yearbook, volume 1: The approaching Lewis turning point and its polity implications*, eds. Cai Fang and Du Yang, xix–xli. Leiden and Boston: Brill.
Chen, Edward K.Y. 1997. "The total factor productivity debate: Determinants of economic growth in East Asia." *Asia-Pacific Economic Literature* 11, no. 1: 18–39.
Du, Yang. 2009. "The potentials of labour supply and policy reactions to the Lewis turning point." Chapter 10 in *The China population and labour yearbook, volume 1: The approaching Lewis turning point and its polity implications*, eds. Cai Fang and Du Yang, 177–194. Leiden and Boston: Brill.
Garnaut, Ross, and Yiping Huang. 2006. "Continued rapid growth and the turning point in China's development." Chapter 2 in *The turning point in China's economic development*, eds. Ross Garnaut and Ligang Song, 12–34. Canberra: The Australian National University E-Press.

Helpman, Elhanan. 2004. *The mystery of economic growth*. Cambridge, MA and London: The Belknap Press of Harvard University Press.

Howitt, Peter. 1999. Steady state growth with population and R&D inputs growing. *Journal of Political Economy* 107: 715–730.

Kindleberger, Charles P. 1967. *Europe's postwar growth: The roll of labour supply*. Cambridge, MA: Harvard University Press.

Kuznets, Simon. 1955. Economic growth and income inequality. *American Economic Review* 45: 1–28.

Lewis, W. Arthur. 1954. Economic development with unlimited supplies of labour. *Manchester School of Economic and Social Studies* 22, no. 2: 139–191.

Lewis, W. Arthur. 1955. *The theory of economic growth*. London: Unwin University Books.

Lewis, W. Arthur. 1958. Unlimited supplies of labour: further notes. *Manchester School of Economic and Social Studies* 26, no. 1 (January): 1–32.

Lucas, Robert E., Jr. 1988. On the mechanics of economic development. *Journal of Monetary Economics* 22: 3–42.

McKay, Huw, and Ligang Song. 2010. China as a global manufacturing powerhouse: Strategic considerations and structural adjustment. *China & World Economy* 18, no. 1: 1–32.

Meadows, Donella H., Dennis L. Meadows, Jorgen Randers, and William W. Behrens III. 1972. *The limits to growth, a report for the club of Rome's project on the predicament of mankind*. London: A Potomac Associates Book, Earth Island Limited.

Minami, Ryoshin. 1966. A model of economic development from classical to neo-classical stages. *Weltwirtschaftliches Archive* 97, no. 2: 345–54.

Minami, Ryoshin. 1973. *The turning point in economic development: Japan's experience*. Tokyo, Japan: Kinokuniya Bookstore.

Mohnen, Pierre. 1996. R&D externalities and productivity growth. *Science Technology Industry Review*, no. 18: 39–66.

Romer, Paul M. 1986. Increasing returns and long-run growth. *Journal of Political Economy* 94: 1002–1037.

Romer, Paul M. 1990. Endogenous technological change. *Journal of Political Economy* 98: S71–S102.

Song, Ligang, Jiang Wu, and Yongsheng Zhang. 2010. Urbanization of migrant workers and expansion of domestic demand. *Social Sciences in China* 31, no. 3: 194–216.

Thirlwall, A.P. 2006. *Growth & development with special reference to developing economies*. New York: Palgrave Macmillan.

Wang, Dewen, and Cai Fang. 2009. The demographic dividend and sustainability of China's economic growth. Chapter 4 in *The China population and labour yearbook, volume 1: The approaching Lewis turning point and its polity implications*, eds. Cai Fang and Du Yang, 65–83. Leiden and Boston: Brill.

Wang, Meiyan. 2009. Educational return and resource allocation between rural and urban areas. Chapter 12 in *The China population and labour yearbook, volume 1: The approaching Lewis turning point and its polity implications*, eds. Cai Fang and Du Yang, 211–244. Leiden and Boston: Brill.

Young, Alwyn. 1995. The tyranny of numbers: Confronting the statistical realities of the East Asian growth experience. *Quarterly Journal of Economics* 110: 641–680.

Labor market conditions and the growth models: China's transition toward 'normal development'

Yiping Huang[a] and Fang Cai[b]

[a]*China Center for Economic Research, National School of Development, Peking University, Beijing,*
[b]*Institute of Population and Labor Economics, Chinese Academy of Social Sciences, Beijing, China*

Huang Yiping and Cai Fang
National School of Development, Peking University and Institute of Population and
Labor Economics, Chinese Academy of Social Sciences

1. China's new transition

The Chinese economy is in the middle of a new transition. China's economic performance during the reform period is sometimes described as the 'China puzzle' (Huang 2010). Many economists call it the 'China miracle' because of its extraordinary economic growth (Lin, Cai, and Li 1995). Others, including former Premier Wen Jiabao, argue that this growth model is not sustainable due to its growing imbalance, inequality and inefficiency problems (Wen 2006). During the past decade, the government made a series of policy efforts trying to change the growth model by improving quality of growth but achieved little direct result.

Most recently, however, important changes started to occur – some are well documented but others are unrecognized. Steady deceleration of economic growth in 2012 was not accompanied by the much feared deterioration of labor market condition. Structure of the economy also began to improve, with narrowing current account surplus, rising importance of consumption, and improving income distribution. We describe such new conditions, including slower growth, higher inflation pressure, more equal income distribution, more balanced economic structure, accelerated industrial upgrading and more dramatic economic cycles as the 'normal development' of the Chinese economy (Huang 2012).

We argue that the Lewis turning point (LTP) of China's labor market is one of the most fundamental triggers of Chinese economy's transition from economic miracle to 'normal development'. China has been known for its abundant labor and low wages, which helped turn China into a global manufacturing center within a relatively short period. Over time, however, labor market conditions shifted, as a result of rapid economic growth, the one-child policy, and other factors. For instances, the sex ratio at birth became quite extreme. And the trend of dependency ratio switched from falling to rising, following declining of fertility rate and ageing of population.

The subject of LTP – the turning point at which a labor market transitions from surplus to shortage – has been a controversial one in China. Our analyses of this issue in early years encountered widespread skepticism and even incredulity (Huang 2004; Cai and Wang 2005; Garnaut and Huang 2006). Objections to our proposition that

China is rapidly approaching the LTP are often based on the observation that China has 1.3 billion people, is known for its cheap labor, and still has a large rural population. Over the years, economists at the Institute of Population and Labor Economics (IPLE) of the Chinese Academy of Social Sciences (CASS) and their collaborators made continuous efforts in further building the case for the LTP in China (see, for instances, Cai 2007; Cai and Wang 2008; Huang and Cai 2010).[1]

However, economists and officials remain divided on some important issues:

1. How many farmers are left in the countryside?
2. What is the remaining potential for rural-urban migration?
3. Is there still a significant urban-rural gap in labor productivity?
4. Is the rising wage evidence of labor shortage?

Hopefully, what happened in 2012, especially persistent labor shortage and wage increase across the country at a time of economic downturn, changed some economists' mind. At the least, it has become a widely accepted expectation that increases in labor cost are secular, not cyclical.

We now firmly believe that China has passed the LTP (Cai, in introduction to this volume). In this concluding chapter, we focus on the macroeconomic implications of the LTP. We make three propositions. First, unlimited labor supply and low wage rates, alongside low costs of other inputs, lead to the so-called 'China puzzle' – extraordinary growth performance but growing structural risks. Second, emerging labor shortage and rising labor costs contribute to the transition of the Chinese economy toward 'normal development'. And, third, improving labor quality will be critical for China in order to avoid the 'middle-income trap' as it loses competitiveness in labor-intensive, low value-added industries.

2. Labor cost and the 'China puzzle'

The so-called 'China puzzle' refers to a unique phenomenon whereby growth acceleration makes optimists more upbeat, but pessimists more depressed about the future of the Chinese economy (Huang 2010). On the one hand, China's extraordinary economic success during its reform period is sometimes described as the 'China miracle' (Lin, Cai, and Li 1995). The reform policies transformed the country from a closed, poor agrarian society into an open, dynamic global economic power within three decades. GDP growth averaged 10% and GDP per capita increased from $220 in 1980 to $6,000 in 2012. China is already the second largest economy in the world and may overtake the US economy in the coming decade or so.

On the other hand, growing structural risks lead some to believe that collapse of the Chinese economy is inevitable (Chang 2001). Even some senior leaders argue that the Chinese growth model is 'uncoordinated, imbalanced, inefficient and unsustainable'.[2] For instance, the investment share of GDP rose from 25% at the beginning of the reform period to close to 50% after the global financial crisis. Such a situation is unsustainable because, mathematically, this share cannot go up to 100%. In the meantime, export share of GDP also surged, current account surplus expanded, consumption share of GDP dropped, and income inequality worsened.

Economists have developed various analytical frameworks to explain changes in the Chinese economy during the past decades. One of the best known books is *The China miracle* (Lin et al. 1995), in which the authors argue that the key to the success was the transition from the heavy industry-oriented development strategy to comparative advantage-oriented development strategy. This enables the factories to significantly improve efficiency of resource allocation by producing what they do best and what the market needs.

Barry Naughton titles his award-winning book *Growing out of the plans* in describing the essence of the Chinese reform – allowing incremental growth of the market-orien-ted, private sector activities, while maintaining support to the old central planned activities and the SOE (Naughton 1995). Chinese economists use the term 'dual track strategy' (Fan 1995). Although continued support to planned activities may be efficiency negative, it helps maintain economic stability and, more importantly, reduces political opposition to reform. As the market-oriented parts of the economy grow rapidly, the planned activities decline on relative terms.

Jeffery Sachs and Wing Thye Woo, however, point out that Chinese economic success can be explained mainly by its convergence to the typical market system of East Asia (Sachs and Woo 2000). While Chinese growth has been spectacular, it can be accounted for by increased inputs and improved productivity. The East Asian economies such as Japan, Korea, Taiwan, Hong Kong and Singapore all achieved similar performance in the past.

Despite the differences in their approaches and perspectives, these economists all appear to agree that the key to the reform is the transition from a centrally planned to a market system. This is certainly correct but may still be only part of the story. In a series of recent research papers, we argue that the fundamental reason behind the 'China puzzle' is its *asymmetric market liberalization* approach during the reform period (Huang 2009, 2010; Huang and Tao 2010; Huang and Wang 2010). Free markets for products ensure that production decisions are based on demand and supply conditions in the economy, and resources are allocated efficiently. Distortions in factor markets are a way of providing incentives for economic entities and, sometimes, overcoming market failures.

One good example is China's FDI policy. In the early years of economic reform, the Chinese government designed a range of preferential policies to attract FDI, including tax holidays, free use of land, subsidized credit, cheap inputs such as energy and water. Government support for FDI projects also reduced problems related to an undeveloped legal system for property rights protection. In typical economic textbooks, such policies are described as policy distortions. But there is no doubt that they have been successful. By 2010 cumulated FDI inflows into China had reached $1.5 trillion. But China provided such 'subsidies' not only to foreign investors but also to domestic investors during past decades by broadly depressing factor costs.

Factor market distortions include the household registration system limiting labor mobility between rural and urban areas, direct controls of bank deposit and lending rates, set of energy prices, especially oil prices, by state agencies, and offering discounted land use fee to investors. In most cases, these distortions depress input costs.

However, labor is a special case, as it is unclear if labor market segmentation lowers or increases labor cost. But labor cost was low for a long time because of because of abundant agricultural labor or unlimited labor supply in a typical Lewis dual economy. Although cheap energy, cheap capital, and cheap land were important in driving development of the manufacturing activities, unlimited labor supply and cheap labor cost were arguably the most important factor determining China's competitiveness in international markets. Most Chinese industries are concentrated in labor-intensive areas.

The low input costs, including low labor cost, contribute to the 'China miracle' and the 'China puzzle'. They are like subsidies to the companies but taxes on the households. They boost profits from production, increase returns to investment and improve international competitiveness of Chinese exports. Low input costs also serve as a special mechanism redistributing income from households to the companies. Over the years, corporate profits grew much faster than household income, as household income was largely capped by stagnant wage rate.

But they also contribute to the structural problems. One, the extraordinary incentives lead to continuous rise of the shares of exports and investment in GDP. Two, the rise in the share of corporate profit in national income increases the national saving rate, as corporate saving rate is generally higher than household saving rate. Three, income inequality among household deteriorates as low-income households rely more on wage income while high-income households rely more on corporate profits and investment returns. Four, consumption share of GDP declines over time as household income grows slower than GDP. And, five, the unusually low costs of energy, capital, and other resources probably also resulted in some waste behavior.

In the end, the 'China puzzle' might not be so special. Many East Asian emerging market economies, such as Korea and Taiwan, experienced very similar changes in their early stages of economic development. Cheap labor and cheap credit were common. Rising investment/export shares, falling consumption share, and deteriorating income distribution also occurred in Korea and Taiwan before they reached their respective LTP. But the problems are certainly more extreme in China because it not only had more surplus labor but also had greater distortions in other inputs costs.

Realizing that the growth model could soon endanger serious risks of sustainability, Premier Wen Jiabao vowed to change the growth model by shifting the focus from quantity to quality of growth and rebalancing external and internal sectors, shortly after taking office in early 2003. Unfortunately, that effort did not pay off. In retrospect, there are probably two reasons for this outcome. One, the government has at least three macroeconomic policy objectives – supporting growth, controlling inflation, and adjusting structure. If there is a conflict among the three, officials would be most likely to sacrifice the last one because growth and inflation could directly affect economic and political stability and might affect senior officials' chances of promotion.

And, two, the government used mainly administrative measures to adjust economic structure. For instance, the National Development and Reform Commission (NDRC) tried to control the overinvestment problem by approving fewer projects. However, since low-cost advantage implied high investment returns, investors would not reduce their investment activities in spite of controls imposed by the NDRC. This suggests that if the government really wants to change economic structure, the best way would be to alter economic agencies' behavior by adjusting the incentive structure.

3. Labor shortage and the 'normal development pattern'

In recent years, however, the Chinese economy has started to show significant transformation. These include steady downward shift of trend growth and rebalancing of economic structure. Some structural changes, such as narrowing of the current account surplus, are well documented in official statistics. Some improvement, such as rising share of consumption in GDP, is not yet reflected in government data. Yet some other adjustments, such as improvement in income distribution, are confirmed by official estimation by strongly rejected by many economists. We think that the structural improvements are real, driven primarily by changes in factor markets, especially an emerging labor shortage.

Downward shift of the growth potential

GDP growth started to decelerate in 2011, partly due to the authorities' tightening policies. Toward the end of the first quarter in 2012, however, it became clear that growth might soon fall below 8% level. From March that year, the government undertook a number of steps trying to stabilize economic growth, including support to ongoing infrastructure projects in the areas of water, power, and transportation. Despite this policy effort, GDP growth decelerated continuously from 8.1% during the first quarter to and 7.4% during the third quarter.

In retrospect, two special factors probably contributed to this continuous slowdown. One, export growth fell from close to 8% during the first half of the year to around 2% during July–August. And, two, housing purchase restriction (HPR) introduced in April 2011 led to slowing of residential property investment growth to below 10% during the third quarter of 2012 from above 30% the year before. Growth deceleration caused renewed fears of a hard landing of Chinese growth among international investors. Many financial market participants repeatedly called for aggressive policy actions to support growth by arguing that the policy-makers were 'way behind the curve'.

The policy-makers, however, stayed relatively calm and appeared to be willing to tolerate somewhat slower growth for three reasons (Huang 2012). First, many government officials became reluctant to adopt aggressive measures supporting growth after implementation of the 4 trillion yuan stimulus package during the global financial crisis. The package was successfully turning around economic growth in 2009. Many economists, however, argued that it increased fiscal risks, created nonperforming loans, contributed to overcapacity in some infrastructure areas and caused inflation and asset bubbles. When growth slowed again from late 2011, the policy-makers were cautious not to overstimulate the economy.

And, second, economic studies estimate China's current growth potential at 6–8%. The World Bank's estimates were 8.6% in 2011–2015 and 7% in 2016–2020 (WB & DRC 2012). Cai Fang and Lu Yang (2012) estimate China's growth potential at 7.2% during 2010–2015 and 6% during 2016–2020 (Figure 1). In a recent multi-country review of growth performance, Eichengreen et al. (2011) project China to grow by 6.1 to 7.0% per year in the decade from 2011 to 2020 and by 5.0 to 6.2% in the period 2021–2030. Similarly, the joint report by the Asian Development Bank and Peking University estimates the growth potential at 8% in 2011–2020 and 6% in 2021–2030 (Zhuang et al. 2012).

And, third, economic indicators such as employment and inflation also suggested no need for aggressive policy easing, despite deceleration of GDP growth to below 8% levels. CPI inflation first eased, from 4.5% in January down to the trough of 1.7% in October, but then picked up slowly to above 2% in the following months. The labor market was also surprisingly resilient. In 2012 the economy created 12.7 million new jobs despite growth slowdown. The number of migrant workers reached 163 million, up 4.7 million from the year before. Total number of farmers employed in non-farm jobs increased to 263 million, with an increase of 9.8 million within the year. Twenty-five provinces adjusted their minimum wages, lifting the national average by 20.2%. And migrant workers' monthly wages averaged 2,290 yuan or $363, up 11.8% from the year before.

Therefore, policy-makers are no longer keen to support above 8% growth. This is mainly because growth potential is already much lower, due to higher level of economic development and tightening condition of labor market. For instance, in 2012, the working age population declined by 3.5 million. The purpose of the cautious macro-economic policy can be viewed as a strategy to allow growth to settle around its new potential. Of course, if the unemployment rate rises unexpectedly, the government likely will engage in more aggressive policies again supporting economic growth.

Rebalancing of the economy already underway

The so-called 'normal development', however, is more about growth slowdown. The economy also shows clear signs of rebalancing in recent years. For instance, the current account surplus narrowed from 10.8% of GDP in 2007 to 2.8% in 2011 and 2.6% in 2012 (Figure 2). Mainly because of this, the People's Bank of China (PBoC) Deputy Governor Yi Gang argued that the yuan exchange rate was near equilibrium, while US President Obama's former top economic advisor, Lawrence Summers, noted in January 2013 that the yuan was not as undervalued as it had been five years earlier. In recent years, two-way movement of the exchange rate and bidirectional capital flows actually started to emerge in China.

Another rebalancing in recent years relates to regional disparity, with the rural-urban income gap narrowing notably (Figure 3). This is the result of combination of stronger policy support to agriculture, faster increases in agricultural prices and steady improvement in rural productivity. In addition, China's reform success was until recently a story of the coastal regions. However, inland economies are now growing more quickly than the coastal economies, thanks to the government's 'go west' policy, the migration of manufacturing industries, and rich resource endowments in western China (Figure 4).

In mid-January, the National Bureau of Statistics (NBS) reported estimates of Gini coefficients for 2003–2012, which show a steady deterioration of income distribution from 0.479 in 2003 to 0.491 in 2008 and steady improvement after that, to 0.474 in 2012 (Figure 5). This, if confirmed, could mark another important turning point in China's economic development, although many Chinese economists are still skeptical about the results. For instance, a recent study by Southwest University of Economics

Figure 1. Growth potentials, estimated by Cai and Lu (%)

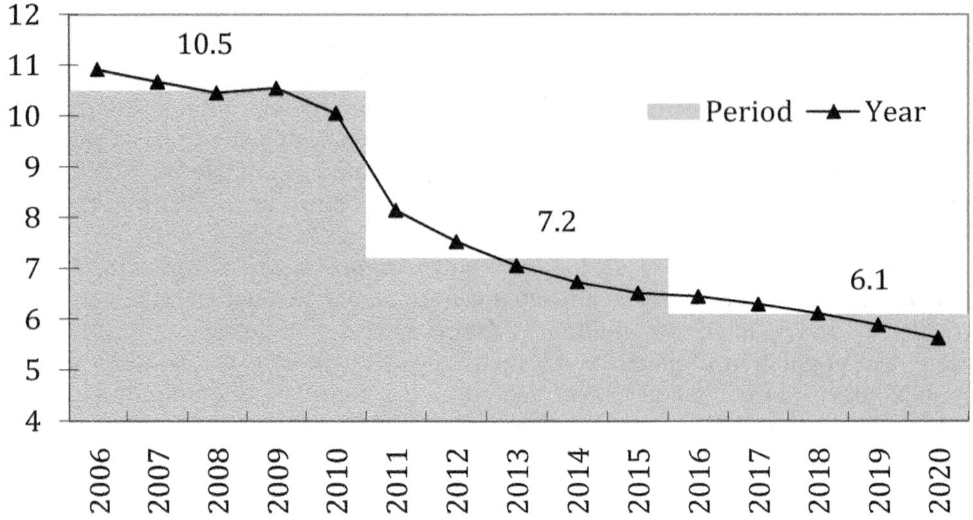

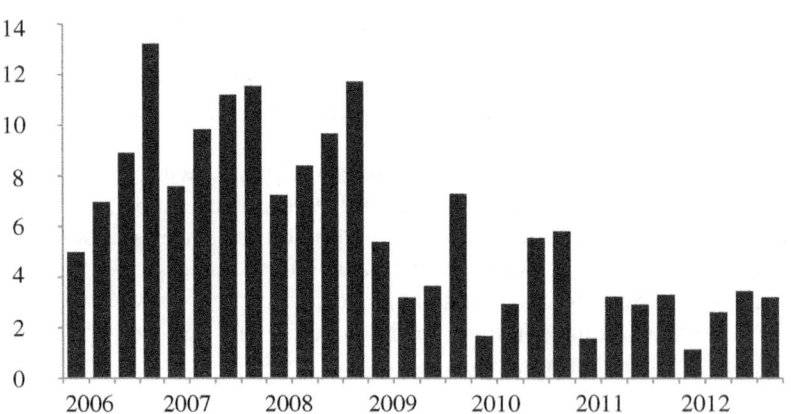

Source: Cai and Lu (2012)

Figure 2. Current account surplus as a share of GDP, 2006–2012 (%)

Source: National Bureau of Statistics

Figure 3. Urban-rural income ratio narrowed, 1987–2012 (%)

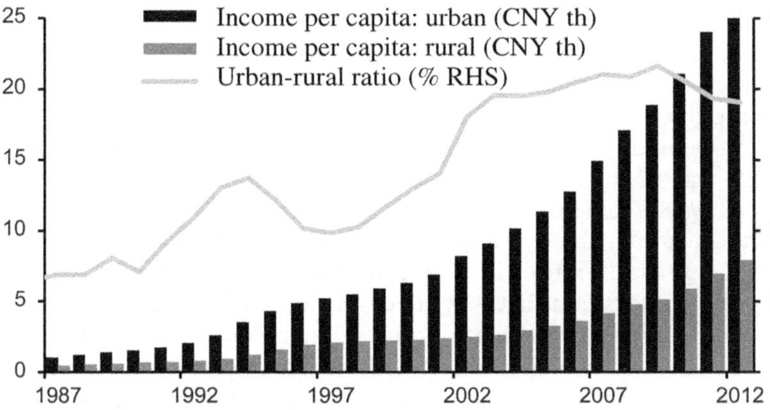

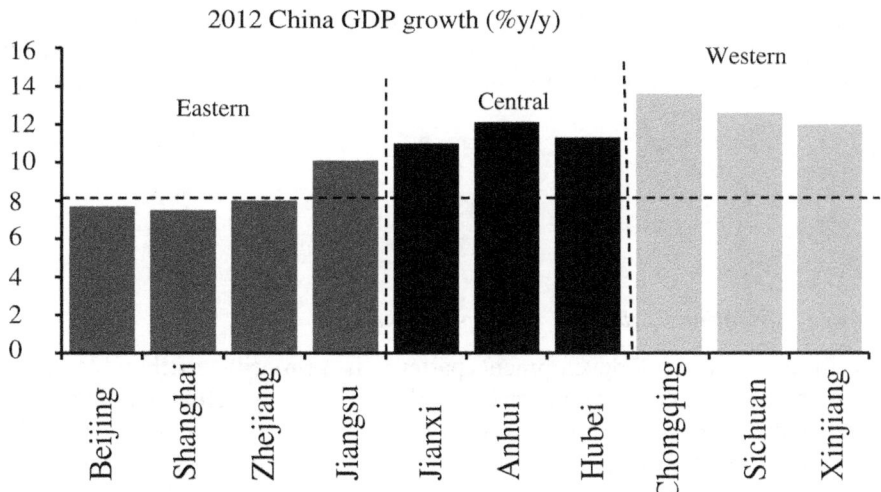

Source: CEIC Data Company

Figure 4. Growth in eastern, central, and western China, 2012 (%)

Source: CEIC Data Company

and Finance reported a Gini coefficient of 0.61 in 2010. One criticism of the official NBS finding was ignorance of income equality in household wealth, such as property. Another was under-reporting of income at the high end.

Official data also suggest that the contribution of consumption to GDP growth increased from about one-third in 2007 to 52% in 2012 (Figure 6). Two Chinese economists, Tian Zhu and Jun Zhang of Shanghai, have gone further, arguing that China's consumption share is grossly underestimated as a result of under-reported residential spending, consumption covered by institutional spending and technical issues in the household survey method. They note that the consumption share estimated by the Penn World Table was 60.9% in 2010, compared with the official figure of 47.4% and 58.9% in the Penn World Table in 1990.

Recent research finds that the consumption share of GDP began to rise after 2008, although this is not yet fully reflected in official statistics (Huang et al. 2012, 2013). Huang and his collaborators find that it is difficult to reconcile accelerating retail sales and decelerating consumption in official statistics after 2008. By calculating a new growth rate for consumption, which is a weighted average of consumption-related retail sales growth and service sales growth, they reveal that the consumption share of GDP fell during much of the past decade, as suggested by official data, but rebounded from 48% in 2008 to 52% in 2010, compared with the official estimate of 47% in that year (Figure 7).

The analysis thus far examined encountered skepticisms after its initial dissemination. Some commentators found it difficult to accept our finding given their strong impression of sharply worsened structural problems following the CNY 4 trillion stimulus package adopted in late 2008. Others argued that structural improvement was impossible since the government had not undertaken more decisive reforms. However, David Li published a similar study applying a different approach (Li and Xu 2012). By recalculating Chinese household consumption expenditure, he concludes that household consumption share rebounded from 36% in 2007 to 38.5% in 2011 (Figure 8).

Key factors contributing to the new development pattern

The transition to 'normal development pattern' is primarily attributable to recent changes in factor markets, among various other factors. As Huang points out, low production costs are primarily responsible for the unique performance of the Chinese economy during the reform period, including strong economic growth and growing structural risks (Huang 2010). For the same reason, he predicts that the reversal of such a cost structure should make China more likely other rapidly growing emerging market economies. The normal development pattern should include slower growth, higher inflation pressure, more equal income distribution, more balanced economic structure, accelerated industrial upgrading, and more dramatic economic cycles. We think these were exactly what happened during the past years.

In the study 'China's next transition', Huang et al. (2011) anticipate several changes in factor markets. Labor market already shows clear signs of supply shortage,

Figure 5. Gini coefficients estimated by the National Bureau of Statistics, 2003–2012

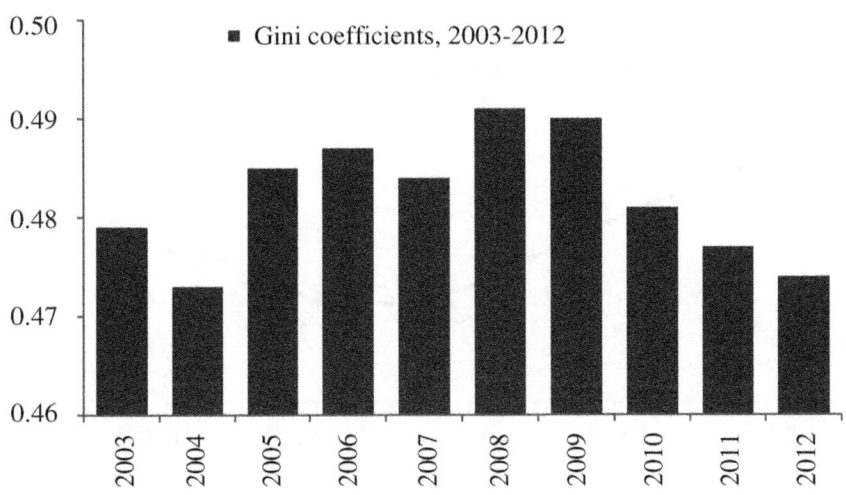

Source: National Bureau of Statistics

Figure 6. Contribution to GDP growth, 1995–2012 (%)

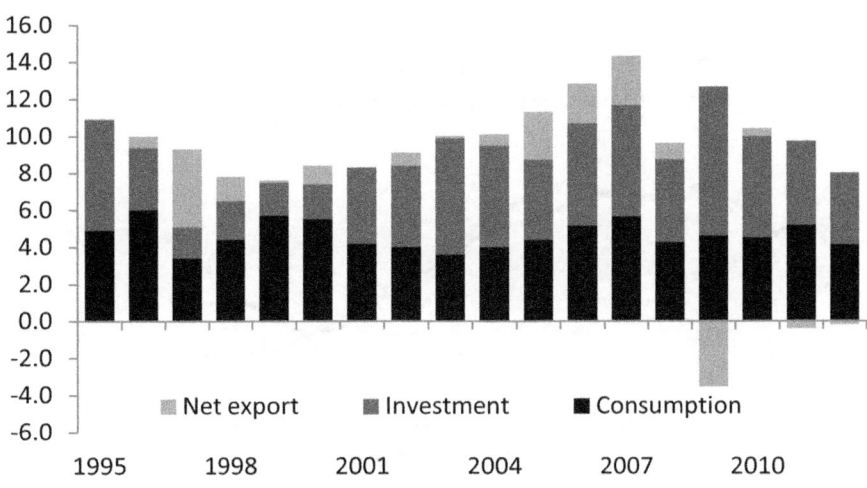

Source: CEIC Data Company

Figure 7. Total consumption share of GDP, estimated by Huang et al. (%)

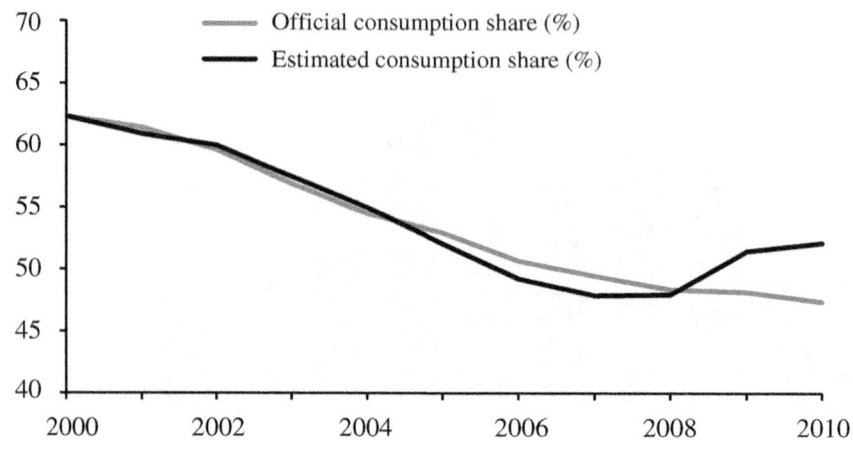

Source: Huang et al. (2012, 2013)

Figure 8. Household consumption share of GDP, estimated by Li and Xu (%)

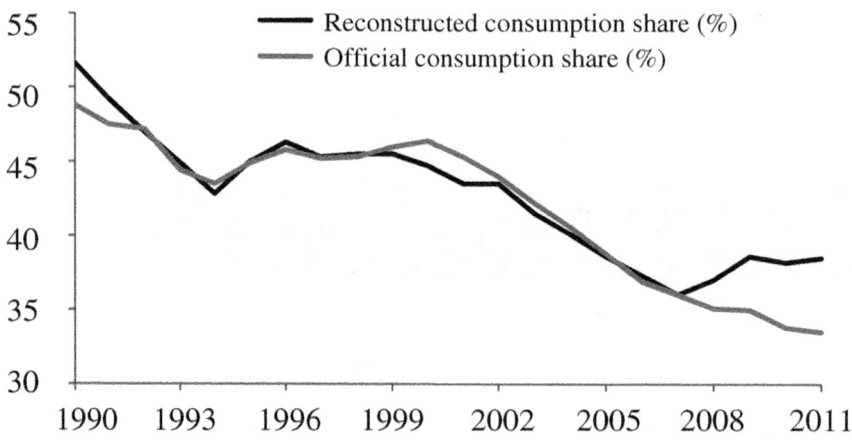

Source: Li and Xu (2012)

evidenced by accelerating wage increases in recent years (Figure 9). Development of shadow banking businesses also opens the door for '*de facto* interest rate liberalization'. The government has also been trying to reform prices of energy, water and other resources. In short, the low-cost advantage, one of the two main contributors to China's economic success during the past decades alongside the reform policy, is rapidly diminishing. For the moment, the most significant changes occur in the labor market, especially the LTP.

The LTP has important implications for China's macro economy and growth model by reversing the past impacts on growth and economic structure. Rapid wage growth, especially that at the lower end of the market, cuts into profit margin. Therefore, it reverses past redistribution of income from households to corporates. As these implicit subsidies for Chinese companies are reduced, export and investment activities soften and, therefore, the economy rebalances. Applying a computable general equilibrium model of the world economy, Huang and Jiang (2010) analyze detailed economy-wide consequences of the LTP in China.

Perhaps it is relatively easy to understand why growth potential declines in recent years. It is a universal phenomenon that growth slows as an economy develops. This is because the narrowing gap caused by global technological developments means fewer people suffer the disadvantage of backwardness (Lin 2012). But the growth slowdown is accelerated in China by changing demographics, including labor shortage and falling working age population. For the same reason, rapidly increasing wages also create inflation pressures, as rising costs can only be absorbed by higher output price, narrower profit margin or faster productivity growth or a combination of these factors.

So, what contribute to rising consumption share of GDP in recent years? The answer is household income. When an 'unlimited labor supply' exists, rapid industrialization is accompanied by a stable wage rate and, therefore, a declining share of wage income in GDP. This is reversed when a labor shortage emerges: wages rise rapidly and the share of wage income in GDP starts to grow. In fact, labor income also picked up from 41% in 2007 to 47.1% in 2009 (Figure 10), which, in turn, boosted consumption relative to GDP. This was also exactly what happened in Korea and Taiwan in the mid-1980s, when their consumption shares started to recover following their respective LTP (Figure 11).

Rapid wage growth was probably also behind the recent improvements in income distribution highlighted by the NBS, since low-income households rely more on wage income and high-income households rely on investment returns or corporate profits. If the past trend was households subsidizing corporations, then the new trend is redistribution of income from corporations to households as rising labor costs increase wage income but squeeze corporate profits. This is probably why, in rapidly developing economies, the so-called Kuznets turning point (when income distribution shifts from deteriorating to improving) often follows the Lewis turning point (Huang and Cai 2010).

It is interesting that the real boost to consumption in recent years came from changing labor market conditions and associated wage increase, not from government policies. This is, however, consistent with our argument that factor costs might be one of the most important factors behind the growing structural risks. Therefore, correction of factor costs should also help alleviate some of the structural problems.

Figure 9. Migrant workers' wages have been rising rapidly

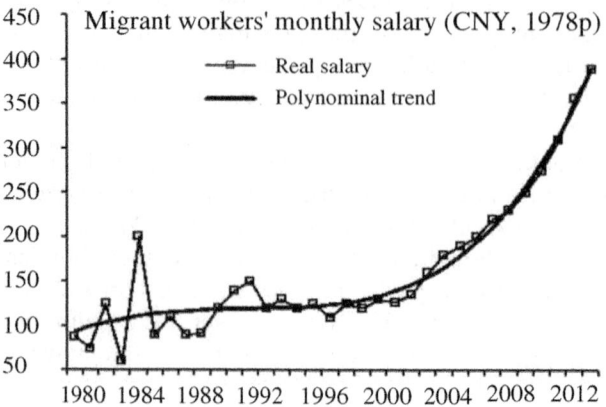

Source: created by authors based on Lu Feng (2011) "Employment expansion and wage growth (2001–2010)", China Macroeconomic Research Center, Peking University, Beijing, 12 June 2011 and National Bureau of Statistics of China

Figure 10. Labor income and consumption share of GDP, estimated by Li and Xu (%)

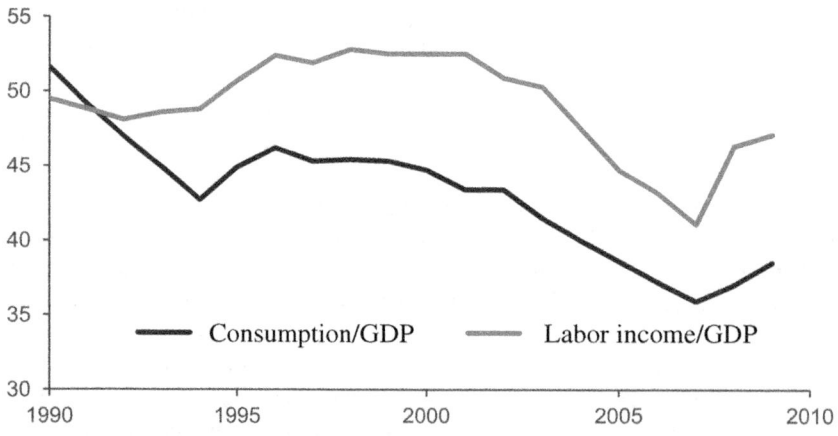

Source: Li and Xu (2012)

Figure 11. Private consumption share of GDP in Korea and Taiwan (%)

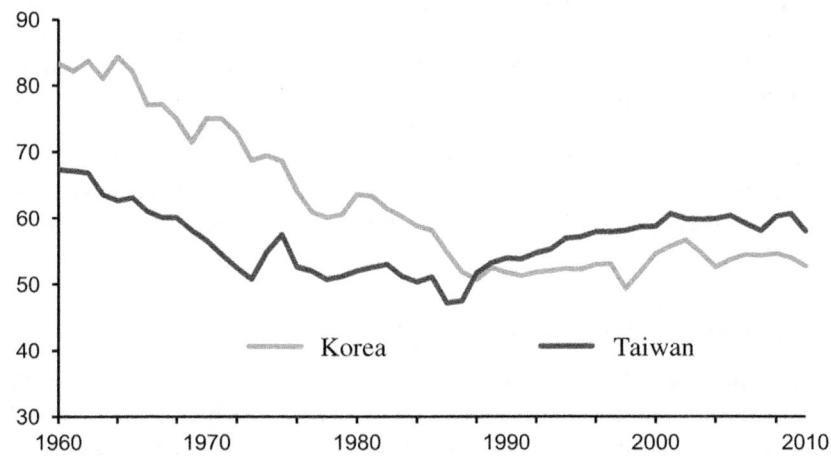

Source: CEIC Data Company

Clearly, rebalancing is still at an early stage. For instance, the consumption share of GDP, at 52% in 2010, on our estimates, was significantly below the 70–90% range that occurs in most developing and developed economies. This gap may be narrowed, in part, through continuous wage adjustment. Expected interest rate liberalization, which will likely lead to high deposit rates, at least, should further facilitate rebalancing. Further changes may also be required to transform the development pattern completely. This could involve measures to improve income equality beyond the primary round of income distribution, development of social welfare systems such as pension, medical insurance and education, and financial and capital account liberalization.

4. Labor quality and the 'middle-income trap'

As the economy shifts toward 'normal development', it immediately faces the challenge of the 'middle-income trap' as its GDP per capita reaches high middle-income level and its labor cost rises rapidly. The 'middle-income trap' may be defined as the situation in which an economy loses competitiveness in low value-added industries but fails to move up to high value-added industries (Zhuang et al. 2012). Chinese industries, especially those in the coastal region, are now under significant pressure as the three important conditions that facilitate their extraordinary growth in the past – unlimited labor supply, low-cost advantage, and rapid export expansion – all diminish steadily.

Clearly, the rise of the 'middle-income trap' is closely associated with changes in labor cost, among others. Globally, only 13 economies succeeded during the past half century in making the jump to high-income economies (World Bank 2012). Skepticism about China's ability to continue relatively rapid economic growth is based on several concerns. One main worry is that the current growth model is 'uncoordinated, unbalanced, inefficient and unsustainable'. Although China maintained close to 10% average GDP growth during the first three decades of economic reform, problems of imbalance, inequality, and inefficiency deteriorated significantly.

These, if not reversed quickly, could seriously dampen the outlook of the Chinese economy. Unfortunately, as some analysts argue, the policy efforts trying to improve growth quality achieved little, at least according to the official statistics (Lardy 2012). Others believe a change of the growth model is possible but it necessarily requires substantially slower growth (Pettis 2013).

Another concern relates to the lack of progress in political reform, alongside market-oriented economic reform. This pattern of reform has led to what prominent Chinese economist Wu Jinglian calls 'state capitalism'.[3] To a large extent, this explains the growing problems of monopoly, corruption and disparity. The SOE, for example, are a typical example of extractive institutions – they extract monopoly profits by controlling cheap inputs and prohibiting entry by others. More importantly, China might be locked into following this path as it will be hard to reverse course except through extreme social turmoil. Without those political reforms necessary to improve political and economic institutions, Chinese growth would sooner or later collapse (Acemoglu and Robinson 2012).

A third difficulty is Chinese industry's ability to innovate and upgrade. So far, Chinese growth has been driven mainly by low-cost advantage, increasing input and productivity gain through resource reallocation, such as rural-urban migration. But growth based on resource mobilization is, by definition, not sustainable (Krugman 1994). But can technological innovation replace resource mobilization to become the main driver of economic growth in China? One obvious hurdle is the low education level of hundreds of millions of migrant workers. If they lose low-skills manufacturing and construction jobs, they might not be able to work in high technology and high value-added sectors. Foreign companies also complain that the environment is not conducive to technological innovation because of lack of proper protection of intellectual property rights in China.

We think these three concerns are real issues but also that they should not be overstated. As we discussed earlier, the rebalancing of the Chinese economy is already underway, although this is not yet fully appreciated by investors and economists. Of course, many of the changes have just begun and the government will need to undertake further reforms in at least three areas to complete transformation of the growth model. First, if China had a no-market economy during the pre-reform period and a half-market economy during the first three decades of the reform period, it is now time to complete the transition to a market economy by removing all the remaining distortions, especially those in factor markets. Second, China needs to establish a macroeconomic policy framework compatible with an emerging market economy, including an accountable budget system and professional monetary policy-making mechanism. And, third, the government's role should shift from directly supporting production and investment through resource mobilization to facilitating innovation and upgrading via supporting physical and soft infrastructure development.

Political reform will be necessary to eradicate corruption and maintain political stability. But we doubt that China will adopt western style democracy any time soon and that the current political regime has already exhausted the growth potential. Institutions matter for longrun growth. But perhaps optimal institutions are different for economies at different stages of development. The post-war experiences of imposing developed economies' institutions on developing countries, such as the Washington Consensus, were largely unsuccessful. One important reason could be that technological innovation and technological catch-up require different types of institution – with GDP per capita at $6,000, China still has huge potential to gain through technological catch-up.

Even in terms of innovation, China has been doing well. It saw science and technology take off much earlier than most other developing countries – its share of R&D expenditure of GDP reached 1% when its GDP per capita was only $3,000, while an average developing country's reaches the same level of R&D expenditure when its GDP per capita is $8,000. Globally, China is already a leader in terms of total R&D spending, patent filing, and R&D productivity (measured by number of patent filing divided by R&D expenditure). Continuous technological innovation and industry upgrading are also observed in a large number of industries including automobiles, large machinery, and information technology. Protection of intellectual property rights (IPR) is a key drag on China's anchor. But China already has a nationwide IPR court system and the number of IPR cases is increasingly rapidly. According to international experiences, IPR protection likely will strengthen significantly indigenous innovation becomes a dominant phenomenon.

The biggest challenge might be labor quality or human capital. As China moves toward high-income country, industrial upgrading will likely shift employment from labor-intensive to capital-intensive to technology-intensive sectors continuously. The Chinese experiences suggest that shifting workers from labor-intensive to capital-intensive sectors in the secondary industry requires, on average, 1.3 years of additional education. Workers shifting further to technology-intensive sectors in tertiary industry require 4.2 years' additional education, on average. However, human capital accumulation can take place only gradually. For instance, the average number of years of education for the population aged 16 years and above increased from 62.4 years in 1990 to 7.56 years in 2000, a net increase of 1.32 years. It further increased to 8.9 years in 2010, another net increase of 1.34 years.

Currently, China has a total of 260 million migrant workers, most of whom only finished junior high school. As wages rise rapidly, whether or not these migrant workers will be able to find employment in higher value-added industries will be a critical test for China's 'middle-income trap' challenge. If not, China may end up in not only growth stagnation but also massive unemployment problems. Therefore, improving labor quality through education and training should be a top policy priority in the coming decades.

5. Concluding remarks

The Chinese economy is in the middle of a major transformation from economic miracle to normal development. The years of 10% average growth are over. Currently, growth is stabilizing at around 8%. But it could go down further in the coming decade. In the meantime, inflation pressure is trending up and may settle at around 5% eventually. These changes constitute what some call the 'new normal' of the Chinese economy (Huang 2012). These growth and inflation rates are, however, not so unique compared with experiences of other emerging market economies during similar stages of economic development.

What is not yet fully recognized by economists, market participants, and the public is that rebalancing toward a consumption-led economy is already well underway. This is clearly reflected in narrowing current account surplus, rising consumption share of GDP, declining urban-rural and regional disparities, and improving income distribution. Of course, most of these adjustments are at their early stages. Further policy actions are necessary in order for China to complete the transition toward a more balanced, more efficient, and more sustainable economy.

We attribute the ongoing transition mainly to changes in the labor market, especially the LTP. LTP has been a controversial subject among Chinese economists and policymakers. During the past six years, we advocated the proposition that China was rapidly approaching the LTP. What happened in 2012, labor shortage at the time of steady growth slowdown, led us to confidently make the case that China has already passed the LTP. Labor market liberalization, such as reform of the household registration system, may affect supply of rural labor to certain extent. But we do not believe that it would reverse the general situation of labor shortage in China.

While the new growth model will certainly be more sustainable compared with the old one, it does not make the tasks easier to fulfill. For instance, it is no longer possible to expand manufacturing production by increasing inputs. China needs to innovate and upgrade in order to stay competitive. Similarly, even with passage of the LTP, China still faces important employment pressure. One important reason is that as it loses competitiveness in the low-end industries, it is unknown if there will be enough new jobs for the labor force. These are two important aspects of the so-called 'middle-income trap' challenge facing China now.

In order to help China avoid the 'middle-income trap', new reforms should center on the theme of redefining the relationship between government and market. Specifically, they should include policy measures in three areas. One, it is time to remove all remaining distortions and complete China's transition to a market economy. Two, China needs to construct a macroeconomic policy framework consistent with an emerging market economy. And, three, the government's role in the economy should shift from supporting economic activities through direct resource mobilization to facilitating innovation and upgrading by supporting physical and soft infrastructure development.

One critical factor that will determine China's success or failure is the quality of the labor force – its education, skill, and experience. Currently, unskilled workers dominate China's labor force and are mainly employed in two sectors – labor-intensive manufacturing and construction. The loss of employment in labor-intensive industries may be partly offset by expansion of service employment. But still a large number of workers need to find jobs in high value-added industries. This requires significant efforts supporting education, training, and research in the coming years.

Endnotes

1 The National School of Development at the Peking University and the Institute of Population and Labor Economics at the Chinese Academy of Social Sciences jointly hosted the workshop *Debating China's Lewis turning point* in April 2010. Papers presented at that workshop were later published as a special issue of the *China Economic Journal* and are included in this volume (Huang and Cai 2010).
2 Wen Jiabao, 2006, Government work report, delivered at the National People's Congress meeting, March 5, 2006.
3 'Fast-track China is on the wrong path'. Interview with Wu Jinglian by Hu Shuli, *Wall Street Journal*, Asia Edition, July 28, 2011. http://online.wsj.com/article/SB10001424053111904800304576471393143140106.html.

References

Acemoglu, Daron and James A. Robinson. 2012. *Why nations fail: The origins of power, prosperity and poverty.* New York: Crown Publishers.

Cai, Fang (ed.). 2007. *Reports on China's population and labor, no. 8: The Lewisian turning point and policy challenges* [in Chinese]. Beijing, China: Social Sciences Literature Press.

Cai, Fang and Lu, Yang. 2012. At what rate can Chinese economy grow in the next 10 years? [in Chinese]. In *Chinese economy blue cover book*, eds. Jiagui Chen et al. Beijing, China: Social Science Literature Press.

Cai, Fang and Wang, Dewen. 2006. Employment growth, labor scarcity and the nature of China's trade expansion. In *The turning point in China's economic development*, eds. Ross Garnaut and Ligang Song. Canberra; Asia Pacific Press.

Cai, Fang and Wang, Meiyan. 2008. A counterfactual analysis on unlimited surplus labor in rural China. *China & World Economy* 16, no. 1: 51–65.

Eichengreen, Barry, Donghyun Park, and Kwanho Shin. 2011. When fast growing economies slow down: International evidence and implications for China. NBER Working Paper 16919.

Garnaut, Ross and Huang, Yiping. 2006. Continued rapid growth and the turning point in China's economic development. In *The turning point in China's economic development*, eds. Ross Garnaut and Ligang Song. Canberra: Asia Pacific Press.

Huang, Yiping. 2004. A labor shortage in China. *Wall Street Journal*, A7, August 6–8.

Huang, Yiping. 2010. Dissecting the China puzzle: Asymmetric liberalization and cost distortion. *Asia Economic Policy Review* 5, no. 2: 281–295.

Huang, Yiping. 2012. The 'new normal' of Chinese growth, October 14, East Asia Forum. http://www.eastasiaforum.org/2012/10/14/the-new-normal-of-chinese-growth/.

Huang, Yiping and Cai, Fang (guest eds.). 2010. Debating China's Lewis turning point. *China Economic Journal* 3, no. 2.

Huang, Yiping, Chang Jian, and Yang Lingxiu. 2011. *China: Beyond the miracle – China's next transition*. Hong Kong: Barclays.

Huang, Yiping, Chang Jian, and Yang Lingxiu. 2012. *China: Beyond the miracle – great wave of consumption upgrading*. Hong Kong: Barclays.

Huang, Yiping, Jian Chang, and Lingxiu Yang. 2013. Recovery of consumption and rebalance of the economy in China. *Asian Economic Papers*.

Huang, Yiping and Jiang Tingsong. 2010. What does the Lewis turning point mean for China? A computable general equilibrium analysis. *China Economic Journal* 3, no. 2: 191–208.

Huang, Yiping and Tao Kunyu. 2010. Factor market distortion and the current account surplus in China. *Asian Economic Papers* 9, no. 3: 1–36.

Huang, Yiping and Wang, Bijun. 2010. Cost distortions and structural imbalances in China. *China and World Economy* 18, no. 4: 1–17.

Krugman, Paul. 1994. The myth of Asia's miracle. *Foreign Affairs* 73, no. 6 (November–December): 62–78.

Lardy, Nicholas R. 2012. *Sustaining China's economic growth after the global financial crisis*. Washington DC: Peterson Institute of International Economics.

Li, David and Sean Xu. 2012. The rebalancing of the Chinese economy. CCER-NBER Conference on the Chinese economy, Peking University, June 25–26, Beijing.

Lin, Justin. 2012. *The quest for prosperity: How developing economies can takeoff?* Princeton, NJ: Princeton University Press.

Lin, Justin, Cai Fang, and Li Zhou. 1995. *The China miracle: Development strategy and economic reform*. Hong Kong: Chinese University of Hong Kong Press.

Naughton, Barry. 1995. *Growing out of the plan: Chinese economic reform, 1978–1993*. Cambridge: Cambridge University Press.

Pettis, Michael. 2013. *Great rebalancing: Trade, conflict, and perilous road ahead for the world economy*. Princeton, NJ: Princeton University Press.

Sachs, Jeffrey D. and Wing Thye Woo. 2000. Understanding China's economic performance. *Journal of Policy Reform* 4, no. 1: 1–50.

Wen, Jiabao. 2006. Government work report. Delivered at the National People's Congress meeting, March 5, Beijing.

World Bank and the Development Research Center of the State Council (WB & DRC). 2012. *China: 2030: Building a modern, harmonious, and creative high-income society*. Washington, DC and Beijing.

Zhaung, Juzhong, Paul Vandenberg, and Yiping Huang. 2012. Growth beyond low-cost advantages: Can the People's Republic of China avoid the middle-income trap? Manila and Beijing: Asian Development Bank and Peking University.

Index

Note: Page numbers in **bold** type refer to figures
Page numbers in *italic* type refer to tables
Page numbers followed by 'n' refer to notes